The Future of the
Public University in America

THE JOHNS HOPKINS UNIVERSITY PRESS

The Future of the Public University in America

Beyond the Crossroads

James J. Duderstadt
Farris W. Womack

The Johns Hopkins University Press
Baltimore and London

The Johns Hopkins University Press
2715 North Charles Street
Baltimore, Maryland 21218-4363
www.press.jhu.edu

Library of Congress Cataloging-in-Publication Data
Duderstadt, James J., 1942–
The future of the public university in America: Beyond the Crossroads /
James J. Duderstadt and Farris W. Womack.
p. cm.
Includes bibliographical references and index.
ISBN 0-8018-7218-9 (hardcover : alk. paper)
1. Public universities and colleges—United States. I. Womack, Farris W.
II. Title.
LB2328.62.U6 D83 2003
378′.05′0973—dc21
2002009868

A catalog record for this book is available from the British Library.

Contents

Preface

Stimulated by federal initiatives such as the land grant acts and the GI Bill and supported and sustained by the investments of the states, the American public university has evolved into one of the most significant social institutions of contemporary society. Our nation's public colleges and universities have democratized higher education, extending the opportunities for a college education to all citizens, applying scholarship and research to serve the diverse needs of society, and engaging with local communities and regions to provide the knowledge and services critical to economic prosperity, public health, and national security.

Throughout the latter half of the twentieth century public higher education flourished, sustained by strong social policies and public investment aimed at providing educational access and opportunity to a growing population. Yet today public higher education faces numerous challenges. A changing student population, far more diverse in age, ethnic background, and economic circumstance than ever before, is demanding change in our institutions. An exponential increase in new knowledge coupled with intensifying needs for advanced education in the workplace are challenging traditional disciplines and methods of instruction. The rapidly evolving technologies of computers and the Internet are eroding constraints posed by the traditional college curriculum and stimulating new market forces for educational services. Furthermore, despite the growing educational needs of a knowledge-based society, public higher education frequently falls behind other social priorities such as health care, corrections, and K-12 education in its capacity to compete for limited tax dollars. Public policies aimed at access and opportunities have been replaced by concerns about educational cost, quality, and accountability.

More broadly, as we begin a new century, the public university faces the challenge of adapting to an era of rapid social, economic, and technological change. This book considers the future of the public university in America from the perspective of two individuals who have served, respectively and together, as president and chief financial officer of one of the nation's leading public institutions, the University of Michigan. Beyond that, the two of us have spent our entire academic careers in public universities, jointly accumulating over sixty years of experience as faculty members, administrators, and leaders at the Universities of Michigan, North Carolina, and Arkansas.

The challenge of leading a public university during a time of great change is considerable, particularly when the institution has the prominence of a flagship state university. These institutions touch the lives of millions of people—students, parents, patients, alumni, sports fans, and, of course, taxpayers. Few, indeed, were the days at Michigan without a new crisis challenging the university and its executive leadership, whether arising from the complex activities and viewpoints of students and faculty or from the intensely political agendas of state legislatures, governing boards, and the media. To be sure, such crises were usually relatively minor within the broader context of the educational mission of the university and its long history of serving the state and the nation. Yet each had the potential to destabilize the institution or damage its reputation, and each required the immediate attention of the administration, even if that resulted in diverting attention from the core missions of the university—teaching, research, and service—and from high-priority yet long-term agendas such as the quality of educational programs. And each arose within the complex and unforgiving public policy and political environment characterizing the public university.

In this book we consider the challenges and issues facing the public university from strategic and reflective perspectives, no longer driven by the hour-to-hour pace of the pager and cellular phone. But we go beyond simply identifying challenges to provide a series of recommendations and strategies for the leaders and patrons of public universities. It is our hope that our perspectives will also be of interest to the broader audience of all those concerned about higher education in America. In this sense this book is intended as an operating manual for the public university, a treatise on lessons learned, shaped and fired in the furnaces of public university leadership.

Consistent with this objective, we have chosen an approach that is more personal and subjective in style than that adopted and preferred by many of our faculty colleagues. Furthermore, the issues and perspectives discussed in this book are heavily influenced by our experiences in leading public research universities, that is, those with substantial graduate and professional programs. Of particular concern are the great state universities, which have served as models of truly public institutions, responsible for and responsive to the needs of the citizens who founded and supported them even while seeking to achieve quality comparable to that of the most distinguished private colleges and universities. Although sometimes different in scale and intensity, most of the challenges of public higher education in America are to be found in these flagship state universities. Hence, we believe our discussion will have relevance to other types of public colleges and universities. In any event the diversity of public higher education in America, from local community colleges to regional four-year institutions to doctoral universities to research universities, makes it difficult for us to deal in any but a very general fashion with the entire enterprise.

We begin with a brief introduction to the complexities of public higher education, considering the forces driving change in our society and in higher education in general but focusing on the challenges particular to the public university. Here we believe it is important to consider the characteristics that define the nature of the public university: its public purpose, legal status, governance, public accountability, and financing. We contrast public and private higher education and discuss the relationship between the two. In particular, we discuss the social contract between American society and the public university as higher education has evolved from being regarded as a public good, supported primarily by tax dollars, to being viewed increasingly as a private benefit, dependent upon a diverse array of stakeholders with unique and disparate needs. We also introduce a recurring theme that appears throughout the book: the declining role of public policy in determining the evolution of the public university, as first politics and then market forces have played increasingly dominant roles in shaping our public institutions.

Individual chapters focus on recommendations, strategies, and lessons learned concerning the various challenges and opportunities facing the public university. We begin by considering how the changing needs of our society are redefining the educational, scholarly, and service missions of the university and provide a framework for addressing these shifting roles. Both economic realities and rapidly evolving technology provide a particular challenge to the public university, and we provide a series of recommendations for how universities might finance their activities and prepare for the digital age. Key in this effort is learning to cope with the rapidly intensifying market forces that threaten to erode the conventional monopolies of the higher education enterprise in America.

Much of the remaining discussion concerns the challenge of leading and governing the public university during this period of change. We identify and discuss the characteristics of the public university which make change particularly difficult: the diverse nature of its various campus communities—students, faculty, staff, and administration; the archaic manner in which it is governed; the ponderous nature of its management and decision-making processes; and the weakness of its leadership, particularly at the presidential level. Here we make the case for rethinking how the public university is governed and led, to make it possible for it to continue to serve our society. We go further to consider the difficult but essential process of university transformation.

Finally, we turn to the future of the public university in America. Here we draw from our experience to consider possible scenarios for the evolution of public higher education. We suggest a proactive approach that will enable public universities both to understand the challenges and opportunities before them and to determine their own paths to the future. In a similar spirit we suggest strategies at the state and federal level which we believe can strengthen public higher education as a resource for future generations.

We are convinced that, while the public university is more important than ever to the future of our nation, it can only maintain its long tradition of service by undergoing significant changes. It is time to move beyond simply analyzing the forces driving change in higher education and to focus instead on strategies that will enable our public universities to serve a rapidly changing America.

Acknowledgments

As we stress time and time again in this book, universities are profoundly human endeavors. Good things happen because good people make them happen, through talent and dedication, especially when they are provided with the support, encouragement, and freedom to push to the limits of their abilities. Our many colleagues among the University of Michigan's faculty, students, and staff who have influenced this book are too numerous to mention individually without running the risk of overlooking important contributions. But there are several groups that deserve special mention.

The University of Michigan has long had a tradition of highly decentralized leadership. Executive officers, deans, directors, and department chairs all enjoy unusual autonomy. While these leaders are provided significant authority, they also accept considerable responsibility, both for the welfare of their units and for the progress of the university more generally. This culture of delegating authority, flexibility, and accountability to the appropriate levels has allowed Michigan to attract and cultivate some truly extraordinary leaders. They, in turn, have been successful in recruiting and developing a faculty, student body, staff, and programs of similarly high standards. During the decade we served as executive officers at the University of Michigan, we had the great privilege of working with a truly remarkable leadership team whose members have continued on to other significant leadership roles in higher education. We wish to acknowledge the impact of their experience, their wisdom, and their guidance on this book, just as we acknowledge their great impact on the university itself.

Next, we wish to acknowledge the exceptional staff support we enjoyed in our administrative roles. The offices of the president and the vice president and chief financial officer are complex and demanding environments, generally closely involved in all critical university issues. Both authors of this book benefited greatly from truly remarkable staff—secretaries, administrative assistants, and office managers—who managed to keep us from sinking beneath the waves of administrative demands.

Finally, we would like to express our deep gratitude to our two "Anns of Ann Arbor," Ann Womack and Anne Duderstadt. The upper reaches of university administration require a team approach in which spouses are frequently called upon to make sacrifices and provide leadership, not to mention pastoral care, for the university community. Furthermore, the challenges and complexities of executive positions, and the inevitable stresses they bring to bear upon their occupants, mean that the advice, counsel, and wisdom of spouses can be invaluable. For this essential support we are deeply grateful and indebted.

The Future of the
Public University in America

CHAPTER ONE

A New Century

Many people regard the public university as among our nation's most significant social institutions. It is through public colleges and universities that the educational, intellectual, and service resources of higher education have been democratized and extended to all citizens. The missions of these institutions reflect some of society's most cherished goals: opportunity through education, progress through research, and cultural enrichment. Public colleges and universities are bound closely to society, responsible to and shaped by the communities that founded them. These institutions have grown up with the nation. They have responded to the changing needs and aspirations of its people as the United States expanded to the frontier and have played key roles in agricultural development and the transition to an industrial society. Public universities were important partners in national defense during two world wars and continue to be important contributors of human and intellectual resources critical to national security. They have expanded and diversified to serve an ever-changing population and its evolving needs.

Today America's public colleges and universities enroll over 75 percent of all college students, currently numbering some eleven million. Nearly 66 percent of all bachelor's degrees, 75 percent of all doctoral degrees, and 70 percent of the nation's engineering and technical degrees are awarded by public universities.[1] Public universities conduct the majority of the nation's campus-based research. They produce most of the country's doctors, lawyers, engineers, teachers, and other professionals and public leaders. They provide critical services such as agricultural and industrial technology, health care, and economic development. They enable social mobility, providing generations of students with the stepping-stones to more rewarding careers and more meaningful lives.

As we begin a new century, Americans can take pride in having built the finest system of higher education in the world, both in terms of the quality of its colleges and universities and the breadth of society served by these institutions. American universities lead the world in the quality of their academic programs; they earn a disproportionate share of international awards such as the Nobel Prize, and they attract students from around the globe. Two-thirds of today's high school graduates seek some level of college education, and U.S. colleges and universities have responded to these needs by providing educational opportunities on an unprecedented scale. The American university is more deeply engaged in society than ever before, playing an increasingly critical role in shaping the economy, culture, and sense of national well-being.

Yet this is a time of change for society and for its institutions. The forces driving change in higher education today are many and varied: the intensifying, lifelong educational needs of citizens in a knowledge-driven economy; the increasing diversity of the population and the growing needs of underserved communities; the globalization of commerce, culture, and education; the impact of rapidly evolving technologies such as the computer and telecommunications; and the exponential growth in both the magnitude and commercial value of the new knowledge created on the nation's campuses.

We live in an "audit" society, in which accountability and performance matter. Concerns about the cost of a college education appear to have replaced earlier concerns about access and opportunity. Furthermore, as society places ever more confidence in the economic forces of the marketplace rather than the policy and programs developed by governments, there is a sense that the evolution of higher education in the twenty-first century will be fueled by private dollars and that the influence of public policy will increasingly be replaced by market pressures. There are growing signs that current paradigms for higher education, the nature of academic programs, the organization of colleges and universities, and the way we finance, conduct, and distribute the services of higher education may not be able to adapt to the demands and realities of the times.

While all of higher education faces a period of change as we enter a new century, the challenges it presents are particularly intense for public universities. The complex political and social environments in which these institutions function, the rapidly changing character of their financing, their public responsibilities and accountability, and the political nature of their governance, among other characteristics, make confronting change not only a great challenge but also a compelling necessity for the public university.

Beyond the Crossroads

This book is based on the belief that we have already moved far beyond the crossroads of considered reflection and contemplative debate about whether change is necessary in the public university. Already the pace of change in public higher education is relentless and accelerating, just as it is in the rest of society. Universities have already traveled down the road toward a dramatically different future than we expected, and there is no turning back. Rather, the challenge today is to develop effective strategies to shape the evolution of public universities so that they will play key, albeit different, roles in responding to the needs of a changing world.

Hence, this book has been written not as an analysis of the various forces driving change in today's public university but, rather, as a consideration of various strategies for shaping the public university of the future. We seek to assist public higher education in shifting from its current tendencies simply to react to the challenges and opportunities of the moment to developing proactive strategies that will allow it to control its own destiny. We ask, for example, how academic programs of universities should be restructured to serve most effectively a student cohort that continues to become more diverse, not only in terms of socioeconomic background but also in terms of age, employment and family responsibilities, and even physical presence (e.g., on campus or in cyberspace). How do we finance public universities, enhancing quality and controlling costs at a time when traditional sources of public support are likely to be restrained or declining? How do we prepare universities for the digital age, a world characterized by increasingly powerful information and communications technologies? How should we govern, lead, and manage public institutions, particularly during a period that will likely require substantial transformation? Can we learn to view the need for change not as a threat but as an opportunity, managing and shaping it to help these institutions better serve society?

Public universities need to pay careful attention to the rapidly changing demographics of students with respect to socioeconomic background, age, family, and employment situations. Both the different learning styles of the "plug-and-play" generation as well as the lifetime learning demands of the high-performance workplace will likely drive a shift from "just-in-case" education, based on degree programs early in one's life, to "just-in-time" education, in which knowledge and skills are obtained during a career, to "just-for-you" educational services, customized to the needs of the student. Similarly, as learning needs become more pervasive in a knowledge-driven economy, national priorities will shift from selectivity and exclusivity (e.g., focusing most resources on educating the "best and brightest") to the universal education of the workforce. The increasing commercial value of the intellectual property produced by campus research and instructional activities coupled with the highly nonlinear process of technology transfer from the campus laboratory to the commercial marketplace are driving changes in the faculty culture. Public universities need new policies to assist them in balancing their traditional responsibilities for teaching, research, and service with the demands of a knowledge-driven economy.

Universities face a particular challenge in adapting to the extraordinarily rapid evolution of information and communications technology. Modern digital technologies such as computers, telecommunications, and networks are reshaping both society and its institutions. Of course, the United States has experienced other periods of dramatic change driven by technology, but never before have we faced a technology that has evolved so rapidly, increasing in power by a hundredfold every decade, obliterating the constraints of space and time, and reshaping the way we communicate, think, and learn. Digital technology will not only transform the activities of the university—teaching, research, and outreach—but it will also transform how we are organized, financed, managed, even whom we regard as students and faculty. The development and execution of effective strategies for addressing the challenges and opportunities presented by digital technology are particularly critical tasks for public universities, which have long been committed to broad access and to reaching beyond the campus to serve society and yet are also constrained by public support and accountability to operate in a cost-effective manner with limited resources.

The market pressures of a knowledge-driven economy are attracting new for-profit providers of educational services and challenging the traditional monopolies of colleges and universities. Although perhaps alien to many sectors of the academy, market competition will demand different strategies for public universities, in which concepts such as "core competence" and "strategic intent," along with business practices such as mergers, acquisitions, and restructuring, will become increasingly important.

Closely related will be the need for new business models capable of adequately financing the complex array of university missions at a time when public support is becoming more limited. It is important to consider strategies such as diversifying the revenue base of the university, building substantial reserves (including endowments), and dramatically reworking the current practices of resource allocation, financial management, and financial accountability. Some public universities will be motivated to consider privatizing their financial operations, becoming, in effect, privately funded but publicly committed universities.[2]

Leading and managing the public university is challenging enough during quiescent times, but the period of rapid change which is upon us may quickly make obsolete many of the traditional approaches to university leadership and demand a serious reconsideration of decision-making and management processes. Similarly, the traditional mechanisms of university governance, such as the use of lay governing boards determined through political means or shared governance with elected faculty bodies, may simply be incapable of dealing effectively with either the pace or the nature of the changing higher education enterprise. It is important to consider not only new forms of but entirely new principles for the leadership and governance of the public university.

Most public colleges and universities will find themselves facing a period of institutional transformation, proceeding at a pace and to an extent that exceeds institutional experience and the capacity of traditional mechanisms. Although universities have changed dramatically in the past, they have generally done so over periods of decades or longer, compatible with the time scales dictated by length of tenure of faculty careers. Yet today public institutions face the need to transform themselves every few years, or even more frequently, in key areas such as finance, technology, and academic programs. This transformation requires entirely new strategies.

Institutions, states, and the nation need to think broadly about the future of the public university. Here we question whether many of the current practices and stereotypes of the public university will remain relevant in the future. Perhaps entirely new concepts, such as "learning ecologies" and "ubiquitous learning," will replace the current national educational infrastructure of colleges and universities.[3] Although speculation about the future can be hazardous and is frequently wrong, it is nevertheless useful to provide a context of possibilities for current decisions.

Finally, it is important in all of these considerations to remember that the public university in America is a social institution, created and shaped by public needs, public policy, and public investment to serve a growing nation. In the past the policies and programs concerning public higher education have been driven by social values and needs: extending educational opportunity to the working class and serving a growing industrial nation (as evidenced in the land grant acts); the commitment to make higher education accessible to all Americans, regardless of socioeconomic background; and the recognition of the importance of universities in creating the knowledge essential to national security, quality health care, economic competitiveness, and an array of other national and regional priorities. These policies and programs provided both the guiding principles for the evolution of the public university and the commitment of public resources necessary to enable it to serve the nation. It remains an open question today whether new social needs and priorities will drive the public policy and investment that define the public university of the twenty-first century or whether market forces, instead, will reshape these institutions, perhaps leaving them disengaged from the public interest.

The Changing Social Contract

Service to society and civic responsibility are among the unique and most important themes of higher education in America. The bonds between the university and society are particularly strong in this country. The public university provides a model of how social institutions, created by public policy and supported through public tax dollars, evolve in response to changing social needs. They exist to serve the public interest. As the needs and aspirations of society have changed, so too have public universities. In a very real sense these institutions have grown up with the nation as each generation has established a social contract with its public universities, redefining the relationship between them and the society they serve.[4]

The historical rationale for public higher education, its raison d'être, is that, since education benefits all of society, it deserves to be supported by public tax dollars.[5] The Carnegie Commission on Higher Education of the 1960s and 1970s framed this idea best when it posed the classic formulation of the questions that shape public policy in higher education: "What societal purposes does higher education fulfill? Who pays? Who benefits? Who should pay?" The commission answered these questions by stating its belief that higher education benefits not just the individual but society as a whole. The return on this societal investment is not just an educated citizenry but also a more vital and productive workforce.[6]

This position underscores the principle that the public university, established by public action and supported through general taxation for the benefit of all of society, is a *public good*. Society benefits from the services of public institutions as well as from the contributions (including future tax payments) made by educated citizens. Because of societal support, the services provided by universities should be available to all who are qualified, without respect to academically irrelevant criteria such as gender, race, religion, and socioeconomic status. Since it is supported by society, the public university is obligated both to be responsible to the needs of society and to be publicly accountable for the use of tax funds.

For most of the history of public higher education, the themes of its evolution have been opportunity through access and service to society enabled by the strong public investment of tax dollars. Each generation has attempted to provide the benefits of higher education to a broader segment of the U.S. population by launching a new array of public institutions: the state universities and the land grant colleges of the nineteenth century, the technical and normal schools of the early twentieth century, the community colleges and statewide university systems in the postwar years, and the virtual and cyberspace universities of today. The federal government has played a major role in the development of public higher education through important legislation such as the land grant acts, the GI Bill, an array of federally funded student financial aid programs, and the direct support of campus-based activities such as research and health care. The primary support for the public university has come from the states and local government, sometimes guided by major policy efforts such as the Wisconsin Idea or the California Master Plan.[7]

Today, however, significant elements of the social contract between society and the public university are changing rapidly. Public resistance to taxes has limited the availability of tax revenue at the local, state, and federal level.

Higher education has become less effective in competing with other social priorities such as health care, K-12 education, and crime prevention and incarceration. Perhaps most significant of all, there has been a subtle shift in policy away from the public principle. Higher education has increasingly become viewed as an individual benefit rather than a societal right. The concept of publicly supported colleges and universities providing free education of high quality to a broad segment of the population (i.e., access through opportunity) has certainly eroded if not disappeared entirely.

As we begin a new century, there is an increasing sense that the social contract between the public university and U.S. society needs to be reconsidered and perhaps renegotiated.[8] The university's multiple stakeholders have expanded and diversified in both number and interest, drifting apart without adequate means to communicate and reach agreement on priorities. Public higher education must compete with an increasingly complex and compelling array of other social priorities for limited public funding. Both the public and its elected leaders today view the market as a more effective determinant of social investment than government policy. Perhaps most significant of all, the educational needs of our increasingly knowledge-intensive society are simultaneously changing and intensifying.

It is easy to see why, as key economic, political, social, and cultural institutions, universities have become both more visible and more vulnerable. The American university has become, in the minds of many, just another arena for the exercise of political power, an arena susceptible to the pull of special interests and open to much negative media attention and even exploitation. It is also understandable that public sympathy toward the university was greater in decades past, when the role of the university was primarily centered around undergraduate education and when only a small fraction of the population had the opportunity for a college education. Part of today's challenge arises from the multiplicity and complexity of the roles that contemporary society has asked the university to assume. Many critics may be asking public universities to return to their earlier and narrower roles, which are more familiar and less threatening.

It is increasingly clear, however, that the public university cannot return to its earlier forms. It long ago passed the point where its earlier, simpler roles and character would be adequate to serve the nation. The knowledge-intensive world has become too dependent upon modern universities. If public universities were to retreat from social engagement and return to their more restricted role of simply educating the young, society would have to invent new social institutions to expanded roles.

A Time for Leadership

History suggests that the American public university as a social institution must change and adapt in part to preserve its traditional roles. For two centuries this extraordinary social institution has not only served as a custodian and conveyor of knowledge, wisdom, and values, but it has transformed the very society it serves, even as social forces have transformed it in turn. It is true that many people, both within and outside the academy, believe that significant change must occur not simply in the higher education enterprise but in all of our institutions. Yet even these people tend to see change as an evolutionary, incremental, long-term process, compatible with the values, cultures, and structure of the contemporary university.

The decade of the 1990s was a time of significant transformation in higher education, as public universities attempted to adapt to changing resources and to respond to new public concerns. As a result, undergraduate education has been significantly improved. Costs have been cut and administrations streamlined. Campuses are considerably more diverse today with respect to race, ethnicity, and gender than they were even a decade ago. Faculties are focusing their research efforts on key national priorities. Public universities have streamlined their operations and restructured their organizations in efforts to contain the rising cost of a college education.

These changes in the public university, while important, have been largely reactive rather than strategic. Yet today the public university does not have the luxury of continuing at this leisurely pace, nor can it confine the scope of changes under way. We are witnessing a significant paradigm shift in the very nature of the learning and scholarship—indeed, in the creation, transmission, and application of knowledge—both in the United States and worldwide, which will demand substantial rethinking and reworking on the part of public institutions. As public higher education enters a new era, the powerful forces of a changing world have pushed universities beyond the crossroads of leisurely choice and decision making and toward a future that we can only dimly perceive and are being challenged to understand.

For the most part public universities still have not grappled with the extraordinary implications of entering an age of knowledge, and this society of learning will likely constitute the future. Academic structures are too rigid to accommodate the realities of rapidly expanding and interconnected bases of knowledge and practice. Higher education as a whole has at times been divided and internally competitive when it needs to speak with a single unequivocal voice. Entrenched interests have blocked paths to innovation and creativity. Perhaps most dismaying, public colleges and universities have yet to come forth with a convincing case for themselves, a vision for their future, and effective strategies for achieving it.

Public higher education in America has a responsibility to help show the way to change, not simply to react to it. Its voice must be loud, clear, and unified in the public forum. At the same time, it must engage in vigorous debate and experimentation, putting aside narrow self-interest and accepting without fear the challenges posed by these extraordinary times.

CHAPTER TWO

The Public University

A visit to the campuses of a distinguished private university conveys an impression of history and tradition. The ivy-covered buildings and the statues, plaques, and monuments celebrating important people and events of the past convey a sense that these institutions have evolved slowly, in careful and methodical ways, to achieve their present forms.

In contrast, a visit to the campus of a great state university conveys dynamism and impermanence. Most of the buildings look new, even hastily constructed, in order to accommodate rapid growth. The icons of the public university tend to be football stadiums or the smokestacks of central power plants rather than ivy-covered buildings or monuments. Campus leaders at public universities may give the impression that the history of these institutions is not greatly valued or recognized. Perhaps this is due to the egalitarian nature of the institutions or, conversely, to the political (and politicized) process that structures their governance and all too frequently informs their choice of leadership. The public university evolves through layers, each generation paving over or obliterating the artifacts and achievements of earlier students and faculty with a new layer of structures, programs, and practices.

So, just what is a *public* university? Many people think of public institutions as large undergraduate teaching factories, supported primarily by tax dollars while providing broad educational opportunities of modest quality at nominal cost. Public universities are also expected to provide an array of services such as health care, agricultural extension, continuing education, and economic development. Yet attempting to distinguish between public and private universities based on their funding source, size and mission, or responsibilities to society can be misleading.

All colleges and universities, for example, receive some degree of public funding from local, state, or federal taxes. Although public universities are unique in the support they receive from direct state appropriations, private universities also receive substantial public support from both state and federal government in the form of research grants, student financial aid, and their tax-exempt status. Like private universities, today many public universities draw the bulk of their support from nonpublic sources such as student tuition, industrial research grants and contracts, private gifts, and income from auxiliary activities such as health care or intercollegiate athletics.

Another contrast between public and private universities, at least in the popular view, is their size. The perception of education in large public universities is that of thousands of students wandering in and out of huge lecture courses taught by foreign teaching assistants. Campus images are of football stadiums, fraternity and sorority parties, or student protests. We think of undergraduate students in these institutions as identified only by their ID numbers until the time of their graduation, when they are asked to stand and be recognized along with thousands of other graduates. Here, again, one must temper this image by recognizing that many public colleges and universities are relatively small, with no more than a few thousand students. Furthermore, many private universities are comparable in size to large state universities.

One might also consider the degree of public responsibility and accountability as a way to distinguish between public and private institutions. Yet here, too, there are more similarities than differences, since both types of institutions have accepted significant social obligations to serve broad and diverse constituencies and provide public service. Both are supported by society and are obligated to be responsive to the needs of society and to be publicly accountable for the use of tax funds. Because all colleges and universities, public and private, receive some degree of public support, they are subject to state and federal laws governing issues such as equal opportunity, environmental impact, and occupational safety.

Thus, public support requires public accountability, responsibility for service to all without discrimination, and dedication to the public interest. To be sure, private universities have considerably more latitude in deciding just how they will serve society, while the roles of public universities are usually dictated by constitutional language, legislative statute, and funding constraints. Yet in reality all of America's colleges and universities, whether public or private, are public assets and are influenced by public policy and constrained by state and federal laws. All receive some form of public subsidy, whether through direct support through government programs such as research grants or student financial aid or through indirect means such as tax benefits.

Probably the greatest distinction between public and private institutions involves their legal status and governance. Public universities are creatures of the state, clearly owned by the taxpayers and governed by public process. They are held accountable to myriad state regulations and laws, as reflected in the rules and regulations governing their operations, such as the sunshine laws that open their meetings and their records to the press or the constraints on personnel policies or expenditures. Even their governing boards are generally selected through partisan political mechanisms such as gubernatorial appointment or popular election and viewed as representing the public's (i.e., the taxpayers') interests rather than serving as trustees for the institution. In fact, since public and private universities are increasingly similar in size, mission, and financing and most sharply distinguished by their ties to government, it has become common to refer to private universities as "independent" universities.

The Public Higher Education Enterprise

Higher education in the United States is distinguished by a remarkable diversity of institutions. Many nations have approached mass education by creating a uniform educational system determined by the lowest common denominator of quality. In the United States we have allowed a diverse system of colleges and universities to flourish in response to the complex and heterogeneous nature of American society. From small colleges to big state universities, from religious to secular institutions, from single-sex to coeducational colleges, from vocational schools to liberal arts colleges, from land grant to urban to national research universities, there is a rich diversity both in the nature and the mission of America's roughly four thousand colleges and universities.

Public higher education reflects this great diversity in mission, character, and stakeholders. For example, community colleges and regional comprehensive public universities tend to serve students from local communities who typically commute to classes on campus or at regional centers and may be enrolled on a part-time basis. Flagship state universities tend to favor a residential educational experience, in which students live on or adjacent to campus and enroll full-time in their academic programs. Some public colleges and universities focus almost entirely on undergraduate education, while others stress graduate study or education for the professions (e.g., law, medicine, and engineering) and research. Some public universities compete for students, faculty, and resources only in local or regional markets. Others, particularly public research universities, compete in national and global markets for people, resources, and reputation.

The great diversity in U.S. society leads not only to variations in the character of our institutions but also to remarkable differences in how institutions respond to a changing society. For example, community colleges and regional four-year public universities tend to be closely tied to the needs of their local communities. They are the most market-sensitive institutions in higher education, and they tend to respond very rapidly to changing needs. When the population of traditional high school graduates declined in the 1980s and 1990s, community colleges moved rapidly into adult education, with a particular emphasis on providing training programs that would support regional economic development. Many four-year regional universities have developed specialized programs to meet key regional needs such as for teachers, health care practitioners, and engineering technologists.

Because of the complexity of their multiple missions, their size, and their array of constituencies, public research universities tend to be most challenged by change. While some components of these institutions have undergone dramatic transformations in recent years, notably professional schools that are tightly coupled with society such as medicine and business administration, other programs such as the liberal arts continue to function much as they have for decades. They have been largely insulated from the effects of a changing society both by the intellectual character of their activities (e.g., based in the humanities) and by their academic culture (e.g., the tenure system and the long tradition of academic freedom). But here, too, change will eventually occur, although perhaps with more difficulty and disruption than in other programs.

It is tempting to compare the university with other types of social institutions, such as corporations, government agencies, or educational institutions in other countries. Here one must take care, however, since the differing objectives, roles, values, and constraints make comparison difficult. For example, during days of concern about the rising costs and prices of higher education in the face of limited resources, one is frequently tempted to compare the university to the business sector. In fact, one of the frequent complaints business leaders raise about higher education is its reluctance to adopt business practices such as total quality management, strategic planning, or go-to-market strategies. To be sure, there are lessons to be learned from the experience of corporations over the past two decades as they have increased productivity and quality while reducing costs. Yet it is also misleading to think that one can impose business methods on the academy.

Clearly, the roles and missions of the university differ from those of a corporation. The latter seeks to make a profit, to increase shareholder value. As a result, most of its decisions are short term, focused on the quarter-by-quarter earnings statements and stock price. In contrast, the university not only serves society through ongoing activities such as education, research, and teaching, but it also has a responsibility to act as a steward for the achievements of past generations while preparing to serve future generations. A profit-loss statement or a balance sheet simply cannot capture the nature of its activities and impact.

So, too, the university—particularly the public university—operates under constraints that would be unthinkable for the private sector. Its most valuable and costly human resource, its faculty, is isolated from traditional management by academic practices such as academic freedom and tenure. Its pricing structure, tuition, is largely fictitious, determined not by market forces but by public subsidy, political constraints, and public sentiment. And public universities face a wide range of additional constraints such as sunshine laws, state regulations, and political pressures.

To compare the public university and a government agency is also complicated. To be sure, some public universities are defined by statute or constitution as a branch or agency of state government, subject to all of the same constraints in terms of personnel policies, purchasing and contracting, and legal practice as any other government body. Yet here too there are very significant differences. Few government agencies are forced to compete in the intense marketplace for talented professionals which characterizes faculty recruitment and retention; instead, they rely primarily on civil service or political appointments. Most expenses of government agencies are met through appropriations from tax revenues. In contrast, appropriations from public funds constitute only a small fraction (averaging 30 percent) of the resources that must be generated by public universities to cover their expenses. Ironically, despite their public character, many government bodies, such as state legislatures, have exempted themselves from intrusive regulations mandating equal opportunity hiring, employee workplace protections, and sunshine laws.

One must also take care in comparing U.S. universities with their counterparts in other nations. American colleges and universities are compelled to provide a general education to young students, while most other nations believe this role to be more appropriate for secondary schools.[1] European universities are viewed primarily as knowledge institutions, with the creation of knowledge as their most important task and teaching and learning designed to build upon these research foundations. They are not asked to accept a major role in the emotional or intellectual growth of young students through general education programs, assuming that those entering their institutions already possess the maturity to move directly into more focused degree programs. Hence, they are also not subject to concerns about the incompatibility of research and teaching, since at the advanced level these activities converge.

Furthermore, no other nation has the diversity of colleges and universities, the array of private and public, large and small, educational institutions as the United States. Most nations utilize strong central planning and coordination to determine the mission, quality, and support of their institution, rather than relying upon the competitive pressures of the marketplace for faculty, students, and resources in the way that America does. Finally, few educational institutions in other countries are as responsive to the needs of society as American colleges and universities, which have both the incentive and the autonomy to take on an ever-growing set of missions to serve society.

Legal Structure

The legal relationship between public universities and government is a complex one. By constitution and statute, states have distributed the responsibility and authority for the governance of public universities throughout a hierarchy of governing bodies: the legislature, state executive branch agencies or coordinating boards, and university governing boards and administrations. Some universities are structurally organized as components of state government, subject to the same hiring and business practices constraining other state agencies. Others are classified as independent public corporations and possess a certain degree of autonomy from state government through constitutional or legislative provision. All are influenced by the power of the public purse—by the strings attached to appropriations from state tax revenues.

All universities require some degree of autonomy to insulate their academic programs from political interference. While private institutions are generally distant enough from such interference, public institutions rely on a more fragile autonomy from the society—and the government—which supports them. In a few states, such as Michigan and California, there is an explicit provision in the state constitution vesting exclusive management and control of the public university in its governing board, presumably to the exclusion of influence from state executive and legislative officials. In other cases institutional autonomy is provided in a much less effective form through statute or practice.

Constitutional or statutory autonomy usually refers, however, only to those matters clearly designated as within the exclusive control of the university's governing board. Powers clearly within the prerogatives of the legislature (e.g., the power to appropriate) or the executive branch (e.g., the governor's budget recommendation and veto power) are exercisable even over constitutionally autonomous institutions. For example, state regulations concerning workplace safety or collective bargaining clearly apply to colleges and universities. Public institutions are subject to oversight by state audit and regulatory agencies, regardless of their legal autonomy by constitution or statute.

Furthermore, no matter how formal the autonomy of a public university—whether constitutional or statutory—other factors can impinge on their independence. For example, in many states sunshine laws that relate to open meetings of public bodies and freedom of information have been extended to the point where they can paralyze the operation of public institutions. Public attitudes, as expressed through populist issues such as control of tuition levels or admission standards, also hinder public institutions from time to time. As we will consider in more detail later, the political nature of the governing boards of public colleges and universities bind them to the political process and can undermine university autonomy. It is not unusual for a governor to pressure politically appointed or elected trustees in an attempt to interfere with what should be an independent institutional decision. State governments and political parties have pressured trustees to remove the president of public universities for political reasons. Such is the political nature of governance in public higher education.[2]

Governance

Most other nations rely on government control of higher education through structures such as a ministry of education. Government ministers or bureaucrats have substantial authority over universities, and institutional leadership (e.g., presidents, rectors, and vice chancellors) is relatively weak. In contrast, the American device for "public" authority in university governance has been a governing board of lay members, either self-perpetuating in the case of private institutions or selected by political appointment or election in the case of public institutions.[3]

Although such governing boards may share some of their power with campus administrators and faculty bodies, in the end they have final authority and responsibility for the welfare and integrity of the institution. In this way the lay governing board is intended to shield U.S. colleges and universities from the government control and political interference those in many other nations face.[4]

In theory, at least, the governing board of a university is expected to focus primarily on policy and to serve as trustees acting on behalf of the welfare of the institution. The detailed management of the institution is delegated to the president, who is selected by the board, and other members of the university administration. Academic policy is delegated to the faculty. The governing boards of private universities have the additional responsibility of fund raising, in which trustees are expected to "give, get, or get off," although recently this responsibility has fallen to many public university governing boards as well.

Nevertheless, there are notable philosophical differences between the governing boards of public and private universities. Trustees of private university governing boards tend to view their roles as stewards and usually attempt to act in the best interest of their institutions. In sharp contrast, the political nature of the process used in selecting the governing board members of public universities frequently leads them to regard their first responsibility to the electorate rather than to the institution. In fact, many public board members tend to focus on narrow forms of accountability to particular political constituencies. They act more as "governors" or "legislators" of their institution than as "trustees." This contrast between the trustee philosophy of the governing boards of private universities and the watchdog stance assumed by public governing boards is both one of the most significant differences and greatest challenges in public higher education today.

Whether the members of governing boards of public colleges and universities are elected or appointed, they are usually selected based more upon their political ties than their knowledge or experience with or commitment to higher education. Furthermore, the political process used to determine public governing boards can be quite distasteful to many of those who possess the broad experience from public or private life necessary to understand the complex nature of the modern university. The general quality of public university governing boards tends to lag considerably behind that of private boards. As a result of their relatively inexperienced and highly political composition, many public governing boards enjoy neither high visibility nor respect on the campus, which can lead to a significant credibility gap between the board, the faculty, and the student body.

Financing

One might be tempted to use the sources of funding as another possible distinction between public and private universities. Many public university presidents wince when they hear the fund-raising pitch to donors used by their private university colleagues: "You folks give to public higher education on April 15. The rest of the year you should give to private colleges and universities." To be sure, state governments provide about 45 percent of the support for public colleges and universities, subsidizing their very low tuition levels, compared to only about 3 percent for private universities, primarily through state-based financial aid programs. In contrast, private universities generate roughly 50 percent of the revenue for their instructional programs from tuition, compared to 25 percent for public universities. Gifts and endowment income represent another difference, amounting to 17 percent for private compared to 6 percent for public universities.[5]

Yet differences between the ways public and private universities are financed are diminishing. As the subsidy provided from state appropriations has eroded, many public universities have responded by increasing tuition levels and launching major private fund-raising campaigns. At the same time, private universities have become increasingly effective in competing for public funding, particularly from the federal government. For example, the private research universities receive very substantial federal support in the form of research grants and contracts. Their students also are eligible for financial aid from both federal and state governments, which in part allow private universities to sustain their relatively high tuition levels. And, perhaps most significant of all, private universities benefit very significantly from the favorable tax treatment of private gifts and earnings on endowment.

Private colleges and universities have been remarkably successful in shaping state and federal higher education policy to their advantage. For example, some would contend that state and federal financial aid programs have been designed in part to subsidize the very high tuition levels of private colleges and universities. [6] Furthermore, state and federal tax policies represent a significant subsidization of private higher education. When the investment corporations created by many private universities to manage their endowments make profits on a business venture, that profit is tax-exempt, and, in effect, the forgone tax revenue must be replaced by tax dollars paid by other citizens, including those sending their students to the local public community college. Not that such public support of private institutions is unusual or necessarily inappropriate. But it should be recognized that most private colleges and universities receive very substantial public subsidies.

Of course, public universities are becoming increasingly dependent upon nonpublic sources for their funding as state support has deteriorated. Most public universities are now heavily involved in private fund raising, with several having launched successful billion-dollar fund-raising campaigns rivaling those of leading private universities. Both public and private universities alike are increasingly dependent upon the revenue generated through auxiliary activities such as health care and continuing education. And most research universities, public and private, are actively engaged in technology transfer activities, ranging from licensing and royalty income to equity interest in spin-off companies.

Missions and Roles

Because of their service mandate, public universities tend to have broader missions and serve more diverse constituencies than private universities. Their instructional activities encompass both the general education and liberal arts programs offered to undergraduates as well as the most highly specialized graduate and professional education. Their research activities range from fundamental investigations to highly applied knowledge services such as agricultural extension and economic development. As the needs of society evolve in complexity, the public university mission similarly broadens. While this multipurpose and comprehensive mission can pose challenges, particularly during periods of constrained resources, most public universities are reluctant to focus their missions for fear of cutting their bonds to the large segments of the society which support them.

The Core Missions

To many students and families the educational role of the university is best symbolized by the university's power in granting degrees. Beyond formal education in the traditional academic disciplines and professional fields, the university has been expected to play a much broader role in the social and intellectual maturation of students. Colleges provide not only the structured learning and discipline necessary for advanced education but also a secure environment, where the young can spend their first years away from their families, learning and exploring without concern for the risks posed by the "real world." The first core mission of the public universities, then, is education, both of a general nature and within the academic disciplines.

The second traditional role of colleges and universities has been scholarship: the discovery, integration, evaluation, and preservation of knowledge in all forms. While the academy would contend that knowledge is important in its own right and that no further rationale is required to justify this role, it is also the case that scholarship and research have been essential to the university's related missions of instruction and service. Furthermore, universities play important roles in preserving our cultural heritage for future generations.

The third traditional mission of the university has been to provide service to society. American higher education has long been concerned with furnishing special expertise to address the needs and problems of society. Public universities' commitment to the development of professional schools in fields such as medicine, nursing, dentistry, law, and engineering are adequate testimony to the importance of this role. So, too, are the major efforts of public universities to serve the public interest through activities such as agricultural extension, economic development, and health care.

Although it is customary to identify the primary activities of the university as the triad of teaching, research, and public service—or in more contemporary terms, as learning, discovery, and engagement[7]—from a more abstract perspective, each of the activities of the university involves knowledge.

The Periphery

If the core missions of the public university are education, research, and public service, then what activities would we identify as on the periphery? In many ways the public university today has become one of the most complex institutions in modern society—far more complex, for example, than most corporations or governments. It comprises many activities, some nonprofit, some publicly regulated, and some operating in intensely competitive marketplaces. The contemporary university teaches students; it conducts research for various clients; it provides health care; it engages in economic development; it stimulates social change; and it provides mass entertainment (as evidenced by the size of its football stadium). In systems terminology the modern university is a loosely coupled, adaptive system, with a growing complexity, as its various components respond to widespread changes. It has become so complex, in fact, that it is increasingly difficult to articulate the nature, mission, or even the fundamental values of the university to those it serves.

In part the modern university has become a highly adaptable knowledge conglomerate because of the interests and efforts of its faculty. Faculty members have been provided with the freedom, encouragement, and incentives to move toward their personal goals in highly flexible ways. Universities have developed a transactional culture, in which everything is up for negotiation. The university administration manages the modern university as a federation. It sets some general ground rules and regulations, acts as an arbiter, raises money for the enterprise, and tries—with limited success—to keep activities roughly coordinated.

Yet in the case of the public university this continual expansion of its peripheral missions also reflects an effort to respond to the ever more diverse needs of society. Public universities were created, in part, to address the needs of their states and the nation. Through long-standing programs such as cooperative extension, adult education, health care, and applied research as well as new endeavors such as online education and technology transfer, public universities continue to become ever more engaged with society. Although there continue to be complaints that higher education is unresponsive to the needs of society, quite the opposite is true, since the competitiveness of American universities causes them to pay close attention to their multiple constituencies.

This intense desire to respond has led many institutions to reallocate limited resources away from their primary responsibilities of teaching and research in an effort to generate more direct public awareness and support. By attempting to respond to unrealistic public aspirations and expectations, to be all things to all people, higher education has whetted an insatiable public appetite for a host of service activities of only marginal relevance to its academic mission. A quick glance around any community with a local university provides numerous examples, from agricultural extension offices to medical clinics to incubation centers for high-tech business formation to athletic camps for K-12 students.

There is little doubt that the need for and the pressure upon universities to serve the public interest more directly will intensify in the years to come. The possibilities are endless: economic development and job creation; health care; environmental quality; the special needs of the elderly, youth, and the family; peace and international security; rural poverty and urban decay; and the cultural arts. There is also little doubt that, if higher education is to sustain both public confidence and support, it must demonstrate its capacity to be ever more useful and relevant to a society under stress.

These peripheral activities play an important role in connecting the public university to the public that it was created to serve. Public service and engagement must be a major institutional obligation of the public university. The public supports the university, contributes to its finance, and grants it an unusual degree of institutional autonomy and freedom, in part because of the expectation that the university will contribute not only graduates and scholarship but also the broader efforts of its faculty, staff, and students in addressing social needs and concerns. Moreover, while education and research are its core missions, these academic activities rarely engage the broader tax-paying public in a compelling way. In a sense it is the service role of the public university through activities such as health care, agricultural extension, and even intercollegiate athletics which builds the necessary level of public understanding and support for the teaching and research mission of the public university.

The Tensions

There is an inevitable tension among the more immediate services sought by society and the long-standing roles of the university in terms of education and scholarship.[8] The complex multidimensional roles and missions of the contemporary public university are driven both by societal need and by the willingness of entrepreneurial faculty to respond to this demand. Public universities are compelled both by character and by political pressures to respond to the rapidly changing needs of society by adding more and more missions at the periphery. Expanding academic health centers into comprehensive health care systems, developing industrial extension services to assist in economic development, creating charter schools and managing K-12 education systems, and even building highly professional athletics programs to provide commercial entertainment are not only accepted but are demanded as appropriate roles of the public university.

Yet such responsiveness to the needs—indeed, even the whims—of society by higher education may in the long run be counterproductive. Not only has it fueled an inaccurate public perception of the primary mission of a university and an unrealistic expectation of its role in public service, but it has also stimulated an increasingly narrow public attitude toward the support of higher education. Powerful forces of parochialism compel institutions to spread themselves ever more thinly as they scramble to justify themselves to their elected public officials. Faculty and administrators alike feel under intense pressure to demonstrate their commitment to public service, even when they recognize that these efforts frequently come at the expense of their primary academic missions.

This situation is compounded by the limited ability of public universities to shed missions in an effort to protect their core activities of education and scholarship and to say no to the ever more numerous demands for public service. In fact, the new missions that public universities are pressured to undertake are almost invariably distant from their core activities. This "mission creep" is one of the greatest challenges to the public university, since the missions that enterprising faculty add to its portfolio are generally reactive and opportunistic rather than strategic. Beyond the resources required for each new mission taken on by the university—since rare indeed is the activity that does not require some degree of subsidy—there is also a concern about the risks associated with these peripheral activities. For example, the financial risks associated with operating large health care systems are considerable, as are the public relations risks associated with big-time college sports and the legal and financial complexities of technology transfer. Most corporations would make certain that the risk of new ventures was appropriately managed and perhaps even isolated from the parent organization through financial firewalls. But such a strategy is difficult, if not impossible, within public institutions, in which both legal requirements and politics require public involvement in all activities.

Society, too, often seeks additional services from public institutions, which can compete with their core missions of education and research. Public universities must develop the capacity to focus and refine their service activities to bring them more in line with their core mission of learning. To do so, they will have to shed some of the missions that have outlived their usefulness to society or their relevance to the academic mission and to ask some difficult questions—for example, are most universities really qualified to operate massive health care systems in today's intensely competitive and high-risk financial marketplace? Do universities have any business operating quasi-professional athletic franchises simply to entertain "armchair America"?

While many of the programs sought from the public university by society may be both useful and appropriate, they must not be allowed to distract the institution from its primary activity of learning. Put another way, those roles and missions at the periphery of the university should not be allowed to degrade its core missions of teaching, learning, and research.

The Interaction between Public and Private Higher Education

Despite their differences in governance and funding, public and private colleges generally cooperate in advancing the cause of higher education. They come together in various organizations such as the American Council on Education and the Association of American Universities to work on behalf of important agendas, including federal research support and student financial aid.

Public and private higher education occasionally part company, although this usually occurs over priorities and emphases rather than substance. For example, for years private universities have pushed hard for federal programs to subsidize major capital facilities as one of their top priorities. While public universities have supported this effort, they have generally not viewed it as a high priority, since they have had access to state appropriations for capital facilities. Likewise, the tax policies governing public and private universities are somewhat different and thus receive different attention.

There is one area, however, in which public and private higher universities come into more direct conflict: the competition for outstanding faculty and students. Although one might think that there is a sharp difference between the student admissions selectivity of public and private colleges and universities, in reality flagship state public universities have generally been able to attract many of the most outstanding students from their region. Such a cohort of outstanding students is particularly important to large public universities, since these students set the pace, the academic standards, for the rest of the student body.

Today, however, several factors are converging which threaten the quality of students enrolling in public universities. Part of the challenge is perception, since students and parents are increasingly influenced by popular college rankings such as those published by *U.S. News and World Report* based upon criteria such as endowment per student and expenditure per student which are clearly biased toward smaller, private institutions. It is worth noting that, because of their large size, even outstanding public universities such as the University of California and University of Virginia do not make the top twenty in the magazine's rankings, although clearly the academic and instructional resources of these institutions dwarf those of many institutions listed higher on the list.

A second factor has to do with more aggressive efforts by the most selective private colleges and universities to buy the "best and brightest" students through generous financial aid using the vast wealth they accumulated as a booming economy swelled private giving and endowment growth. Despite the fact that these institutions have become more selective than ever, now accepting only 10 to 20 percent of those who apply, they are increasingly using financial aid not simply to meet the needs of less fortunate students but also to outbid offers from other institutions. As Harvard's admission brochures state: "We expect that some of our admitted students will have particularly attractive offers from institutions with new aid programs, and those students should not assume we will not respond."[9] Needless to say, despite their relatively low tuition levels, public universities have a difficult time competing with such an aggressive stance.

The faculty-recruiting practices of several of the wealthiest private universities raise a similar concern. Most colleges and universities build their senior faculty ranks from within, by hiring and developing junior faculty. Yet several elite private universities prefer instead to build their senior faculty by raiding established faculty members from other institutions. Their vast wealth allows them to make offers to faculty members which simply cannot be matched by public universities. Most deans of major public universities can readily testify to the great effort expended to fend off raids on their top faculty by wealthy private universities.

The growing disparity in the resources available to public and private colleges and universities has made this competition even more of a challenge. As F. King Alexander notes, the past three decades of growth in federal and state direct student aid policies have favored institutions that rely heavily on student tuition.[10] Indeed, this was an original intent of federal student aid programs, to provide public funding to students so that price disparities between higher-cost and lower-cost institutions were eliminated. As a result, private institutions have been able to increase tuition revenue substantially, subsidized in part by generous federal financial aid programs that cover roughly 40 percent of their high tuition pricing. Political constraints and public perception have limited most public colleges and universities from taking full advantage of the fiscal incentives provided by state and federal direct student aid programs. When coupled with a 25 percent decline in state appropriations as a proportion of the revenue of public institutions over the past two decades and the surge in endowments and private giving during the bullish equity market of the late 1990s,[11] it is not surprising that public universities have fallen further behind their private university counterparts in expenditures per enrolled student.

One important manifestation of this fiscal disparity is provided by the most significant component of instruction-related expenditures: faculty salaries. Since 1980 salary disparities in all faculty ranks have increased significantly favoring private research universities. Faculty salaries in the late 1960s and early 1970s were relatively consistent between public and private research universities and only slightly favored private university faculty, with the average differences across all professorial ranks amounting to less than $2,000 (in 1998 constant dollars). After 1980 public-private university salary disparities began to increase dramatically and have continued through the 1990s, to over $14,000 in 1998. Alexander notes that only three public "Research I" universities have improved upon their faculty salary market position since 1980 when compared to the average salaries of faculty at private research universities.[12] Even among the nation's most distinguished public universities such as the University of California at Berkeley and the University of Wisconsin the gap has widened between average faculty salaries and those of private universities.

To illustrate the problem, it is instructive to think of higher education as a complex ecosystem, composed of a wide variety of life forms. Most are benign and pastoral, such as the community colleges, comprehensive universities, and liberal arts colleges, which serve particular constituencies in a largely non-competitive environment. In this ecosystem the public research universities would be competitive but probably akin to elephants, slow of foot and seldom directly combative. At the top of the food chain are the intensively competitive predators, carnivores such as Harvard and Princeton, which tend to feed on the rest, using their vast wealth to lure away other universities' best faculty and students and leaving behind depleted, if not decimated, academic programs in public universities.

Of course, when challenged about their faculty raids on public universities, the elite private institutions generally respond by suggesting a trickle-down theory. Such free market competition, they argue, enhances the quality of all faculties, accepting the fundamental premise that the very best faculty members should be in the wealthiest institutions. They usually do not acknowledge that in their predatory recruiting they are generally attempting to lure outstanding senior scholars who have already benefited from years of support by public universities during their scholarly development. Nor do they admit, although they certainly realize, the damage that is done to the academic programs of public universities by their raiding practices.

Yet, as in all ecosystems, evolutionary adaptation does occur. As we noted earlier, the vast wealth of the elite private universities depends in part upon public largesse, in this case through very generous tax policies that benefit both charitable giving and endowment investments. As the faculty-raiding practices of these predatory institutions become more aggressive and intrusive, the large public universities may eventually be forced to unleash their most powerful defensive weapon: political clout. After all, influential as the elite private universities may be, they are no match for the political influence of flagship state universities, which are able to build and coordinate considerable political pressure in every state and within Congress. One can imagine a situation in which the pain from irresponsible faculty raids by wealthy private universities becomes so intense that the public universities are compelled to unleash the *T* word, *tax policy,* and question the wisdom of current tax policies that sustain vast wealth and irresponsible behavior at a cost to both taxpayers and to their public institutions. Needless to say, such a move could damage both private and public higher education. But it could happen if the very wealthy private universities do not behave in a more responsible fashion by curtailing their current faculty recruiting practices.

Evolutionary Paths

Since all colleges and universities are subject to many of the same forces driven by economic, social, and technological change, it is not surprising to find that in many respects public and private institutions are converging. After all, they must compete with one another for students, faculty, and financial resources. The competitive market for faculty members, particularly among the leading research universities, drives convergence in appointment policies such as tenure and promotion. Academic and professional programs are evaluated and accredited by similar bodies, which encourages uniformity in academic offerings and culture.

We have noted that the constraints on state appropriations have compelled many public universities to launch major fund-raising efforts to go after private giving, just as private colleges and universities have done for many years. So, too, private institutions seek not only public support through federal programs such as sponsored research and student financial aid, but they are increasingly shaping legislation at the state level which allows them to access state tax dollars as well. In fact, they increasingly portray their mission of teaching, research, and service, along with their commitment to access and engagement, in language essentially indistinguishable from those of public institutions.

Yet, while the competitive marketplace encourages similarities in strategies and missions, commitments to serve the public interest are voluntary for private universities, while they are fundamental to the character of public universities. Furthermore, public universities operate under quite different constraints than private institutions. They are governed by lay boards of a decidedly political nature. They are constrained by state regulations and policies concerning issues such as public access, procurement, and employment. Their public character demands a philosophy of providing low-cost education to a broad range of students. It also requires them to take on a far broader spectrum of missions, including more utilitarian activities such as practical education, applied research, and extension services. And, perhaps most important for this discussion, it constrains their capacity to adapt to rapid change to a considerable extent.

CHAPTER THREE

Responding to the Changing Needs of Society

The contemporary university is defined, in part, by the many roles it plays in an ever-changing society. Universities provide educational opportunities. They produce scholars, professionals, and leaders. Universities transfer culture from one generation to the next. They perform the research necessary to generate new knowledge critical to the progress of the nation and the world. And they provide service to society across a number of fronts, including health care and economic development, which draw on their unique expertise.

Yet the same powerful economic, social, and technological forces driving change in society are also transforming its needs and expectations for the contributions of the university. Although the university's traditional roles of educating the young, creating new knowledge, preserving and transmitting cultural resources to future generations, and providing knowledge-intensive services to society will continue to be needed, society will require much more from its institutions. The high-performance workplace is creating new needs for adult education provided in a form that is compatible with career and family responsibilities. Universities are increasingly seen as sources of commercially valuable intellectual property arising from their research and instructional activities. Local communities, states, and the nation itself seek new knowledge-intensive services from the university requiring deeper engagement and partnership.

New forms of organizations are evolving to meet society's changing knowledge needs, for example, for-profit colleges, cyberspace universities, telecoms, dot-coms, collaboratories, all specializing in providing society with knowledge-intensive products and services, many once the prerogative of the university alone. Traditional universities face increasingly intense competition in this new knowledge marketplace. In effect we are seeing the emergence of a global knowledge and learning industry that will challenge the traditional higher education enterprise. Most colleges and universities, including the public university, will find themselves in an increasingly competitive market for both traditional and new products and services. They will have to demonstrate anew that they are the best qualified to define the substance, standards, and process of higher education.

Changing educational needs raise important issues concerning access, affordability, diversity, and selectivity of educational opportunity. The changing role of the research university in providing knowledge-intensive products and services raises important issues concerning the balance between responding to the commercial pressures of the marketplace and protecting the public interest. In this chapter we will examine the changing needs of society for the multiple roles of the public university and suggest possible strategies for responding.

Education in the Age of Knowledge

The university has long played both a personal development and a civic role in the lives of students, providing each new generation of students with the opportunity to better understand themselves, to discover and understand the important traditions and values of the past, and to develop the capacity to cope with the future. Despite the dip in the postwar baby boom, enrollments in public universities have risen 30 percent since 1980 and are projected to increase another 17 percent in the decade ahead.[1] Today 65 percent of U.S. high school graduates seek some level of college education, and this number could well increase as a college degree becomes the entry credential to the high-performance workplace. There is an increasingly strong correlation between the level of one's education and personal prosperity and quality of life. Even those with college degrees will find themselves hard-pressed to keep pace in a future that will in all likelihood demand frequent career changes. The ability to continue to learn and to adapt to—indeed, to manage—change and uncertainty will become among the most valuable skills of all.

Eighteen- to twenty-two-year-old high school graduates from affluent backgrounds no longer dominate today's undergraduate student body. Indeed, only 16 percent of today's students attend school full-time, live on campus, and are between the ages of eighteen and twenty-two.[2] Today one-third of undergraduate students work full-time, and over half attend college on a part-time basis. We now see increasing numbers of adults from diverse socioeconomic backgrounds, already in the workplace, perhaps with families, seeking the education and skills necessary for their careers. They seek convenience, service, quality, and low cost rather than the array of course electives and extracurricular activities characterizing today's undergraduate programs. This demand for adult education may soon be greater than that for traditional undergraduate education.[3] Today's universities will have to change significantly to serve the educational needs of adults, or new types of institutions will have to be formed.

Most of the attention American universities devoted to improving the quality of undergraduate education during the 1990s focused on the general education experience of the first two years. While this approach has certainly improved the quality of large introductory courses, providing additional opportunity for small seminars, writing experiences, and, when necessary, remedial instruction, it has largely proceeded within the traditional classroom paradigm. Yet the students entering college today both seek and require a different form of education in which interactive and collaborative learning will increasingly replace the passive lecture and classroom experience. Students have become more demanding consumers of educational services, although frequently their efforts are directed at obtaining the skills needed for immediate career goals.

Increasingly, educators are realizing that learning occurs not only through study and contemplation but even more effectively through the active discovery and application of knowledge. There is a certain irony here. When asked to identify the missions of the university, university faculty and administrators generally respond with the time-tested triad: teaching, research, and service. Undergraduate education, however, is usually thought of only from the perspective of the first of these missions, teaching. Clearly, the academy should broaden its concept of the undergraduate experience to include student involvement in other aspects of university life.

For example, although public research universities possess a rich array of intellectual resources, through their scholars, laboratories, and libraries, too few of them are utilized in the current undergraduate curriculum. Perhaps every undergraduate should have the opportunity, or even be required, to participate in original research or creative work under the direct supervision of an experienced faculty member. The few students who have been fortunate enough to benefit from such a research experience usually point to it as one of the most valuable aspects of their undergraduate education. There is ample evidence to suggest that significant learning also occurs when students participate in community or professional service. Such activities provide students with experience in working with others and applying knowledge learned in formal academic programs to community needs. Many students arrive on campus with little conception of broader community values, and the experience of doing something for others can be invaluable.

The undergraduate experience should be reconsidered from a broader perspective, encompassing the multiple missions of the university. All too frequently each mission of the university is associated with a different component—a liberal education and teaching with the undergraduate program, research with the graduate school, and practical service with professional schools. In reality all components of the university should be involved in all of its missions.

In these new learning paradigms the word *student* becomes largely obsolete, at least in the sense that it describes a passive role of absorbing content selected and conveyed by teachers. Instead, we should probably begin to refer to the clients of the twenty-first-century university as active *learners,* since they will increasingly demand responsibility for their own learning experiences and outcomes. In a similar sense the concept of a faculty member as a "teacher" may also be outdated. Today the primary role of most faculty members in undergraduate education is to identify and present content. In these new paradigms the role of the professor becomes that of nurturing and guiding active learning, not of identifying and presenting content. That is, they will be expected to inspire, motivate, manage, and coach students.

It is not surprising that during these times of challenge and change in higher education the nature and quality of graduate education has also come under scrutiny. The current highly specialized form of graduate education may no longer respond either to the needs of students or society. The majority of Ph.D. programs have traditionally seen their role as training the next generation of scholars or, even more limited, as cloning the current cadre of dissertation advisors. To be sure, the process of graduate education is highly effective in preparing students whose careers will focus on academic research. Yet the specialized research training provided to most graduate students leaves them ill prepared for the broader teaching responsibilities they are likely to encounter in the higher education enterprise.[4] More than half of new Ph.D.s will find work in nonacademic, nonresearch settings, and graduate programs must prepare them for these broadened roles.[5]

Although undergraduate education in the liberal arts remains the core mission of most public universities, their commitment to professional education is considerable.[6] In fact, an analysis would show that many public research universities devote a significant fraction, and in some cases the majority, of their faculty and financial resources to education in the professions, including business, engineering, law, and medicine. Furthermore, even many undergraduate degree programs are designed primarily to prepare students for professional careers, such as engineering, nursing, teaching, and business. This is also the case for "pre-professional" undergraduate majors designed to prepare students for professional programs at the graduate level, such as pre-med or pre-law. Even traditional disciplinary majors are based on sequences of courses designed to prepare students for further graduate study in the field, for possible careers as academicians or scholars. In this sense the contemporary public university is based heavily upon professional education and training. Of course, this is nothing new, since even the medieval university was based on the learned professions of theology, law, and medicine.

The rapid growth of the knowledge base required for professional practice has overloaded the curricula of many professional schools. This has been particularly serious in undergraduate professional degree programs such as engineering and premed, since the tendency is to include more and more specialized material at the expense of the liberal arts component of an undergraduate education. In a world of continual change we should no longer assume that a professional education can provide sufficient knowledge for a substantial portion of a career. Some professional schools are now taking action to restructure their curricula by providing early but limited exposure to professional practice and stressing the development of skills for lifelong learning rather than mastering a sequence of highly specific subjects, with the intent of relying more heavily on "just-in-time" education, practical knowledge provided in modules and perhaps even through distance learning paradigms to practitioners when and where they need it.

For example, some business schools now find their faculty more heavily involved in nondegree continuing education programs such as executive education than in traditional master of business administration (M.B.A.) programs. They find that learning in such programs is more efficient, since older students are more mature and highly motivated. Furthermore, since both the students and their employers can more accurately assess the value of the program, they are more willing to pay tuition levels that reflect the true cost.

Today's college graduates will face a future in which the need for education will be ongoing. They are likely to change jobs, even careers, many times during their lives. Educational goals need to be reconsidered from this lifetime perspective. In a world driven by knowledge, learning can no longer be regarded as a once-is-enough or on-again, off-again experience. Rather, people will need to engage in continual learning in order to keep their knowledge base and skills up to date. Undergraduate and graduate education are just steps—important steps to be sure—down the road toward a lifetime of learning. They should ensure a person's ability and desire to continue to learn, to become attuned to change and diversity and adaptable to new forms of knowledge and learning of the future. To prepare for a future of change, students need to acquire the ability and the desire to continue to learn, to become comfortable with change and diversity, and to appreciate both the values and wisdom of the past while creating and adapting to the new ideas and forms of the future. These objectives are, of course, precisely those one associates with a liberal education.

Since the need for learning will become lifelong, perhaps the relationship between a student/graduate and the university will similarly evolve into a lifetime membership in a learning community. Just as the word *student* may no longer be appropriate to describe an active learner, perhaps the distinction between *student* and *alumnus* may also no longer be relevant. There is an increasing interest on the part of alumni in remaining connected to their university and to learning opportunities throughout their lives.

There are already signs of both subtle and profound transitions in how some universities conceive the fundamental nature of their educational programs. With rapidly evolving communications and information technology,

learning experiences are no longer confined to the campus or highly structured degree programs for the young but, rather, are increasingly tailored to
the time, place, and individual needs of the public. The terminology is shifting
from students to learners, from faculty-centered to learner-centered institutions, from classroom teaching to the design and management of learning
experiences, and from student to a lifelong member of a learning community.[7]

Access, Affordability, Selectivity, and Diversity

A growing number of college-age students, the intensifying educational
needs of adults demanded by a knowledge-driven economy, and the increasing
diversity of the U.S. population have made the issue of access to educational
opportunity once more a central concern. Largely ignored since the college
days of the baby boomers in the 1950s and 1960s, the linked issues of access,
affordability, selectivity, and diversity once again require careful attention and
reconsideration.

The Cost of a College Education

A key determinant of access is affordability. Certainly, the cost of a college
education is among the more contentious issues in higher education today.
Students and parents, taxpayers and politicians, and the media and the public
have all raised concerns about spiraling tuition levels and the affordability of
a college education. Many believe that college tuition is out of control, essentially pricing higher education out of the reach of all but the wealthy.
Some even suggest that the price of a college education is no longer worth its
benefits.[8]

To separate myth from reality, we need to examine carefully two issues
relating to the cost of a college education. First, we must understand the
relationship between what it costs a university to operate, the price a student
actually pays, and the value received by students through this education. Second, we need to consider the issue of just who should pay for a college education: parents, students, state taxpayers, federal taxpayers, private philanthropy,
or the ultimate consumer (employers in business, industry, and government).
It is important to realize that quality in higher education does not come cheap.
Someone must pay for it. The real debate in U.S. society is less about cost than
about who should pay for higher education.

A variety of factors determine the cost of a college education to students and their parents: the tuition charged for instruction, room and board, the cost of books, travel, and other incidental expenses. The most immediate concern here is tuition, since this represents the price that the institution charges for the education it provides and over which it has (or should have) the most control.

At the outset it must be recognized that no student pays the full cost of a college education. *Every* student at every university is subsidized to some extent in meeting the costs of his or her education through the use of public and private funds.[9] With the help of private gifts and income on endowment, many private institutions are able to set tuition levels (prices) at one-half or one-third of the true cost of the education. Public institutions manage to discount tuition "prices" even further to truly nominal levels—to as low as 10 percent of the real cost—through public tax support and financial aid programs.

In 2000–2001 tuitions in public four-year colleges and universities averaged $3,500, compared to $16,332 in private institutions. But there is considerable variation. For example, at the University of Michigan, one of the more expensive public universities, instate undergraduate tuition is about twice the national average, at $7,000 per year.[10] Yet even this represents only 25 percent of the estimated costs of educating an undergraduate student, with most of the subsidy coming from state taxpayers and private philanthropy. Furthermore, when this tuition is discounted by the financial aid available to all instate undergraduates with demonstrated need, the average net price for a year's education drops to less than $3,000.

This is a very important point. Even though tuition levels have increased at all institutions, public and private, they remain moderate and affordable for most colleges and universities. It is the very high tuition at a few highly selective private institutions such as Harvard, Stanford, and MIT, where tuition has soared to $25,000 per year or more, which has generated the most attention. Yet less than 1 percent of all college students attend such elite institutions.[11] Nearly 80 percent of all students attend public colleges with annual charges for tuition which average only $3,500. Despite the increases in the tuition charged by public colleges and universities to compensate for the erosion in funding from public tax dollars, public higher education remains affordable for most families, particularly when augmented by student financial aid programs.

There is another, more substantive reason for the current concerns about the rising costs of a college education. For almost a century the costs of higher

education generally increased somewhat more rapidly than inflation. Fortunately, however, average family income also increased substantially over this
period. As long as family income increased at about the same rate as tuition,
the costs of a college education were tolerated, since they remained at roughly
the same fraction of family expenses. Yet in the 1980s, just at about the time that
the growth in state appropriations for public higher education began to slow,
triggering corresponding hikes in college tuition levels, the rate of increase of
family income began to decline as well.[12] As a result, the share of annual family
income required to pay for a year of college has grown for most income groups
over the past two decades. Only the wealthiest 20 percent of Americans have
seen family income keep pace with tuition increases. The shift of the burden
for meeting the costs of a college education from the taxpayer to the family
occurred at a most inopportune time, when the family budget was coming
under increasing stress.

While many families can still afford the costs of a college education for their
children at public or even private universities, others are not so fortunate. Yet,
despite increasing tuition levels, today a college education is more affordable to
more Americans than at any period in the nation's history, as evidenced by the
fact that enrollments have never been higher. This is due in part to the availability of effective need-based financial aid programs. In truth the real key to
providing access to a college education for Americans has not been through
low tuition but, rather, through need-based financial aid programs. For low-
income students attending a public university, the average contribution of
federal, state, and institutional financial aid typically exceeds the gross tuition
price so that they, in effect, pay no tuition at all.

As state and federal subsidizing of the costs of education has declined,
whether through declining support of institutions or financial aid programs,
tuition charges have understandably increased. Much of this new tuition revenue has been used to protect the financial aid programs critical to low-income
families. Put another way, public universities, like private universities, have
asked more affluent families to pay a bit more of the true cost of educating
their students—although not the full costs, to be sure—so that they can avoid
cutting the financial aid programs that enable economically disadvantaged
students to attend.

The financial aid programs established by the Higher Education Act of 1965
and its subsequent amendments and reauthorizations significantly changed
the mechanism for federal support of higher education. Rather than allocating

funds directly to institutions, the federal government channeled funds directly to students through a complex system of financial aid programs. This policy shift gained momentum in the 1970s, when the Nixon administration expanded federal financial aid programs still further, thereby encouraging colleges and universities to move to a high tuition, high financial aid model in which tuition was set at levels more comparable to actual educational costs, while financial aid programs were used to provide access.

Such federal financial aid programs were first based upon need and focused on low-income students. During the late 1970s and early 1980s, however, political pressures extended eligibility to middle- and upper-middle-class students through efforts such as the Middle Income Assistance Act, thereby providing, in effect, even further public assistance to high tuition private colleges and universities. Furthermore, during the 1980s federal programs began to emphasize student loan aid over federal grant aid by again expanding student eligibility for loans. For example, in 1979 two-thirds of federal assistance to students came in the form of grants and work-study jobs, with the remaining one-third in the form of subsidized loans.[13] Today the reverse is true; grants typically constitute only one-third of a student's federal aid award, and the remaining two-thirds is extended in the form of loans. The percentage of tuition covered by federal financial aid for low-income students has decreased over time, while institutional grants have increased rapidly for students from both low- and middle-income groups.

The nature of the federal loan program shifted once again in 1997 with a major new series of tax credits and deductions, the Hope Scholarships and Lifetime Learning tax credits, designed to help middle-class students and families meet the cost of a college education.[14] While this legislation was portrayed as a $40 billion national investment in higher education, many contend that the credits represent instead a massive middle-class entitlement program, politically very popular but not strategically well aligned with the needs of the nation.[15] Although the size of the Pell grants to economically disadvantaged students has also been increased, there is concern that the major impact of the tax benefits will be on middle-class consumption and not on expanding the opportunity for a college education.

Today federal financial aid programs provide over $50 billion a year to college students.[16] Currently over 55 percent of undergraduates receive some level of student aid from federal, state, or private sources, averaging $6,256 per student. The participation rate for financial aid is even higher at the graduate level, with over 60 percent receiving some form of financial aid averaging $13,255. These programs have shifted, however, from an emphasis on expanding access to higher education to a goal of reducing the cost burdens of a college education on the middle class. Put another way, the higher education tax benefits contained in the Taxpayer Relief Act of 1997 represent yet another step away from the concept of higher education as a social investment. In a sense, by shifting student financial aid first from grants to loans and then from loans to tax credits that benefit primarily the middle and upper classes, federal policy has shifted away from the view that higher education is a public good and toward the view that education benefits primarily the individual. By channeling federal support through tax assistance rather than need-based grants, the government has also indicated a preference for investing in the marketplace rather than in students most in need or in the capacity of colleges and universities. It also clearly suggests that middle-class votes have become more important to federal leaders than the access of low-income students to educational opportunities.

These shifts in federal financial aid programs also represent the increasing priority given to the support of private higher education at the federal level. Public universities are at somewhat of a disadvantage in benefiting from these federal financial aid programs. Since there are no tuition limits on federal financial aid support, private universities have been able to raise tuition to capture an increasing share of federal dollars (now amounting to roughly 40 percent, despite the fact that they enroll less than 20 percent of college students). Lower-cost public universities, constrained in pricing by state policy and governing board politics, have been unable to move to the high tuition–high financial aid models most benefited by federal programs. Ironically, while most state government have sought to control costs in order to expand access, limiting tuition growth to the consumer price index (CPI) or less, the federal government has given economic incentives to private colleges and universities to raise tuition, since the high tuition–high aid approach to federal programs tends to reward institutions charging disproportionately higher tuition.

It should not be surprising that the policy shifts characterizing public support of higher education have impacted the access of various socioeconomic groups in different ways.[17] During the past two decades a large discrepancy has appeared in college participation with respect to family income. The growth in college enrollments during these periods has occurred primarily from the top three income quartiles, in which college participation has increased to 70 percent. There has been little additional participation in the lowest income quartile, still amounting to less than 30 percent. Although one could argue that the major increase in student financial aid programs should offset the impact of raising tuition in public colleges and universities, in reality access from low-income groups is determined very much by the perception of costs, causing a very sensitive relationship between tuition level and enrollment in the lower income quartile. Similarly, the shift of financial aid policies from grants to loans and now tax benefits further tends to discourage lower-income students.

Some states have aggravated these income disparities even further by intentionally diverting resources away from need-based financial aid programs designed to enhance access to low-income students and instead channeling these funds to middle- and upper-income students in an effort to buy votes. Of most concern is the recent trend to provide merit awards to high school students who score well on standardized examinations, since students from lower-income families are less likely to succeed on such tests because of their limited access to high-quality K-12 education and extracurricular learning opportunities. For example, the State of Michigan has used the majority of its tobacco settlement funds to provide $2,500 merit scholarships to students who score highest on the statewide Michigan Education Assessment test. In 2000, 63 percent of white high school students taking the test qualified for such a merit scholarship, while only 2 percent of African American students who took the test qualified. Most of the white students were in the upper two economic quartiles of the population, while the African American students were in the lowest quartile, demonstrating the clear political intention of the program to buy middle- and upper-class votes rather than providing access to educational opportunity to those most in need of assistance.

Clearly, there is a compelling need to focus the attention of the nation once again on providing access to quality higher education regardless of financial ability. Indeed, this is one of the most fundamental purposes of the public university. The highest priority for public funding should be given to those most in need. The tragedy is that public leaders at the state and federal level are targeting student financial aid programs to benefit the middle and upper classes to the neglect of those less fortunate, who will simply not have the opportunity for a college education without financial assistance. Ironically, many governing boards of public colleges and universities take the same tack when they hold tuition levels down to unrealistically low levels rather than using additional tuition revenue to fund strong financial aid programs. To some degree this represents a profound misunderstanding of the fact that educational access and opportunity are achieved not through subsidizing those who can afford to pay but, rather, by providing financial assistance to those who cannot. But there is also a very pragmatic element to these policies, since middle- and upper-class voters are more influential than those at the low end of the income scale. Finally, there is a certain element of hypocrisy inherent in these policies, since those governing board members and public leaders most insistent upon low tuition and educational benefits for the middle class are themselves usually in the upper income brackets.

Three decades of shifting public policies have tended to aggravate the economic stratification in society, the gap between rich and poor, by allowing widening inequalities of income and wealth to determine access to educational opportunity. It is also the case that we have relatively little understanding, and little empirical data, about the impact of various public subsidies on the access to higher education, despite the fact that this country currently spends over fifty billion dollars within the states to subsidize the low tuition in public colleges and universities and a similar amount at the federal and state level on student financial aid programs. As Patrick Callan, director of the National Center for Public Policy and Higher Education, has observed, there is no other public policy issue in higher education in which expert opinion is so completely at odds with public perceptions. Most higher education experts overwhelmingly favor high-tuition/high–financial aid strategies as the most effective way to expand educational opportunity since they focus public subsidies on those least able to afford a college education. The general public and their elected representatives, however, consistently favor low tuitions and increasingly prefer to determine financial aid on the basis of student academic qualifications rather than financial need.[18]

Excellence, Selectivity, and Exclusivity

Although access to quality higher education should be a significant, if not the primary, priority of U.S. colleges and universities, many are instead driven by a culture of selectivity and elitism which has characterized much of American higher education during the past several decades. One of our colleagues refers to this circumstance as the "Harvardization" of higher education in America, in which the highly selective approach to admitting students (and recruiting faculty) of the Ivy League colleges has set the gold standard for all colleges and universities, whether they be elite private universities, public universities, or small liberal arts colleges. In the highly competitive market-place for students, faculty, resources, and reputation, there is a common perception that the more selective an institution is, the better its student body and academic programs. Popular rankings of colleges and universities such as those published by *U.S. News and World Report* make it clear that academic ranking and reputation are directly correlated with selectivity.

This emphasis on selectivity, indeed, elitism, has been pushed to extreme limits. The most elite institutions, such as Harvard, Stanford, and Yale, accept only about one out of every ten applicants. Even leading public universities such as the University of California, Michigan, and Virginia today admit only a small fraction of applicants. Yet, in truth, not only do the majority of applicants rejected by these elite institutions have the academic ability to both succeed and benefit from their academic programs, but in many cases they have academic credentials comparable to or even better than those students who have been accepted (particularly when the latter are athletes, alumni legacies, or the relatives of influential donors). Put another way, selectivity in many institutions has reached the stage where admissions decisions are made more on the basis of subjective evaluations than empirical data.

Not only should one question the admissions process that leads to such high selectivity, but one might also question the wisdom of students and parents striving for admission to such highly selective institutions. Although there appears to be little correlation between admissions selectivity and career earnings or achievement, parents and students hold tight to the belief that the more selective an institution one attends, the better their chances for success later in life. Brand name has high value in college applications.

As the admissions policies of elite institutions become increasingly selective and their costs for attendance become ever higher, there may eventually come a backlash. In fact, there are already some signs of a shift in public attitudes toward higher education which will place less stress on values such as "excellence" and "elitism" and more emphasis on the provision of cost-competitive, high-quality services, shifting from "prestige-driven" to "market-driven" philosophies. While quality is important, even more so is cost; the marketplace seeks low-cost, quality services rather than prestige. The public is asking increasingly, "If a Ford will do, then why buy a Cadillac?" Why should their children attend an expensive private institution, when they could attend their flagship state university for less than 20 percent of the cost? It could be that the culture of excellence, which has driven both the evolution of and competition among colleges and universities for over a half-century, will no longer be accepted and sustained by the American public.

More generally, the tendency of linking excellence to exclusivity, of spending more and more on fewer and fewer students, may eventually crumble under the weight of its own elitism for another reason. In a knowledge-intensive society ever more dependent upon educated people and their ideas, what are needed are not richer and more selective elite universities but, rather, more institutions capable of providing quality educational opportunities for our citizens. We need to increase our flow of human capital, not refine it. In a sense a knowledge-driven society must shift from elite education to universal education for its very survival. It is time to "de-Harvardize" higher education in America.

Part of the difficulty here is the tendency to focus on "inputs" as indicators of academic quality: the test scores and class rank of entering students, the selectivity of college admissions decisions, the funds spent on educating students. Yet in American today only 55 percent of those entering college will graduate with a degree of any sort within a decade of high school graduation— an appalling waste of talent and effort. Clearly, we should not focus simply on inputs but also on outputs, on the value added by a college education. Access to a college education alone is meaningless unless public institutions are also committed to the success of students.

As a society, we must not be deceived by the myopic focus on the artificial measures of educational quality promoted either by commercial ratings such as those published by *U.S. News and World Report* or by elite institutions. We cannot long tolerate the growing gap between rich and poor in our society, driven increasingly by inequities in educational opportunity. A democratic society in an age of knowledge requires access to education and the opportunity for success for all citizens. No one must be left behind for economic or social reasons.

Diversity

One of the most enduring characteristics of public higher education in the United States has been its ever-broadening commitment to serve all the constituents of the diverse society that founded and supported its colleges and universities. As this nation enters a new century, it grows even more diverse, transformed by an enormous influx of immigrants from Latin America, the Caribbean, Africa, and Asia. Demographers project that by the year 2030 approximately 40 percent of all Americans will be members of minority groups, and by midcentury we may cease to have any majority ethnic group, a milestone reached by California in 2000. As the United States evolves into a truly multicultural society with remarkable cultural, racial, and ethnic diversity, we will clearly require further changes in the nature of higher education.

Although such diversity brings remarkable vitality and energy to the American character, it also poses great challenges, both to the nation and to its institutions. America was once viewed as a melting pot, assimilating first one group and then another into a homogeneous stew. Yet, in reality, many people tend to identify both themselves and others in racial and cultural terms and to resist such assimilation and homogeneity. Universities especially need to understand and accommodate the ways in which new, nontraditional members of our communities think and function, in order to span racial and cultural divides. They must take decisive action to build more diverse institutions to serve an increasingly diverse society.

Yet today's political climate raises serious questions about the nation's commitment to equity and social justice for all Americans. Segregation and exclusivity still plague many communities and social institutions. An increasing number of Americans oppose traditional approaches to achieving diversity such as affirmative action.[19] Federal courts are considering cases that challenge racial preference in admissions, and in state after state voters are taking aim through referenda at an earlier generation's commitment to civil rights.

When one discusses the topic of diversity in higher education, it is customary to focus on issues of race and ethnicity. But it is also important to recognize that human diversity is much broader, encompassing characteristics such as gender, socioeconomic background, and geographical origin, and these, too, contribute to the nature of an academic community. In both the narrow and broader sense it is important to first lay out the rationale for the importance of diversity in American higher education.

Universities are created and designed to benefit society at large, both by advancing knowledge and by educating students who will, in turn, serve others. Therefore, beyond creating knowledge and educating students, universities are also responsible for perpetuating important civic and democratic values: freedom, democracy, and social justice. To achieve these broader goals, colleges and universities may at times be required to take affirmative action to overcome social inequities imposed on people who have historically been prevented from participating fully in the life of the nation. Higher education has an obligation to increase participation by members of racial, ethnic, and cultural groups that are not adequately represented among students, faculty, and staff. Fundamental issues of equity and social justice must be addressed if public universities are to keep faith with national values, responsibilities, and purposes.

Over the years public universities have committed themselves to providing equal opportunity for every individual regardless of race and nationality as well as in terms of class, gender, or belief. This is the university's basic obligation as a democratic institution and as a major source of future leaders of our society. Equity and social justice have been core values of higher education in the United States and are integral to universities' scholarly mission.

Nevertheless, universities are social institutions of the mind, not of the heart. While there are compelling moral and civic reasons to seek diversity and social equity on campuses, the most effective arguments in favor of diversity to a university community tend to be those related to academic quality. Perhaps most important in this regard is the role diversity plays in educating students. Universities have an obligation to create the best possible educational environment for the young adults whose lives are likely to be significantly changed during their college years. The quality of educational programs is affected not only by the nature of the individual students enrolled in institutions but also by the characteristics of the entire group of students who share a common educational experience. To prepare these students for active participation in an increasingly diverse society, universities clearly need to reflect this diversity on their campuses. Beyond that, there is ample evidence from research to suggest that diversity is a critical factor in creating the richly varied educational experience that helps students learn. Especially since students in late adolescence and early adulthood are at a crucial stage in their development, diversity (racial, demographic, economic, and cultural) enables them to become conscious learners and critical thinkers and prepares them to become active participants in a democratic society.[20] Students educated in diverse settings are more motivated and better able to participate in an increasingly heterogeneous and complex democracy.[21]

Diversity is also important to scholarship. Unless scholars draw upon a broad spectrum of people and ideas, they cannot hope to generate the intellectual and social vitality needed to respond to the growing complexities of our world. Perhaps at one time society could tolerate singular answers, when most Americans still imagined that tomorrow would look much like today. But this assumption of stasis is no longer plausible. As knowledge advances, we un-cover new questions that we would not have imagined a few years ago. Society evolves, and the issues we grapple with shift in unpredictable ways. A solution for one area of the world often turns out to be ineffectual or even harmful in another. Academic areas as different as English and sociology have found their very foundations radically transformed as they attempt to respond to current dilemmas.

In addition to these intellectual benefits, including underrepresented groups allows our institutions to tap reservoirs of human talents and experiences from which they have not yet fully drawn. It seems apparent that universities could not sustain such high distinctions in a pluralistic global society without honor-ing diversity and openness to new perspectives, experiences, and talents. In the years ahead they will need to draw on a range of insights to understand and function effectively in the national and world community.

Although U.S. higher education has long sought to build and sustain di-verse campuses, it has faced many challenges in trying to achieve this goal. Prejudice and ignorance continue to exist on the nation's campuses, just as they do throughout the larger society. The United States still faces high levels of racial segregation in housing and education despite decades of legislative efforts to reduce it. Not surprisingly, new students arrive on campuses bring-ing with them a full spectrum of experiences and opinions about race. Most students complete their elementary and secondary education without ever having attended a school that enrolled significant numbers of students of other races and without living in a neighborhood where other races were well repre-sented. It is on campuses that many students have the opportunity to live and learn with students from very different backgrounds for the first time. It is not easy to overcome the legacy of prejudice and fear which divides us.

We cannot fool ourselves into thinking that public institutions will change any more quickly and easily than the societies of which they are a part. Achiev-ing the democratic goals of equity and justice for all has often required intense struggle, and as a nation we remain far from realizing them. In confronting the issues of racial and ethnic inequality in America, universities are probing one of the most painful wounds in American history.

Throughout the latter half of the twentieth century the nation's progress toward greater racial diversity as a society has been made, in part, through policies and programs that recognize race as an explicit characteristic. For example, universities with selective admissions have used race as one of several factors in determining which students to admit to their institutions. Special financial aid programs have been developed which address the economic disadvantages faced by underrepresented minority groups. Minority faculty and staff have been identified and recruited through targeted programs.

Yet affirmative action policies that use race as an explicit factor in efforts to achieve diversity or address inequities have been challenged through popular referenda and legislation and by the courts. Actions taken in several states, for example, now prohibit the consideration of race in college admissions. In such instances alternative approaches such as admitting a certain fraction of high school graduates or using family income to determine access are suggested for achieving diversity. The available evidence suggests, however, that such alternatives may not suffice.[22] Income-based strategies are unlikely to be good substitutes for race-sensitive admissions policies because there are simply too few blacks and Latinos from poor families who have strong enough academic records to qualify for admission to highly selective institutions. Furthermore, standardized admissions tests such as the Scholastic Aptitude Test (SAT), American College Test (ACT), and Law School Admission Test (LSAT) are of limited value in evaluating "merit" or determining the admissions qualifications of all students but particularly so for underrepresented minorities, for whom systematic influences make these tests even less diagnostic of their scholastic potential. There is extensive empirical data indicating that experiences tied to one's racial and ethnic identity can artificially depress standardized test performance.[23] Hence, progress toward greater diversity will likely require significant changes in strategy in the years ahead. Unfortunately, the road we have to travel is neither frequently walked nor well marked. There are very few truly diverse institutions in American society. Universities will have to blaze new trails and create new social models. To do this they will need both a commitment and a plan. Here they must take the long view, one that will require patient and persistent leadership. Progress also will require sustained vigilance and hard work as well as a great deal of help and support.

Here it is useful to consider the University of Michigan's experience in its effort to achieve diversity because it led to measurable progress and because, since it happened on our watch, we can describe some of the victories and pitfalls that occurred along the way. Like most of higher education, the history of diversity at Michigan has been complex and often contradictory. There have been many times when the institution seemed to take a step forward, only to be followed by two steps backward. Nonetheless, access and equality have always

been a central goal of this institution. An early president, James Angell, portrayed the school's mission as providing "an uncommon education for the common man," contrasting it with the role of the nation's private colleges, which served the elite of society. In the early 1800s the population of the state swelled with new immigrants, and by 1860 the regents referred "with partiality" to the "list of foreign students drawn thither from every section of our country." The first African American students arrived on campus in 1860s, and by the turn of the century Michigan's student body reflected a broad diversity with respect to race, gender, nationality, and economic background.

Although the university sustained its commitment to diversity throughout the twentieth century, its progress reflected many of the challenges facing our society during the years of overt discrimination based upon race, religion, and gender. The student disruptions of the 1960s and 1970s triggered new efforts by the university to uphold its commitments to affirmative action and equal opportunity, but again progress was limited, and a new wave of concern and protests hit the campus during the mid-1980s, just prior to the appointment of our administration. In assessing this situation, we concluded that, although the university had approached the challenge of serving an increasingly diverse population with the best of intentions, it simply had not developed and executed a plan capable of achieving sustainable results. More significantly, we believed that achieving our goals for a diverse campus would require a very major change in the institution itself.

In approaching the challenge of diversity as an exercise in institutional change, we began by engaging as many of our constituents as possible in a dialogue about goals and strategies with the hope of gradually building widespread understanding and support on and beyond our campus. Throughout 1987 and 1988 we held hundreds of discussions with groups both on and off campus, involving not only students, faculty, and staff but also alumni and state and civic leaders. Meetings were sometimes contentious, often enlightening, but rarely acrimonious. Gradually, understanding increased, and support for the effort for the evolving plan grew.

It was the long-term strategic focus of our planning which proved to be critical. The university would have to leave behind many reactive and uncoordinated efforts that had characterized its past and to move toward a more strategic approach designed to achieve long-term systemic change. In particular, we foresaw the limitations of focusing only on affirmative action—that is, on access, retention, and representation. We believed that without deeper, more fundamental institutional change these efforts by themselves would inevitably fail, as they had throughout the 1970s and 1980s.

The challenge was to persuade the university community that there was a real stake for everyone in seizing the moment to chart a more diverse future. More people needed to believe that the gains to be achieved through greater diversity would more than compensate for the necessary sacrifices. The first and vital step was to link diversity and excellence as the two most compelling goals for the institution, recognizing that these goals were not only complementary but would be tightly linked in the multicultural society characterizing our nation and the world in the future. As we moved ahead, we began to refer to the plan as "The Michigan Mandate: A Strategic Linking of Academic Excellence and Social Diversity."

The mission and goals of the Michigan Mandate were stated quite simply: (1) to recognize that diversity and excellence are complementary and compelling goals for the university and to make a firm commitment to their achievement; (2) to commit to the recruitment, support, and success of members of historically underrepresented groups among our students, faculty, staff, and leadership; and (3) to build on our campus an environment that sought, nourished, and sustained diversity and pluralism and which valued and respected the dignity and worth of every individual. A series of carefully focused strategic actions was developed to move the university toward these objectives. These strategic actions were framed by the values and traditions of the university and an understanding of its unique culture, which is characterized by a high degree of faculty and unit freedom and autonomy and animated by a highly competitive and entrepreneurial spirit.

The first phase was focused on the issue of increasing the representation of minority groups within the university community. Our approach was based primarily on providing incentives to reward success, encouraging research and evaluating new initiatives, and supporting wide-ranging experiments. Here it is important to note that the plan did not specify numerical targets, quotas, or specific rates of increase to be attained, nor did it modify the university's traditional policies for student admission.[24]

To cite just one highly successful example, we established what we called the "Target of Opportunity Program," aimed at increasing the number of minority faculty at all ranks. Traditionally, university faculties have been driven by a concern for academic specialization within their respective disciplines. This motivation is fundamentally laudable and certainly has fostered the exceptional strength and disciplinary character that we see in universities across the country; however, it also can be limiting. Too often in recent years the university had seen faculty searches that were literally "replacement" rather than "enhancement" searches. To achieve the goals of the Michigan Mandate, the university had to free itself from the constraints of this traditional perspective. Therefore, the central administration sent out the following message to the school's academic units: be vigorous and creative in identifying minority teachers/scholars who can enrich the activities of your unit. Do not be limited by concerns relating to narrow specialization; do not be concerned about the availability of a faculty slot within the unit. The principal criterion for the recruitment of a minority faculty member should be whether the individual can enhance the quality of the department. If so, resources will be made available by the central administration to recruit that person to the University of Michigan.

But there was a stick as well as a carrot to this program. Since we did not have any new resources to fund the Target of Opportunity Program, we simply totaled up our commitments throughout the year and then subtracted this amount from the university-wide budget for the following year, before allocating the remainder to traditional programs. In effect this meant that academic units that were aggressive and successful in recruiting new minority faculty were receiving base budget transfers from programs that were not as active. It took some time for this outcome to become apparent, and during this period some of the more successful academic units made very significant progress (e.g., the departments of English literature, history, and psychology) at the expense of other units that chose a more passive approach to strengthening diversity (e.g., the school of medicine).

From the outset we anticipated that there would be many mistakes in the early stages. There would be setbacks and disappointments. The important point was to make a commitment for the long range and not be distracted from this vision. This long-range viewpoint was especially important in facing up to many ongoing pressures, demands, and demonstrations presented by one special interest group or another or taking a particular stance on a narrow issue or agenda. Nevertheless, it was very difficult at times to maintain a long-term vision, as one issue or another became a litmus test of university commitment for internal and external interest groups. While these pressures were understandable and probably inevitable, the plan would succeed only if university leaders insisted on operating at a long-term strategic rather than on a short-term reactive level.

By the mid-1990s Michigan could point to significant progress in achieving diversity. The representation of underrepresented students, faculty, and staff more than doubled over the decade the effort was first put in place.[25] But, perhaps even more significant, the success of underrepresented minorities at the university improved even more remarkably, with graduation rates rising to the highest among public universities, promotion and tenure success of minority faculty members becoming comparable to their majority colleagues, and a growing number of appointments of minorities to leadership positions in the university. The campus climate not only became more accepting and supportive of diversity, but students and faculty began to come to Michigan because of its growing reputation as a campus that prized diversity. Strikingly, as the campus became more racially and ethnically diverse, the quality of its students, faculty, and academic programs increased to their highest level in history, which reinforced our contention that the aspirations of diversity and excellence were not only compatible but, in fact, highly correlated. By every measure the Michigan Mandate was a remarkable success, moving the university beyond our original goals of having a more diverse campus.

Research

One generally thinks of the research role of the university as a more recent, twentieth-century characteristic of higher education, yet blending scholarship with teaching in American higher education actually took root in the mid-nineteenth century. The public university, through on-campus scholarship and off-campus extension activities, was key to the agricultural development of the United States and then in the transition to an industrial society. World War II provided the incentive for even greater activity, as universities became important partners in the war effort, achieving scientific breakthroughs in areas such as atomic energy, radar, and computers. During this period universities learned valuable lessons in how to develop and transfer knowledge to society and how to work as full partners with government and industry to address critical national needs. In the postwar years a new social contract evolved that led to a partnership between the federal government and the American university which aimed at the support and conduct of basic research.

The basic structure of the academic research enterprise of the past half-century was set out in July 1945 in a wartime study chaired by Vannevar Bush and resulting in the seminal report, *Science: The Endless Frontier*. The central theme of the document was that, since the nation's health, economy, and military security required continual deployment of new scientific knowledge, the federal government was obligated to ensure basic scientific progress and the production of trained personnel. Federal patronage of scientific research was not only essential for the advancement of knowledge; it was also in the national interest. The Bush report stressed a corollary principle—that the government had to preserve "freedom of inquiry," to recognize that scientific progress results from the "free play of free intellects, working on subjects of their own choice, in the manner dictated by their curiosity for explanation of the unknown."[26] Since the federal government recognized that it did not have the capacity to manage effectively either the research universities or their research activities, the relationship became essentially a partnership, in which the government provided relatively unrestricted grants to support part of the research on campus.

The resulting partnership between the federal government and the nation's universities has had an extraordinary impact. Federally supported academic research programs on campuses have greatly strengthened the scientific prestige and performance of American research universities. The research produced on U.S. campuses has had great impact on society, playing a critical role in a host of areas including health care, agriculture, national defense, and economic development.[27] It has made the United States the world's leading source of fundamental scientific knowledge. It has produced well-trained scientists, engineers, and other professionals capable of applying this new knowledge. And it has laid the technological foundations of entirely new industries such as electronics and biotechnology.

The research partnership between the federal government and the universities has also reshaped the academic culture on U.S. campuses. Since most research funding is channeled directly to a single investigator or a small team of investigators, a culture rapidly developed on university campuses in which faculty were expected to become independent "research entrepreneurs," capable of attracting the federal support necessary to support and sustain their research activities. In many areas, including the physical sciences, the capacity to attract substantial research funding became an even more important criterion for faculty promotion and tenure than publication. Some institutions even adopted a freewheeling entrepreneurial spirit, best captured in the words of one university president, who boasted, "Faculty at our university can do anything they wish—provided they can attract the money to support what they want to do!"

The level of sponsored research activity is not only a measure of faculty quality and a source of graduate student support, but it is also frequently a determinant of institutional reputation. Little wonder, then, that university leaders seek ways to increase the external funding for research, particularly from the federal government. Of course, the most direct strategy for success in sponsored research involves increasing the quality of faculty and graduate students, but this takes both time and considerable investment. Many universities have found that they can unleash faculty research entrepreneurism by removing disincentives such as the bureaucracy and paperwork involved in preparing, submitting, and administering research grants and contracts and providing support through administrators knowledgeable about sponsored research opportunities and federal funding agencies. The weight given to sponsored research activity in salary, promotion, and tenure decisions and having discretionary funds indexed to indirect cost recovery can also provide positive incentives.

Because over sixty cents of every federal dollar spent for campus-based research currently goes to the biomedical sciences, corresponding to the staggering growth in the budget of the National Institutes of Health, university medical centers play a key role in expanding research activities.[28] Universities that do not have a medical center are well advised to develop a relationship with one if they wish to compete effectively for funding in key areas of the life sciences. Many universities have taken advantage of their political influence, sometimes through lobbyists, to bypass the competitive peer review process used in most federal research funding and instead persuade their congressional representatives to earmark federal legislation to provide direct funding for a pet project. In fact, such congressional earmarks now amount to over $1.5 billion per year, a substantial fraction of the $20 billion the federal government spends on campus-based research.[29]

While the partnership between the federal government and research universities has had great impact in making the American research university the world leader in both the quality of scholarship and the production of scholars, it has also had its downside. Pressures on individual faculty for success and recognition have led to major changes in the culture and governance of universities. The peer-reviewed grant system has fostered fierce competitiveness, imposed intractable work schedules, and contributed to a loss of collegiality and community. It has shifted faculty loyalties from the university to their disciplinary communities. Publication and grantsmanship have become one-dimensional criteria for academic performance and prestige, to the neglect of other important faculty activities such as teaching and service. During the past two decades there has been a significant shift in university expenditures from instructional activities to faculty research, driven in part by federal research programs but matched to a significant degree by the reallocation of internal university funds.

There has been a similar negative impact on the higher education enterprise as faculties pressure more and more institutions to adopt the culture and value system of research universities. To put it bluntly, there are many more institutions that claim a research mission, that declare themselves "research universities," and that make research success a criterion for tenure than the nation can afford. With hundreds of institutions seeking or claiming this distinction, the public is understandably confused. The immediate result is less willingness to support or tolerate the research role of higher education.

A Question of Balance

Public universities have always responded to the needs and opportunities of American society. In the nineteenth century the federal land grant acts triggered the establishment of professional schools and the development of applied research in essential areas. In the post–World War II years public universities developed a thriving capability in basic research and advanced training in response to the federal initiatives embodied in the federal government–university research partnership. Through the twentieth century public universities have provided the educational opportunities, fundamental research, and knowledge-based services needed by a changing America.

Today public higher education faces greater pressures than ever to establish its relevance to the various constituencies in society. A knowledge-driven society requires a highly skilled workforce, entrepreneurs and innovators, and new ideas and new technology to prosper in an ever more competitive global economy. The increasing pace in the creation, development, and application of knowledge requires forming new relationships with both private industry and government agencies. So, too, does the direct support of university activities by institutions in both the public and private sector. Academic institutions are drawn into new and more extensive relationships with each passing day.

We should be alert and sensitive to the new opportunities open to public higher education in the era of knowledge-driven economies. At every level—undergraduate education, graduate and professional education, research and scholarship, the provision of knowledge-intensive products and services—the public university is uniquely positioned to respond to these developments. In a sense these changes could even come quite naturally, especially considering the individualistic, entrepreneurial nature of the faculty and the loosely coupled, dynamic organizational structure of the contemporary university. Although we know that these institutions take on too many missions, we cannot deny that in doing so they are seeking to respond to the opportunities and challenges occurring in society.

Public universities are also highly vulnerable, however, particularly because they often remain in the grip of tradition, habit, public policy, and politics. It will be their special challenge to identify and protect what has been useful and truly serves the needs of our society while incorporating what is new and vital into their structures. It is certainly the case that the public university is and should be responsible to many constituents. Both the independence and competition of American universities motivate them to pay close attention to a diverse array of groups. In a very real sense an institution's distinction may be determined by its success in managing the tension among the various roles demanded by these diverse constituencies. Given the intense pressures that recent social and economic changes have brought to bear upon the public university, these institutions have a special obligation to hold tight to their core mission: to serve society in the creation, preservation, and dissemination of knowledge by maintaining the quality of their instructional and research activities.

Public colleges and universities must never lose sight of the fact that education and scholarship are the primary functions of a university, its primary contributions to society, and, hence, the most significant roles of the faculty. When universities become overly distracted by other activities, they not only compromise this core mission, but they also undermine their priorities within our society. So, too, when faculty members lose their commitment to the life of the mind, when their interest and involvement in education and research ebbs, when they begin to view their activities as a job rather than a calling, their claim on the important perquisites of the academy such as academic freedom and tenure weakens.

It is clear that a new paradigm is needed for the public university in America in order to meet the numerous challenges confronting higher education today: the rising costs of excellence, changing roles, the tension of relating to various constituencies, the demands of pluralism and diversity, and the need to achieve a new spirit of liberal learning. The new model must integrate and balance the various missions expected of these institutions, which can integrate teaching, research, and public service, just as they do undergraduate, graduate, and professional education. The model must be capable of spanning both the public and private sectors, linking the many concerns and contrasting values of the diverse constituencies served by higher education.[30]

CHAPTER FOUR

Technology

The rapid evolution to a knowledge-based society has been driven in part by the emergence of powerful new digital technologies such as computers, telecommunications, and high-speed networks. Such modern information technologies have vastly increased the capacity to know and to do things and to communicate and collaborate with others. They allow us to transmit information quickly and widely, linking distant places and diverse areas of endeavor in productive new ways. This technology allows us to form and sustain communities for work, play, and learning in ways unimaginable even a decade ago.

Of course, civilization has seen other periods of dramatic change driven by technology, but never before has a technology evolved so rapidly, increasing in power by a hundredfold every decade, obliterating the constraints of space and time, and reshaping the way we communicate, think, and learn.[1] Today information technology (IT) allows us to form and sustain communities for work, play, and learning in ways unimaginable just a decade ago. Information technology changes the relationship between people and knowledge.

The university has survived other periods of technology-driven social change with its basic structure and activities intact. But the changes driven by evolving information technology are different, since they affect the very nature of the fundamental activities of the university: creating, preserving, integrating, transmitting, and applying knowledge. More fundamentally, because information technology changes the relationship between people and knowledge, it is likely to reshape in profound ways knowledge-based institutions such as the university.

The university has already experienced significant change driven by information technology. Management and administrative processes are heavily dependent upon it, as the millions of dollars spent preparing for "Y2K" made all too apparent. Research and scholarship also rely upon information technology. For example, scientists use computers to simulate physical phenomena, networks link investigators in virtual laboratories or "collaboratories," and digital libraries provide scholars with access to knowledge resources. There is an increasing sense that new technology will also have a profound impact on teaching, freeing the classroom from the constraints of space and time and enriching students' learning through access to original materials.

Yet, while this technology has the capacity to enhance and enrich teaching and scholarship, it also poses certain threats to traditional university practices. Powerful computers and networks can be used to deliver educational services to anyone, anyplace, anytime, and are no longer confined to the campus or the academic schedule. Technology is creating powerful market forces as students evolve into active learners and consumers of educational services.

Today we are bombarded with news concerning the impact of information technology on the market place, from "e-commerce" to "edutainment" to "virtual universities" and "I-campuses." The higher education marketplace has seen the entrance of hundreds of new competitors that depend heavily upon information technology. Examples include the University of Phoenix, the Caliber Learning Network, Sylvan Learning Systems, the United States Open University, the Western Governors University, and a growing array of "dot-coms" such as Unext.com and Fathom.com. It is important to recognize that, while many of these new competitors are quite different from traditional academic institutions, they are also quite sophisticated in their pedagogy, their instructional materials, and their production and marketing of educational services. They approach the market in a highly sophisticated manner, first moving into areas that have limited competition, unmet needs, and relatively low production costs, but then moving rapidly up the value chain to more sophisticated educational programs. These IT-based education providers are already becoming formidable competitors to traditional postsecondary institutions.

The implications are particularly serious for the public university, long committed to providing broad access and to reaching beyond the campus to serve society and yet also constrained by public support and accountability to operate in a responsive and cost-effective manner. For example, the relationship between the available resources and scale of most public universities has long been dictated by norms such as student-to-faculty ratio (typically fifteen to twenty-five for most institutions). Yet, as information technology obliterates the constraints of space and time, it is likely to break this relationship. So, too, public universities will be under considerable pressure to use the new technology to expand still further their capacity to serve even broader elements of society with distance education, even if this comes at the expense of their responsibilities for traditional campus-based instruction.

The Evolution of Information Technology

It is difficult to understand and appreciate just how rapidly information technology is evolving. For the first several decades of the information age, the evolution of hardware technology followed the trajectory predicted by "Moore's Law"—that the chip density and consequent computing power for a given price doubles every eighteen months.[2] This rate corresponds to a hundredfold increase in computing speed, storage capacity, and network transmission rates every decade. Other characteristics such as memory and bandwidth are evolving even more rapidly, at rates of a thousandfold every decade or faster. Of course, if information technology is to continue to evolve at such rates, we will likely need not only new technology but also new science. But, with emerging technology such as quantum computing, molecular computers, and biocomputing, there is a significant possibility that the exponential evolution of digital technology will continue for at least a few more decades.

To put this statement in perspective, if information technology continues to evolve at its present rate, by the year 2020 the thousand-dollar notebook computer will have a computing speed of one million gigahertz, a memory of thousands of terabits, and linkages to networks at data transmission speeds of gigabits per second. Put another way, it will have a data processing and memory capacity roughly comparable to the human brain[3]—except it will be so tiny as to be almost invisible, and it will communicate with billions of other computers through wireless technology.

The last comment raises an important issue. The most dramatic impact on our world today from information technology is not in the continuing increase in computing power. It is in a dramatic increase in bandwidth, that is, the rate at which we can transmit digital information. From the three hundred bits-per-second modems of just a few years ago, we now routinely use ten to one hundred megabit-per-second local area networks in our offices and houses. Gigabit-per-second networks now provide the backbone communications to link local networks together, and, with the rapid deployment of fiber optics cables and optical switching, terabit-per-second networks are just around the corner. Fiber optics cable is currently being installed throughout the world at the astounding equivalent rate of over three thousand miles per hour. In a sense the price of data transport is becoming zero, and, with rapid advances in photonic and wireless technology, telecommunications will continue to evolve very rapidly for the foreseeable future.

Already the Internet links hundreds of millions of people. Estimates are that by the end of the decade this number will surge to billions, a substantial portion of the world's population, driven in part by the fact that most economic activity will be based on digital communication. Bell Laboratories suggests that within two decades a "global communications skin" will have evolved, linking together billions of computers that handle the routine tasks of society, from driving cars to monitoring health.

As a consequence, human interaction with the digital world—and with other humans through computer-mediated interactions—is evolving rapidly. We have moved beyond the simple text interactions of electronic mail and electronic conferencing to graphical user interfaces (e.g., the Mac or Windows world) to voice to video. With the rapid development of sensors and robotic actuators, touch and action at a distance will soon be available. With virtual reality it is likely that we will soon communicate with one another through simulated environments, through "telepresence," perhaps guiding our own software representations, our digital agents or avatars, to interact in a virtual world with those of our colleagues.

This is a very important point. A communications technology that increases in power by a thousandfold decade after decade will soon allow human interaction with essentially any degree of fidelity we wish—3-D, multimedia, telepresence, perhaps even directly linking neural networks into cyberspace, à la Neuromancer,[4] a merging of carbon and silicon.

During the decade ahead, we can be reasonably confident that information technology will become "peta-everything" (where *peta* corresponds to 10^{15}, i.e., to one million billion), in terms of processing power (operations per second), data transmission (bytes per second), and storage (bytes). IBM scientists project that within several years we will have over 10^{10} sensors, 10^9 servers, and 10^{12} software agents linked into the net. Put another way, within our lifetimes it will be possible to use a wireless device to reach anyone in the world and have any request for information answered with the touch of a button.

The Impact of Information Technology on the University

The Activities of the University

The earliest applications of information technology in higher education involved using the computer to solve mathematical problems in science and technology. Today problems that used to require the computational capacity of supercomputers can be tackled with the contemporary laptop computer. The rapid evolution of this technology is enabling scholars to address previously unsolvable problems, such as proving the four-color conjecture in mathematics, analyzing molecules that have yet to be synthesized, or simulating the birth of the universe.

The availability of high bandwidth access to instrumentation, data, and colleagues is also changing the way scholars do their work. They no longer need to focus as much on the availability of assets such as equipment or the physical proximity of colleagues and, instead, can focus on hypotheses and questions. It also has changed the way graduate students interact and participate in research, opening up the environment for broader participation. In fact, information technology is "democratizing" research by allowing researchers and institutions that would normally not have access to the sophisticated facilities and libraries of research universities to become engaged in cutting edge scholarship.

The preservation of knowledge is one of the most rapidly changing functions of the university. Throughout the centuries the intellectual focal point of the university has been its library, its collection of written works, which preserves the knowledge of civilization. Today such knowledge exists in many forms—as text, graphics, sound, algorithms, and virtual reality simulations—and it exists almost literally in the ether, distributed in digital representations over worldwide networks, accessible by anyone, and certainly not the prerogative of the privileged few in academe. The computer—or, more precisely, the "digital convergence" of various media from print to graphics to sound to sensory experiences through virtual reality—could well move beyond the printing press in its impact on knowledge.

The library is becoming less a collection house and more a center for knowledge navigation, a facilitator of information retrieval and dissemination.[5] In a sense the library and the book are merging. One of the most profound changes will involve the evolution of software agents, which will collect, organize, relate, and summarize knowledge on behalf of their human masters. The capacity to reproduce and distribute digital information with perfect accuracy at essentially zero cost has shaken the very foundations of copyright and patent law and threatens to redefine the nature of the ownership of intellectual property.[6] The legal and economic management of university intellectual property is rapidly becoming one of the most critical and complex issues facing higher education.

The traditional classroom paradigm is also being challenged by digital technology, driven not so much by the faculty, who have by and large optimized their teaching effort and their time commitments to a lecture format, but by students. Members of today's digital generation of students have spent their early lives immersed in robust, visual, electronic media—home computers, video games, cyberspace networks, and virtual reality. Unlike those of us who were raised in an era of passive, broadcast media such as radio and television, today's students expect, indeed demand, interaction. They approach learning as a "plug-and-play" experience; they are unaccustomed and unwilling to learn sequentially—to read the manual—and, instead, are inclined to plunge in and learn through participation and experimentation. Although this type of learning is quite different from the sequential, pyramidal approach of the traditional college curriculum, it may be more effective for this generation, particularly when provided through a media-rich environment.

For a time such students may tolerate the linear, sequential course paradigm of the traditional college curriculum. They still read what they are assigned, write the required term papers, and pass their exams. But this is decidedly not the way that they learn. They learn in a highly nonlinear fashion, by skipping from beginning to end and then back again and by building peer groups of learners and developing sophisticated learning networks in cyberspace. In a very real sense they build their own learning environments, which enable interactive, collaborative learning, whether we recognize and accommodate this approach or not.

The digital generation's tolerance for the traditional classroom and four-year curriculum model may not last long. Students will increasingly demand new learning paradigms more suited to their learning styles and more appropriate to prepare them for a lifetime of learning and change. They are comfortable living and playing in "e-space," and they will demand that their learning and work experiences adapt to this reality of the digital age.

Sophisticated networks and software environments can be used to break the classroom loose from the constraints of space and time and make learning available to anyone, anyplace, at any time. The simplest approach uses multimedia technology via the Internet to enable distance learning. Yet many believe that effective computer network–mediated learning will not be simply an Internet extension of correspondence or broadcast courses. Since learning requires the presence of communities, the key impact of information technology may be the development of computer-mediated communications and communities that are released from the constraints of space and time. There is already sufficient experience with such asynchronous learning networks to conclude that, at least for many subjects and when appropriately constructed, the computer-mediated distance learning process is just as effective as the classroom experience.[7]

The attractiveness of computer-mediated distance learning is obvious for adult learners whose work or family obligations prevent attendance at conventional campuses. But perhaps more surprising is the degree to which many on-campus students are now using computer-based distance learning to augment their traditional education. Broadband digital networks can be used to enhance the multimedia capacity of hundreds of classrooms across campus and link them with campus residence halls and libraries. Electronic mail, teleconferencing, and collaboration technology are transforming our public institutions from hierarchical, static organizations to networks of more dynamic and egalitarian communities. Distance learning based on computer network–mediated paradigms allows universities to push their campus boundaries outward to serve learners anywhere, anytime.

In the near term, at least, traditional models of education will coexist with new learning paradigms, providing a broader spectrum of learning opportunities in the years ahead. Information technology will accelerate the transitions from student to learner, from teacher to designer/coach/consultant, and from alumnus to lifelong member of a learning community. And with these transitions and new options will come both an increasing ability and responsibility on the part of learners to select, design, and control the learning environment.

The Form and Function of the University

Colleges and universities are structured along intellectual lines, organized into schools and colleges, departments and programs, which have evolved over the decades. Furthermore, the governance, leadership, and management of the contemporary university are also structured to reflect this intellectual organization as well as the academic values of the university, such as academic freedom and institutional autonomy, rather than the command-communication-control administrative pyramid characterizing most organizations in business and government. The "contract" between members of the faculty and the university also reflects the unusual character of academic values and roles, the practice of tenure being perhaps the most familiar example.

Just as the university is challenged in adapting to new forms of teaching and research stimulated by rapidly evolving information technology, so too its organization, governance, management, and relationships to students, faculty, and staff will require serious reevaluation and almost certain change. For example, the new tools of scholarship and scholarly communication are eroding conventional disciplinary boundaries and extending the intellectual span, interests, and activities of faculty far beyond traditional organizational units such as departments, schools, or campuses. This is particularly the case with younger faculty members whose interests and activities frequently cannot be characterized by traditional disciplinary terms.

Beyond driving a restructuring of the intellectual disciplines, information technology is likely to force a significant disaggregation of the university on both the horizontal (e.g., academic disciplines) and vertical (e.g., student services) scale. Faculty activity and even loyalty is increasingly associated with intellectual communities that extend across multiple institutions, frequently on a global scale. New providers are emerging which can better handle many traditional university services, ranging from student housing to facilities management to health care. Colleges and universities will increasingly face the question of whether they should continue their full complement of activities or "outsource" some functions to lower-cost and frequently higher-quality providers, relying on new paradigms such as e-business and knowledge management.

It has become increasingly important that university planning and decision making not only take account of technological developments and challenges but also draw upon the expertise of people with technological backgrounds. Yet all too often university leaders, governing boards, and even faculties ignore the rapid evolution of this technology, treating it more as science fiction than as representing serious institutional challenges and opportunities. To a degree this response is not surprising, since in the early stages new technologies sometimes look decidedly inferior to long-standing practices. For example, few would regard the current generation of computer-mediated distance learning programs as providing the socialization function associated with undergraduate education in a residential campus environment. Yet there have been countless instances of technologies, from personal computers to the Internet, which were characterized by technology learning curves much steeper than conventional practices. Such "disruptive technologies" have demonstrated the capacity to destroy entire industries, as the explosion of e-business makes all too apparent.[8]

In positioning itself for this future of technology-driven change, universities should recognize several facts of life in the digital age. First, robust, high-speed networks are not only becoming available but are also absolutely essential for knowledge-driven enterprises such as universities. Powerful computers and network appliances are available at reasonable prices to students, but they will require a supporting network infrastructure. There will continue to be diversity in the technology needs of faculty, with many of the most intensive needs likely to arise in parts of the university such as the arts and humanities in which strong external support may not be available. All universities face major challenges in keeping pace with the profound evolution of information and its implication for their activities.

The Postsecondary Education Enterprise

The "e-economy" is growing at an annual rate of 175 percent. It is estimated that by 2004 the e-economy will be seven trillion dollars, roughly 20 percent of the global economy.[9] Beyond providing the graduates and knowledge needed by this digital economy, the contemporary university must be able to function in an increasingly digital world, in the way that it manages its resources; relates to clients, customers, and providers; and conducts its affairs. E-commerce, e-business, and the e-economy must become integral parts of the university's future if it is to survive the digital age.

Information technology eliminates the barriers of space and time, and new competitive forces such as virtual universities and for-profit education providers enter the marketplace to challenge credentialing.[10] The weakening influence of traditional regulations and the emergence of new competitive forces, driven by changing societal needs, economic realities, and technology, are likely to drive a massive restructuring of the higher education enterprise. From experiences with other restructured sectors of the economy such as health care, transportation, communications, and energy, we could expect to see a significant reorganization of higher education, complete with the mergers, acquisitions, new competitors, and new products and services that have characterized other economic transformations.

A key factor in this restructuring has been the emergence of new aggressive for-profit education providers that are able to access the private capital markets (over four billion dollars in the last year). Most of these new entrants, such as the University of Phoenix and Jones International University, are focusing on the adult education market. Some, such as Unext.com, have aggressive growth strategies, beginning with addressing the needs for educating corporate employees in the area of business. Using online education, they are able to offer cost reductions of 60 percent or more over conventional corporate training programs, since they avoid travel and employee time off.[11] They are investing heavily (over one hundred million dollars in 2000) in developing sophisticated instructional content, pedagogy, and assessment measures, and they are likely to move up the learning curve to offer broader educational programs, both at the undergraduate level and in professional areas such as engineering and law. In a sense, therefore, the initial focus of new for-profit entrants on low-end adult education is misleading, since in five years or less their capacity to compete with traditional colleges and universities could become formidable indeed.

It is appropriate to make one further comment concerning the "digital divide," the widening gap between those who can afford access to information technology and those who cannot. Such stratification in society among the haves and have-nots would be of great concern if information technology were not evolving so rapidly. This technology, however, is migrating rapidly toward "thin client" systems, in which the personal computer becomes an inexpensive and ubiquitous commodity available to anyone and everyone, like today's television or telephone, while the real investment occurs in the supporting network infrastructure.

In reality the concern should not be with the digital divide but, rather, with the growing gap in prosperity, power, and social well-being between those who have access to quality education and those who do not, because of economic circumstances, jobs, families, or location. From this perspective the development of technology-based methods for delivering educational services such as asynchronous learning networks and virtual universities may actually narrow the educational gap by providing universal access to quality educational opportunities.

This point is important. Rather than further stratifying society, information technology will more likely become a democratizing force. It will distribute learning opportunities more broadly than the currently highly selective education system is able or inclined to do. Moreover, it will also likely democratize scholarship by providing a broader spectrum of institutions, scholars, and perhaps even lay citizens with access to the rich intellectual resources of the most prestigious institutions. Although this democratizing character may threaten both elite colleges and research universities, it may also be key to meeting the mass educational needs of our knowledge-driven society.

Institutional Strategies

We now turn to a series of recommendations for public universities and their leaders, both faced not only with complex and costly decisions concerning the acquisition and use of information technology but, more broadly, with the task of developing institutional strategies to cope with the digital age. Discussions with campus leaders suggest that most attention is being focused on near-term issues—for example, determining what information technology infrastructure for campus-based activities is necessary and how to finance it. Although academic leaders are most concerned with the implications of electronic learning environments and distance learning, many campus administrators and IT professionals are immersed in the challenge of upgrading antiquated administrative computer systems and replacing them with enterprise resource planning, knowledge management, or e-business systems, at rather considerable expense.

What, then, do presidents, trustees, and other leaders of academic institutions need to know? What new technologies are they likely to encounter next? Where are they likely to see the first impact on their institutions? Where will various possible decisions likely take them? Addressing these questions may be a high priority for some university leaders. But a greater number of leaders are more concerned with how they create an academic environment that students and faculty need for quality teaching, learning, and scholarship. They recognize that establishing this environment will require a tradeoff of investments between bricks (conventional physical infrastructure) and clicks (information technology). And, increasingly, many of them realize that they can no longer approach these issues in isolation. They must seek partners, both within the higher education enterprise and beyond, to include the commercial and government sectors and possibly even international collaborators.

It is important that both planning and decisions address the issues and realities of the present. Technology really does not tell us what will happen or what to do next year. The more distant the future, the more exciting and distracting it can become. Universities should always keep in front of them the need to make decisions about issues of today, even as they consider and influence possibilities for the future.

Yet university leaders need a long-term strategic context to enable near-term decisions. It is important to make informed investments and launch creative initiatives today but within a framework for the longer term. Among all of our social institutions universities are particularly obliged to look to the long term, seeking not just the quick fix but also longer-term strategies and necessary commitments.

We have stressed the degree to which digital technology is reshaping both society and its institutions. Its exponential pace of evolution drives rapid, profound, unpredictable, and discontinuous change. It is a disruptive technology that is eroding, even obliterating, conventional constraints such as space, time, and monopoly and reshaping both the structure and boundaries of institutions.[12] More specifically, decisions involving digital technology raise very key strategic issues for colleges and universities requiring both the attention and understanding at the very highest levels of institution leadership. Technology is comparable in importance to other key strategic issues such as finance, government relations, and private fund raising in which final responsibility must rest with the president. The pace of change is too great and the consequences of decisions too significant simply to delegate to others such as faculty committees or chief information officers. Leadership on technology issues must come from the president and the provost, with the encouragement and support of the governing board.

Digital technology is pervasive, affecting every aspect and function of the university, from teaching and scholarship to organization, financing, and management. Yet the challenge on many campuses is that there are too many people doing their own thing. Although many faculty, staff, and students are knowledgeable about the applications of technology in their narrow field of interest, gaining broader awareness is a challenge. Furthermore, many faculty members are simply unaware of the potential applications and implications of technology for their own activities, much less the broader university. There is a digital divide at many levels throughout the contemporary university.

It is difficult to coordinate the various silos of activities in the public university into a coherent structure. A technology strategy must be systemic, drawing together diverse applications such as instruction, research, libraries, museums, archives, academic computing, and university presses. Yet it must also recognize and accommodate the very great diversity among university activities. Like a biological ecology, a technology strategy should be open, complex, and adaptive, with sufficient robustness and diversity to respond and adapt to the varied and ever-changing needs of academic programs.

Yet information and communications technologies are tools for creating and enhancing connectivity, of strengthening the sense of community across distance and time lines. More abstractly, this technology supports the knowledge environment to enable the creation and dissemination of knowledge and the preservation of knowledge communities.

Identifying and implementing the organizational and management structure appropriate for digital technology is a major issue, and barrier, at most institutions. All organizations, whether in higher education, commerce, or government, face a quandary: should they centralize, through growth or mergers, becoming conglomerates to take advantage of economies of scale, standardization, and globalization? Or should they decentralize, seeking autonomy, empowerment, and flexibility at the level of unit execution while encouraging diversity, localization, and customization? Which path should they choose?

Actually, both—yet neither. There is no unique way to organize technology-based activities, although it is likely that most colleges and universities are currently far from an effective or optimal configuration. Furthermore, *flexibility* and *adaptability* are the watchwords for any such organization during a time of extraordinarily rapid technological change. The challenge is to orchestrate and coordinate the multiple activities and diverse talent on campus which explore and transform their activities with information technology. The key to achieving these transformations is to build layered organization and management structures.[13] At the highest, centralized level one should seek a clear institutional vision, driven by broadly accepted values, guided by common heuristics, and coordinated through standard protocols. Below this, at the level of execution, one should encourage diversity, flexibility, and innovation. In a sense institutions should seek to centralize the guiding vision and strategy (i.e., where the institution should head) while decentralizing the decision-making process and activities that determine how to achieve these institutional goals. Universities should seek to synchronize rather than homogenize their activities. Rather than obliterating silos of activity, one should use standard protocols and infrastructure to link them together, creating porous walls between them.

Public universities will face particularly serious challenges, since they are accountable to public authority and therefore averse to risk, and IT is an area in which risk and success are closely linked. A large public university is too big, and its authority too widely dispersed, to make rapid decisions. Individuals and units need to be able to make many small, rapid, risky, and relatively inexpensive decisions from below and to have the opportunities and resources to experiment.

Historically, technology has been seen as a capital expenditure for universities or as an experimental tool to be made available to only a few. In the future higher education should conceive of information technology both as an investment and as a strategic asset for universities, critical to their academic mission and their administrative services, which must be provided on a robust basis to the entire faculty, staff, and student body. Colleges and universities must learn an important lesson from the business community: investment in robust information technology represents the stakes for survival in the age of knowledge. If you are not willing to invest in this technology, then you may as well accept being confined to a backwater in the knowledge economy, if you survive at all.

Just as with the organization and management of the university, administrators need to seek a layered or tiered architecture for digital technology which is characterized by a unified "back end," or centralized infrastructure, and diverse and flexible "front-end" applications. Modularity and tiering are the keys to effective technology acquisition and implementation strategies. Connectedness and interoperability are key criteria in IT infrastructure design.

We are in the very early stages of technology-driven tectonic shifts that will reshape public institutions and their enterprise. Although the university as a social institution has survived largely intact for over a millennium, it has done so in part because of its extraordinary ability to change and adapt to serve society. Beyond vision, organization, and investment, universities need a well-defined set of operational strategies and tactics. Technology-driven transformation should be viewed as steps up a ladder rather down a road, since at each level a new set of challenges will arise. Timing and the pace of change are all-important; if they are incompatible with the capacity of the institution, strong resistance and possibly even chaos can result.

It is important to challenge an institution with high expectations. But leaders should also recognize that for most institutions the limiting factors will be the availability of human resources. There are few among the faculty or administrative staff who fully understand the nature and implications of digital technology. There are even fewer who are capable of leading a process of change. While universities typically look to their IT organizations or libraries for such leadership, it is more likely to exist among the faculty, with those who have actually utilized state-of-the-art digital technology in the fundamental academic activities of the university, teaching and research.

Yet there is another constituency capable of driving change in the university: students. This should not be surprising to those familiar with the history of higher education, since students have frequently taken on this role, from stimulating new academic programs to organizing the institution. Furthermore, many students, particularly at the graduate level, supply much of the intellectual momentum of the university through their research and teaching activities. As we noted earlier, the plug-and-play generation is more comfortable with digital technology than most of the current generation of university faculty and leaders. Young students not only are more adept in applying the technology to their own activities but frequently play key roles in its development, as the numerous IT startups led by undergraduate and graduate students make apparent. With technology, just as with other issues, students are likely to be a powerful force driving change in higher education.

The Challenge of University Leadership in the Digital Age

The digital age poses many challenges and opportunities for the contemporary university, just as it does for society and its other institutions. There is no evidence of slowdown in the pace of evolution of information technology, by any measure or characteristic. In fact, we appear to be on a superexponential technology learning curve that is likely to continue for at least the next several decades. Photonic technology is evolving at twice the rate of computer technology, and miniaturization and wireless technologies are evolving even faster. Furthermore, we are likely to be surprised by unanticipated technologies at more frequent intervals, just as we were with the personal computer in 1980 and the Internet browser in 1994. Getting people to think about the implications of accelerating technology learning curves is important, since the event horizons are much closer than most realize.

For most of the history of higher education in America we have expected students to travel to a physical place, a campus, to participate in a pedagogical process involving tightly integrated studies based mostly on lectures and seminars by recognized experts. Yet, as the constraints of time and space—and perhaps even reality itself—are relieved by information technology, will the university as a physical place continue to be relevant?

In the near term, a decade or less, it seems likely that the university as a physical place, a community of scholars and a center of culture, will remain. Information technology will be used to augment and enrich the traditional activities of the university, in much their traditional forms. To be sure, the current arrangements of higher education may shift. For example, students may choose to distribute their college education among residential campuses, commuter colleges, and online or virtual universities. They may also assume more responsibility for and control over their education. In this sense information technology is rapidly becoming a liberating force in society, not only freeing us from the mental drudgery of routine tasks but also linking us in ways we never dreamed possible. Furthermore, the new knowledge media enables us to build and sustain new types of learning communities, free from the constraints of space and time. Higher education must define its relationship with these emerging possibilities in order to create a compelling vision for its future as it enters the next millennium.

For the longer term, two or more decades from now, the future of the university becomes less certain. Although the digital age will provide a wealth of opportunities for the future, we must take great care not simply to extrapolate about the past but also to examine the full range of possibilities for the future. There is clearly a need to explore new forms of learning and learning institutions which are capable of sensing and understanding the change and of engaging in the strategic processes necessary to adapt or control it.

While the threats posed to traditional roles and practices may serve usefully as the warning shots across the bow of colleges and universities—particularly their faculties—university leadership should not be simply reacting to threats but, instead, be acting positively and strategically to exploit the opportunities presented by information technology. As we have suggested, this technology will provide great opportunities to improve the quality of education and scholarship. It will allow colleges and universities to serve society in new ways, perhaps more closely aligned with their fundamental academic mission and values. It will also provide strong incentives for building new alliances among diverse educational institutions, thereby providing systemic opportunities for improving the quality of higher education in America.

Thus, while college and university leaders should recognize and understand the threats posed by rapidly evolving information technology to their institutions, they should seek to transform these threats into opportunities for leadership. Information technology should be viewed as a tool of immense power to use in enhancing the fundamental roles and missions of their institutions.

CHAPTER FIVE

Market Forces

We generally think of public higher education as a public enterprise, shaped by public policy and actions to serve a civic purpose. Yet market forces also act on public colleges and universities. Students seek educational programs. Government and industry procure and sponsor research. An array of public and private organizations seeks professional services. So, too, academic institutions must compete for students, faculty, and resources. To be sure, the higher education marketplace is a strange one, heavily subsidized and shaped by public investment so that prices are always considerably less than true costs. If prices such as tuition are largely fictitious, even more so is much of the value of education services based on myths and vague perceptions, such as the importance of a college degree as a ticket to success or the prestige associated with certain institutions.

Yet at the same time, in part driven by financial pressures and other priorities, governments at the state and federal level have increasingly accepted the argument that a college education should be viewed less as a public investment in an educated citizenry and more as a consumer good of primary benefit to the student. Today the buzzwords *accountability* and *outcomes* often replace the earlier language of "access" and "opportunity" as the basis for public investment in both students and institutions. At the state and institutional levels it is also the case that those whom the market and now public policy reward through financial aid programs are students who show the greatest promise of academic achievement regardless of need. Yet the determination of academic potential for merit-based financial awards is generally based on simplistic measures such as standardized test scores and high school grade point average, student characteristics that are frequently influenced by socio-economic factors such as family wealth.

In the past most colleges and universities served local or regional populations. Although there was competition among institutions for students, faculty, and resources—at least in the United States—the extent to which institutions controlled the awarding of degrees, that is, credentialing, led to a tightly controlled competitive market. Universities enjoyed a monopoly over advanced education because of geographical location and their monopoly on credentialing through the awarding of degrees. Statewide systems of public universities have operated essentially as cartels, with roles and markets carefully prescribed. Today, however, all of these market constraints are being challenged by greater dependence on market forces and less on regulation. The growth in the size and complexity of the postsecondary enterprise is creating an expanding array of students and educational providers. Technology is allowing new competitors to bypass the traditional barriers to entering the higher education marketplace such as large capital costs and accreditation.

As a result, higher education is rapidly evolving from a loosely federated system of colleges and universities serving traditional students from local communities to, in effect, a global knowledge and learning industry driven by strong market forces. With the emergence of new competitive forces and the weakening influence of traditional regulations, the higher education enterprise is evolving like other "deregulated" industries, such as health care or communications or energy. Yet, in contrast to these other industries, which have been restructured as government regulation has disappeared, the global knowledge industry is being unleashed both by the changing educational needs of a knowledge-driven society and the role of information technology in obliterating the constraints of space and time on human activities. Higher education is breaking loose from the moorings of physical campuses, even as its credentialing monopoly begins to erode. And, as society becomes ever more dependent upon new knowledge and educated people, upon knowledge workers, this global knowledge business must be viewed clearly as one of the most active growth industries of our times.

This perspective of a market-driven restructuring of higher education as an industry, while perhaps both alien and distasteful to the academy, is nevertheless an important framework for considering the future of the university. While the postsecondary education market may have complex cross-subsidies and numerous public misconceptions, it is nevertheless very real and demanding, with the capacity to reward those who can respond to rapid change and punish those who cannot. Universities will have to learn to cope with the competitive pressures of this marketplace while preserving the most important of their traditional values and character.

The Winds of Change

The challenge of meeting the educational needs of a growing and highly diverse population of students is compounded by the need to transform pedagogical methods to accommodate active, collaborative, and technology-based learning. The current people- and knowledge-intensive paradigm of the university appears to be incapable of containing costs and enhancing productivity. Yet, even as the demand for educational services has grown and the operating costs to provide these services have risen, public support for higher education has flattened and declined over the past several decades relative to other public priorities. Rapidly evolving information and communications technologies are obliterating the constraints of space, time, and monopoly, allowing new competitors to provide educational services to anyone at anyplace and anytime, confined no longer to the campus, the academic schedule, or the academic culture. Colleges and universities are caught up in an escalating competition for better students and faculty, more research funding, winning athletic programs, more prestige, and the resources to sustain both their current activities and achieve their ambition.

The experiences of other sectors of the economy such as banking, health care, telecommunications, and energy provide ample evidence that dramatic changes in demand, cost, and technology can drive fundamental change in the marketplace which requires a restructuring of the industry. We believe that such is likely the case with higher education.

Yet, in addition to these forces of change, we should also add public policy, since in recent years, at both the state and national level, public officials have developed legislation, policies, and programs with the clear intent of stimulating a much more competitive marketplace in higher education. At the level of the states the long-standing policy of providing sufficient public funding to enable public universities to offer a college education at only a nominal cost has been replaced by the expectation that universities will charge—and students will pay—tuition and fees that are sufficient to compensate for educational costs beyond what the states are willing or able to provide.

Throughout most of the twentieth century the growth of higher education in America was sustained by growing public commitments. During this period public institutions saw significant growth in their primary source of support, state appropriations from general tax revenues. Tuition and other student fees played a relatively minor role. This situation began to change in the late 1970s, as public support first began to slow and then actually began to decline.[1] At all levels of government—federal, state, and local—public resistance to taxation coupled with shifting priorities led to constraints on tax revenues and the allocation of limited public resources to other priorities such as health care and corrections. As a result, public support of higher education declined throughout the 1980s and early 1990s. Although it recovered somewhat with the strong economy of the late 1990s, state appropriations turned downward again in 2001 as the national economy began to weaken.

During periods of declining appropriations public universities have been forced to tighten their belts, cut programs, and increase productivity. Yet it was impossible for cost containment efforts alone to compensate for the erosion in state support during the 1980s and 1990s. It was necessary to shift a larger share of the burden for the support of higher education in public universities to students and parents through increased tuition and fees, which from an economic perspective was quite a reasonable approach. State tax support of public universities had provided a strong subsidy for higher education, allowing these institutions to charge a price, tuition, considerably below actual costs. As this public subsidy declined, the price of a college education at a public university, as represented by tuition, naturally increased.[2] Of course, in an absolute sense the tuition levels at public universities were still only a small fraction of those at private universities—for example, for the 2000–2001 academic year the average tuition for undergraduates enrolled in public colleges and universities was $3,510 per year, compared to an average of $25,000 for the Ivy League universities.

In many states this shift from the provision of a college education as an essentially free good to one with an associated price, namely tuition, was driven as much by the desire to create market forces in public higher education as to shift state funding to other priorities such as corrections and health care. Whether stated or not, it was the clear intent of public leaders at both the state and national level to shift more of the burden for the support of higher education from the shoulders of the taxpayer to those who benefited most, students and parents. Yet, despite the strong economic rationale for increasing tuition at public colleges and universities in the face of declining public support, this action has stimulated strong concerns from citizens and consequent political action to constrain tuition levels. Even a modest increase in the tuition levels of public colleges and universities triggers strong negative reactions from students and parents, harsh criticism from the press, and political pressure or direct legislative action to limit fee increases. Unfortunately, this concern and activism have not translated back into broad public support for renewed investment in higher education. Today public higher education is caught on the horns of a dilemma, for, although the public expects—indeed, demands—broad access to high-quality public education, it is unwilling to pay for this benefit either through taxes or tuition.

The second example of a shift toward market philosophies is provided by the changing nature of federal student financial aid policies. As we noted in chapter 3, there has been a shift in the emphasis of federal support of higher education, away from institutional grants for academic programs or facilities and toward students and parents through a complex system of financial aid programs. These programs have also evolved over the years from grants to loans and, most recently, to tax benefits. When coupled with the broadening of eligibility for federal aid to middle- and upper-middle-income students, this represents a shift in the priorities of federal financial aid programs away from providing access to educational opportunities to those unable to afford a college education. Equally significant, the shift in federal support from institutions to individuals reflects a conscious effort to let the marketplace determine the allocation of federal dollars through student choice. As F. King Alexander notes, this change from direct federal funding of colleges and universities to funding individuals through financial aid programs represents a deeper philosophical shift, from the view that higher education is a public good benefiting all of society to one in which it is an individual benefit.[3]

The Restructuring of the Higher Education Enterprise

As the need for advanced education becomes more intense, there are already signs that some institutions are responding to market forces and moving far beyond their traditional geographical areas to compete for students and resources. Colleges and universities increasingly view themselves as competing in a national or even global marketplace. Even within regions, such as local communities, colleges and universities that used to enjoy a geographical monopoly now find that other institutions are establishing beachheads through extension services, distance learning, and even branch campuses. With advances in communication, transportation, and global commerce, several universities in the United States and abroad increasingly view themselves as international institutions, competing in the global marketplace.

Beyond competition among colleges and universities there are new educational providers entering the marketplace with the aim of providing cost-competitive, high-quality education to selected markets.[4] Sophisticated for-profit entities such as the University of Phoenix (UOP) and Unext.com are moving into markets throughout the United States, Europe, and Asia. Already more than a thousand virtual universities are listed in college directories with over one million students enrolled in their programs. It has been estimated that today there are over sixteen hundred corporate training schools in the United States providing both education and training to employees at the college level. Industry currently spends over $66 billion per year on corporate training. It is only a matter of time before some of these programs enter the marketplace to provide educational services more broadly.

Although education contributes almost 10 percent of GDP in the United States, strong public subsidy has provided little incentive in the past to access the $16 trillion U.S. capital market. Higher education alone represents a market of $225 billion, of which only $5 billion is served by the for-profit sector. As Stan Davis and Jim Botkin have noted, in the past the principal barrier to private sector entry into higher education has been the huge sunk cost and unprofitability of the traditional campus-based university. Today, however, technology and changing societal needs enable the entrance of new focused, low-cost, and profitable private sector competitors.[5]

In recent years we have seen an explosion in the number of new competitors in the higher education marketplace. It is estimated that in 2001 there were over 650 for-profit and proprietary educational providers in the United States. For the first time in U.S. history the for-profit sector perceives higher education as a significant investment opportunity. As an investment report by NationsBanc Montgomery Securities concluded: "Education represents the most fertile new market for investors in many years. It has a combination of large size (approximately the same as health care), disgruntled users, low utilization of technology, and the highest strategic importance of any activity in which this country engages. Finally, existing managements are sleepy after years of monopoly."[6] Higher education generates an enormous amount of cash, and it is furthermore heavily subsidized by states and the federal government through financial aid programs. It is a very attractive target for for-profit providers.[7]

Many of these efforts target highly selective markets, such as the University of Phoenix, which already operates over one hundred learning centers in thirty-two states, serving over 100,000 students. UOP targets the educational needs of adult learners whose career and family responsibilities make access to traditional colleges and universities difficult. By relying on highly structured courses formatted for the student's convenience and taught by practitioners as part-time instructors, UOP has developed a highly competitive paradigm.

Other for-profit industry-based educational institutions are evolving rapidly, such as Sylvan Learning Systems and its subsidiaries, Athena University, Computer Learning Centers, and the World Learning Network. They join an existing array of proprietary institutions such as the DeVry Institute of Technology and ITT Educational Services. Not far behind are a number of sophisticated industrial training programs, such as Motorola University and the Disney Institute, originally formed to meet internal corporate training needs but now exploring the opportunity to offer educational services to broader markets. Of particular note here are the efforts of information services companies such as Accenture and McKinsey which are increasingly viewing education as just another information service.

An extraordinarily diverse array of new products, services, and providers are entering the e-learning marketplace, from curriculum and content development (OnlineLearning, NYR Online, educational publishers), software learning environments (Lotus, Convene, WebCT, Blackboard.com, Eduprise.com), teleconferencing (Caliber, One-Touch), and educational management organizations (Unext.com, University of Phoenix). Of particular interest is the rapid evolution of higher education Web portals that bring for-profit companies into direct contact with students, through Web sites that link useful information for students with advertising and e-commerce.

Between 1988 and 1998 enrollment in for-profit degree-granting institutions grew by 59 percent to 365,000 students. Nationwide for-profit institutions now constitute 28 percent of the two-year college market and 8 percent of the four-year market. Most focus on career-oriented, hands-on, and customer-focused programs and services that are particularly effective in meeting the needs of nontraditional students.[8] It is important to recognize that, although many of these new competitors are quite different than traditional academic institutions, they are also quite sophisticated both in their pedagogy, their instructional materials, and their production and marketing of educational services. For example, Caliber Learning and the British Open University invest heavily in the production of sophisticated learning materials and environments, utilizing state-of-the-art knowledge concerning learning methods from cognitive sciences and psychology. They develop alliances with well-known academic institutions to take advantage of their brand names (e.g., Wharton in business and MIT in technology). They approach the market in a highly sophisticated manner, as we noted earlier, first moving into areas with limited competition, unmet needs, and relatively low production costs, such as large undergraduate survey courses amenable to mass production and commodification, but then moving rapidly up the value chain to more lucrative, highly customized professional education.

Traditional colleges and universities tend to focus on inputs such as entering student quality and metrics such as expenditure per student as well as upon process dictated by established student-to-faculty ratios, credit hours, and degree programs. The new for-profit providers focus instead on outputs, on measuring student learning and the competency achieved by particular programs, forms of pedagogy, and faculty. They have set aside the factory model of student credit hours, seat time, and degree programs long preferred by the higher education establishment and are moving, instead, to anytime, anyplace, any length, anyone flexibility, customized to the needs of the learner and verifiable in terms of its effectiveness.

In the face of such competition traditional colleges and universities are also responding with an array of new activities. Most university extension programs are moving rapidly to provide Internet-based instruction in their portfolios. University collaboratives such as the National Technological University and the Midwest University Consortium for International Activities have become quite formidable competitors. They are being joined by a number of new organizations such as the Western Governors University, the Michigan Virtual University, and an array of university-stimulated dot-coms such as UNext.com and versity.com which aim to exploit both new technology and new paradigms of learning.

Yet not all such efforts are successful. The Western Governors University, a venture started by seventeen western states, opened its online doors to much fanfare in 1999 but has enrolled only a few hundred students. The British Open University opened a North American subsidiary, the United States Open University, in the late 1990s, only to close it in 2002 as it became clear that the open university paradigm did not adapt easily to the American marketplace. The California Virtual University, a project launched in 1997, folded in 1999, citing financial problems. The Michigan Virtual University, launched by a consortium of public universities in the state, has been somewhat more successful, first targeting the corporate marketplace and more recently branching out into K-12 teacher training; by 2002 it had enrolled over five thousand students.[9]

The academy has long been accustomed to deciding what it wishes to teach, how it will teach it, and where and when the learning will occur. Students must travel to the campus to learn. They must work their way through the bureaucracy of university admissions, counseling, scheduling, and residential living. And they must pay for the privilege. If they navigate through the maze of requirements, they are finally awarded a certificate to recognize their experience—a college degree. This process is sustained by accrediting associations, professional societies, and state and federal governments.

This carefully regulated and controlled enterprise could be eroded considerably by several factors. First, the great demand for advanced education and training cannot be met by such a carefully rationed and controlled enterprise. Second, the expanding marketplace will attract new competitors who will exploit new learning paradigms and increasingly threaten traditional providers. And, perhaps most important of all, newly emerging information technology will not only eliminate the constraints of space and time, but it will also transform students into learners and consumers. Open learning environments will provide learners with choice in the marketplace—access to learning opportunities, knowledge-rich networks, collections of scholars and expert consultants, and other avenues for learning.

The Achilles' heel of the modern university is its overextension, its attempt to control all aspects of learning. Universities provide courses at the undergraduate, graduate, and professional level. They support residential colleges, professional schools, lifelong learning, athletics, libraries, museums, hospitals, and entertainment. They have assumed responsibility for all manner of activities beyond classroom education: housing and feeding students, providing police and other security protection, counseling and financial services—even operating power plants on many midwestern campuses. Yet market competition tends to seek out and exploit weakness and underperformance, a frequent consequence of overextension.

Today's monolithic universities, at least as full-service organizations, are at considerable risk. These institutions have become highly vertically integrated over the past several decades. Yet today we are already beginning to see a growing number of differentiated competitors for many of these activities. Universities are under increasing pressure to spin off or sell off or close down parts of their traditional operations in the face of this new competition and to examine the contributions and cost-effectiveness of other heretofore integral components.

The most significant impact of a deregulated higher education "industry" may be to break apart this monolith, much as other industries have been broken apart through deregulation. As universities are forced to evolve from being "faculty centered" to "learner centered," they may well find it necessary to unbundle their many functions, ranging from admissions and counseling to instruction and certification. Capitalizing on one's strengths and outsourcing the rest is commonplace in many industries. Consider, for example, the computer industry, in which webs of alliances exist among hardware developers, manufacturers, software developers, and marketers of hardware and software. These are constantly being created and modified in response to competitive dynamics.

This idea can be applied to academia. While universities are very good at producing intellectual content for education, there may be other organizations that are much better at packaging and delivering that content, such as the publishing or entertainment industry. While in the past universities have had a monopoly on certifying learning, there may be others, whether they are accreditation agencies or other kinds of providers, more capable of assessing and certifying that learning has occurred. Many other university activities—for example, financial management and facilities management—might be outsourced and better handled by specialists.

Throughout most of its history higher education has been a cottage industry. Individual courses are a handicraft, made-to-order product. Faculty members design from scratch the courses they teach, whether they are for a dozen or several hundred students. They may use standard textbooks from time to time—although most do not—but their organization, their lectures, their assignments, and their exams are developed for the particular course at the time it is taught. Students would be surprised to know that their tuition dollars per hour of lecture at the more elite universities amount to over fifty dollars, the price of a ticket to a college football game.

In a very real sense the industrial age bypassed the university. So, too, social institutions for learning—schools, colleges, and universities—continue to favor programs and practices based more on past traditions than upon contemporary needs. Yet it may be quite wrong to suggest that higher education needs to evolve into a mass production or broadcasting mode to keep pace with civilization. This was the evolutionary path taken by K-12 education, with disastrous consequences. Besides, even industry is rapidly discarding the mass production approach of the twentieth century and moving toward products more customized to particular markets.

Our ability to introduce new, more effective avenues for learning, not merely new media in which to convey information, will change the nature of higher education. This will bring with it new modes of organization, new relationships among universities and between universities and the private sector. The individual handicraft model for course development may give way to a much more complex method of creating instructional materials. Even the standard packaging of an undergraduate education into "courses," in the past required by the need to have all the students in the same place at the same time, may no longer be necessary with new forms of asynchronous learning. Of course, it will be a challenge to break the handicraft model while still protecting the traditional independence of the faculty to determine curricular content. Beyond that, there is also a long-standing culture in which most faculty members assume that they own the intellectual content of their courses and are free to market them to others for personal gain, for example, through textbooks or off-campus consulting services. But universities may have to restructure these paradigms and renegotiate ownership of the intellectual products represented by classroom courses if they are to constrain costs and respond to the needs of society.

Let us return to our earlier example of content preparation. As we have noted, universities—more correctly, faculty—are skilled at creating the content for educational programs. Indeed, we might identify this skill as one of their core competencies. But they have not traditionally been particularly adept at "packaging" this content for mass audiences. To be sure, many faculty members have written best-selling textbooks, but these have been produced and distributed by textbook publishers. In the future of multimedia, Net-distributed educational services, perhaps the university will have to outsource both production and distribution to those most experienced in reaching mass audiences—the entertainment industry.

In such commodity markets brand names can be very important. Traditionally, branding in higher education has been based primarily on prestige—for example, the Harvard paradigm of whoever spends the most on the fewest students (and consequently is most highly rated by *U.S. News and World Report*) becomes the lead brand. Yet it is also possible that in a commodity market brand names could well become more closely related to learning value added. In such a marketplace it could well be that for-profit education providers that establish clear evidence of strong student learning outcomes could begin to compete with and perhaps even dominate traditional elite institutions with brand names based more on institutional reputation and prestige.

Higher education is an industry ripe for the unbundling of activities. Universities, like other institutions in society, will have to come to terms with what their true strengths are and how those strengths support their strategies—and then be willing to outsource needed capabilities in areas in which they do not have a unique advantage. The new learning services are increasingly available among many providers, learning agents, and intermediary organizations. Such an open, network-based learning enterprise certainly seems more capable of responding to the staggering demand for advanced education, learning, and knowledge than traditional approaches. It also seems certain not only to provide learners with many more choices but also to create more competition for the provision of knowledge and learning services.

The perception of the higher education enterprise as a deregulated industry has several other implications. In a sense education today is one of the last remaining sectors of the economy dominated by public control which has failed to achieve the standards of quality, cost-effectiveness, and technological innovation demanded by our knowledge-driven society. Furthermore, compared to other sectors that have been subject to massive restructuring, ranging from utilities to telecommunications to transportation to health care, the education industry represents the largest market opportunity for the private sector since health care in the 1970s.

As we have noted, there are currently 4,048 colleges and universities in the United States (including 672 for-profit colleges), characterized by a great diversity in size, mission, constituencies, and funding sources.[10] Not only are we likely to see the appearance of new educational entities in the years ahead, but, as in other deregulated industries, there could well be a period of fundamental restructuring of the enterprise itself. Some colleges and universities might disappear. Others might merge. Some might actually acquire other institutions. One might even imagine Darwinian "hostile takeovers," in which some institutions devour their competitors and eliminate their obsolete practices. Such events have occurred in deregulated industries in the past, and they are possible in the future we envision for higher education.

Actually, such restructuring of the higher education enterprise has occurred before. As the population of college-age students swelled during the decades following World War II, many public universities evolved into complex systems, spawning regional campuses, absorbing formerly normal schools and technical colleges, and attempting to dominate statewide or regional markets. But this expansion was driven by strong growth of public tax support to respond to the education needs of a growing population. Today we see the possibility of market competition and private dollars driving a rearrangement of higher education.

As much as some resist thinking about education in these terms, taking the perspective of higher education as a postsecondary knowledge industry in a vast network is an important viewpoint that will require a new paradigm for how public universities think about what they have to offer. Internally, it suggests the possibility of radical changes in the academic structure of the university, its educational processes such as teaching and research. Externally, it suggests both competing and collaborating with an array of noneducational organizations such as the telecommunications and entertainment industry. As society becomes ever more dependent upon new knowledge and educated people, this global knowledge business must be viewed as one of the most active growth industries of our times. It is clear that no person, government, or corporation will be in control of the higher education industry. It will respond to forces of the marketplace.

Perhaps the most serious threat of the emerging competitive marketplace for knowledge and education is the danger that it will not only erode but also distort the most important values and purposes of the university. In a highly competitive market economy short-term pressing issues usually win out over long-term societal investments.

The early for-profit entrants into postsecondary education are aiming first at the corporate market for business education. After all, the corporate training market is huge, $66 billion in 2000, and growing by 11 percent a year. Furthermore, online education has the potential of eliminating the considerable costs of employee travel and payment for time spent in training programs, estimated at 60 percent of corporate training costs. David Collis estimates that roughly 60 percent of for-profit education is aimed at corporate clients, and 75 percent of educational content is business education.[11]

As a result, colleges and universities might first be tempted to breathe a bit more easily, since the for-profit sector appears to be going after adult markets that they have not traditionally served. Yet this view may be deceptive. The new entrants are investing at very significant levels in developing education content, improving pedagogical methods, and assessing student learning outcomes. They are moving up the learning curve very rapidly, and it is only a question of time before they broaden outward to provide additional educational services at both the graduate and undergraduate education levels. The threat to incumbents is that they may be overwhelmed, as for-profit providers not only learn how to provide cost-effective, high-quality online education but, furthermore, develop the brand names for quality through demonstrated competence. The impact on traditional colleges and universities may be delayed, but it will be no less dramatic—indeed, traumatic—when it occurs, in part because they are procrastinating on making the necessary investments and activities to learn how to exploit technology-delivered education and the new adult marketplace.

As David Collis puts it, the emerging for-profit, online education enterprise is like a tsunami, with colleges and universities sitting on the beach, sunning themselves in the warm glow of a hot economy while believing that the gentle surf before them is simply the tide coming in. Little do they realize that out over the horizon is a swelling hundred-foot tsunami wave, bearing down upon them, with little chance to outrun it.

Of course, there may be some near-term steps to slow the tsunami of commercial online education. States might apply regulations to constrain offering degree programs or credentials across state lines (although this move could also run afoul of interstate commerce regulations). Nations might do the same. But, as we have learned from e-commerce and other Internet activities, IT-based commercial activities eventually become formidable, irresistible, and pervasive. As the early entrants jockey to define the Amazon.com for e-learning, it seems inevitable that the tsunami will sweep across state and national borders, possibly inundating those colleges and universities in their path which ignore the threat or are slow to respond to it.

As each wave of transformation sweeps through the economy and through society with an ever more rapid tempo, the existing infrastructure of educational institutions, programs, and policies becomes more outdated and perhaps even obsolete. While the pervasive need for advanced education dictated by the high-performance workforce has significantly expanded the student population, it has also transformed it significantly in character and need. While young adults continue to seek the experience of intellectual maturation and socialization associated with undergraduate education, their numbers are now exceeded by working adults, seeking knowledge and skills of direct relevance to careers and expecting a professional, businesslike relationship with learning institutions. For these learners convenience and cost-effectiveness have become comparable to academic quality and institutional reputation in importance. They demand that institutions focus on providing educational services that meet their needs, rather than stressing the scholarly achievement of faculty, public services such as health care or entertainment (intercollegiate athletics), or building institutional prestige (brand name).

Today it is estimated that higher education represents roughly $225 billion of the $665 billion education market in the United States.[12] But even these markets are dwarfed by the size of the "knowledge and learning" marketplace, estimated in excess of $2.2 trillion. Furthermore, with the year 2000 population of eighty-four million students enrolled in higher education worldwide estimated to double by 2020, the size of the global marketplace is considerably larger.

Little wonder that many believe that the market forces created by the workforce skills needs of a knowledge economy and driven by new competitors and technologies will present a formidable challenge to existing colleges and universities. Although the expanding educational needs of a growing population, the high-performance workplace, and developing nations will sustain the size of the market served by traditional higher education, this market share is almost certain to decline as new, technology-based competitors emerge to serve new educational markets.

Market Strategies

How should traditional colleges and universities approach the challenges and opportunities presented by an evolving postsecondary education market?

Clearly, the first objective is to develop a unique strategy that helps an institution focus on and improve in areas of strength or, in business language, identify and stress its core competencies. Every institution, no matter how strong or prestigious, needs a dynamic competitive strategy capable of adapting to a rapidly changing marketplace.

In the effort to develop such a market strategy, every institution must revisit some very basic issues. Should they remain focused on their traditional roles and clients, allowing new competitors to serve the growing marketplace of nontraditional students and educational/knowledge needs without challenge? Or should they develop the capacity to serve these new and growing needs of a knowledge-intensive society? Where would the resources come from to support such an expansion of educational missions—students, taxpayers, corporate clients? Perhaps of even more immediate concern is how colleges and universities can cope with the potential erosion of revenue from high–profit margin activities such as general education and professional education which appear to be the early targets of for-profit competitors?

More generally, how can conventional academic institutions accommodate the likely evolution and integration of education into a global knowledge and learning industry? Should universities seek to establish their traditional academic activities as sufficiently world-class to be competitive in this global marketplace? Or should they outsource world-class services provided by other institutions to their regional market and instead focus their own efforts on homegrown educational products designed for local markets? How important will reputational characteristics such as prestige or brand name be in such a global marketplace? Clearly, there will not be one best educational approach that works for all institutions. The diverse nature of learning and learners will provide many opportunities for differentiation.

From a broader perspective we can see the rapid evolution of a global knowledge and learning industry as a continuation of an ever-expanding role and presence of the university during the past century. From the commitment to universal access to higher education after World War II to the concern about cost and efficiency in the 1980s to the role of the university in a knowledge-driven society, there have been both growth in the number and complexity of the missions of the university and the entry into postsecondary education of new players and competitors. Today we think of the postsecondary education industry as consisting of a core of educational institutions: research, doctoral, and comprehensive institutions; four-year colleges; two-year colleges; proprietary institutions; and professional and specialized institutions. This core is supported, sustained, and augmented by an array of external players, including state and federal government, business and industry, and foundations. The traditional postsecondary institutions will be joined at the core of the emerging knowledge and learning industry by new players: telecommunications companies, entertainment companies, information technology companies, information service providers, and corporate and governmental education providers.[13]

At the top of the food chain are the elite research universities, such as Harvard and Stanford as well as the University of California–Berkeley and the University of Michigan, which provide an intellectually rich—and financially very expensive—educational experience to a relatively small number of students. For example, even a large university such as UC-Berkeley enrolls fewer than 30,000 students compared to the 260,000 enrolled in the California State University System. Harvard and Stanford enroll even fewer, about 10,000 each. And the elite liberal arts colleges such as Amherst and Oberlin are even more focused, with only about 2,000 students participating in their faculty-intensive residential campus experience.

At the other extreme are adult education institutions such as the University of Phoenix and the British Open University which use a combination of standardized regional centers and online technology to reach hundreds of thousands of students. Addressing the educational needs of even larger numbers are the systems of regional state universities and community colleges. Although these institutions do not provide the rich educational experience of a residential campus with low student-to-faculty ratios—indeed, most of their students are commuters and many are part-time with full-time jobs—they do educate the bulk of the roughly fourteen million students enrolled in higher education programs in the United States.

In understanding how these diverse institutions relate to the higher education marketplace, it is important to keep several points in mind. First, most students tend to pay for the credential of a college degree rather than for an educational experience, since they perceive this to be the ticket to satisfying and well-compensated careers. Furthermore, for those who can afford it, the prestige of a college or university is usually viewed as more important than the quality of the educational experience they actually will receive in its academic programs. Of course, university brand names have long been important because of the social networks based upon college and alumni experiences. But branding has become even more important in recent years as federal funding and private giving become increasingly correlated with faculty reputation and as the college ratings provided by publications such as *U.S. News and World Report* have established the rankings of various institutions firmly in the minds of the marketplace.

The educational needs of the nation have evolved from focusing on the leaders of society to providing broad, quality educational opportunities for the entire population—in a sense, universal and pervasive educational opportunities. Society will expect from their educational institutions the production of an educated workforce capable of competing compete in the changing global economic landscape. Institutions that can continually change to keep up with the needs of the transforming economy they serve will survive. Those that cannot or will not change will become less relevant and more vulnerable to newly emerging competitors.

Of course, technology will play a critical role in this development, since digital technology is emerging as a primary delivery mechanism for educational services and intellectual content. The burgeoning use of the Internet and other national and international networks is creating environments in which intellectual capacity, information and knowledge bases, methodologies, and other educational services are made available to learners anywhere, anytime. Almost every function of the contemporary university will be affected by, and possibly even displaced by, digital technology. New competitors will appear, threatening the status quo with more effective and less costly alternatives. With over one hundred million new learners at stake globally, the competition will be keen, indeed. As individuals, business, and government turn to network alternatives, the franchise of the college degree or college credit will face significant challenges. Although it will take a long time for the full impact of technology-driven transformation of the marketplace to be fully appreciated, even small shifts in the core activities of the university could have a dramatic impact.

Although the most prestigious and prosperous institutions will have significant advantages in this restructured marketplace for higher education, they too will face serious challenges. For the most expensive institutions the early impact could well be price pressures. For all but the most elite institutions (i.e., the most prominent brand names) the cost pressure imposed by comparisons of student tuition rates could be enormous. How can a family justify spending $20,000 to $30,000 per year on tuition when a new competitor may be able to provide academic offerings of comparative quality at $5,000 to $10,000, based on actual measurement and comparison of student learning achievements? Similarly, public officials and politicians will also become more conscious of such comparisons during a time when state and federal budgets are under increasing pressure from limited revenues and competing public priorities such as health care, corrections, and K-12 education. Already we see some states beginning to question the need to invest in more campus-based facilities when distance learning may provide lower-cost alternatives.

Perhaps even more immediate will be significant price competition from new competitors in low-cost, high–profit margin academic programs such as business education and general education. Technology-intensive, for-profit competitors such as Jones International University and Unext.com initially target business education for adults in the workplace because they are frequently subsidized by employers, and online education can offer significant cost savings by eliminating travel and time-off-job expenses. But, as experience is gained in these online programs, it is logical to expect them to compete more directly with established business schools both for degree programs and executive education. Moving farther up the learning curve, several for-profit competitors have already announced their intention to enter the general education market, which is also characterized by relatively inexpensive instructional costs and large student populations.

Some of the most elite institutions may adopt a strategy of relying on their prestige and their prosperity to isolate themselves from change, to continue to do just what they have done in the past, and to be comfortable with their roles as niche players in the higher education enterprise. But for most of the larger, more comprehensive institutions the activities of elite education and basic research are simply too expensive to sustain without some attention to the cross-subsidies from activities that are more responsive to the marketplace.

Clearly, colleges and universities should play to their strengths as they develop market strategies. The capabilities of the faculty and student body; the vast physical, financial, and intellectual resources; and the reputation of major research universities represent very considerable assets in competing for the new educational markets. Many public universities already have both a mission and a culture supportive of off-campus activities, particularly land grant institutions with decades of experience in sophisticated extension activities in agriculture, industrial development, and adult education.

The financial pressures of the early 1980s and 1990s taught most universities the wisdom of focusing resources to achieve quality in selected areas of strength rather than attempting to be all things to all people. An increasingly competitive and rapidly changing marketplace will demand even more focus and differentiation. There are strong incentives to meet the broad expectations of various stakeholders through alliances of institutions with particular focused strengths rather than continuing to broaden the institutional mission, with the consequent dilution of resources, since the breadth and extent of the diverse demands of society tend to exceed the resources and capacities of a single institution.

Two examples illustrate the point. Many students and families believe that the teaching-intensive residential campuses of small liberal arts colleges provide a more effective learning environment than the mega-campuses of large research universities. Yet public research universities provide extraordinary resources such as libraries, laboratories, and performance centers, not to mention faculty members who are leading scholars in a broad array of disciplines and professional fields. One might imagine combining the strengths of both types of institutions by forming alliances among liberal arts colleges and research universities. This arrangement might permit the students enrolling at large research universities to enjoy the intense, highly personal experience of a liberal arts education at a small college while allowing the faculty members at these colleges to participate in the type of research activities occurring only on large research campuses.

There are also strong incentives to form alliances involving universities and commercial competitors. Universities can benefit from the experience gained from commercial competitors as well as their ability to access private capital markets to invest in product development and assessment. The corporate partners, in turn, can benefit from the "brand name" of established universities. Past experience from restructured industries suggests that the marketplace rewards suggests those who enter early, adapt rapidly, and are ready to seize opportunities when they arise. While the diversity of the higher education marketplace makes it unlikely that a true monopoly will long survive, the value of having a brand name and the huge fixed cost, low variable cost nature of the new business suggests that early movers will have sustainable advantages.

In a similar sense states and communities are certain to rethink whether their existing higher education infrastructure is strategically positioned to serve their needs in the face of such a rapidly evolving marketplace of new needs and new providers. Does New York really need sixty-four separate state universities? Does California need nine major public research universities? From this perspective the current trend of state and federal governments of shifting public support from institutions to students may make perfect sense from a market viewpoint. It is certainly a possible strategy to increase competition and reduce the burden on the public purse by redirecting funding to consumers.

The Brave New World of Commercial Education

The market forces unleashed by technology and driven by increasing demand for higher education are very powerful. If they are allowed to dominate and reshape the higher education enterprise, we could well find ourselves facing a brave new world in which some of the most important values and traditions of the university fall by the wayside. After all, while universities teach the skills and convey knowledge demanded by the marketplace, they also do much more. They also preserve and convey cultural heritage from one generation to the next, perform the research necessary to generate new knowledge, serve as constructive social critics, and provide a broad array of knowledge-based services to society, ranging from health care to technology transfer. These latter roles are unlikely to be valued in quite the same way by the commercial marketplace for postsecondary education.

Although traditional colleges and universities are likely to continue to play a significant role in this future, they are likely to be both threatened and reshaped by shifting societal needs, rapidly evolving technology, and aggressive for-profit entities and commercial forces. Together, these conditions could drive the higher education enterprise toward the mediocrity that has characterized other mass media markets such as television and journalism. While the commercial, convenience store model of the University of Phoenix may be a very effective way to meet the workplace skill needs of some adults, it certainly is not a paradigm that would be suitable for many of the higher purposes of the university. As we assess these market-driven, emerging learning structures, we must bear in mind the importance of preserving the ability of the university to serve a broader public purpose.

The experience with restructuring in other industries has not been altogether encouraging, particularly with market-driven, media-based enterprises. While the dissolution of the AT&T monopolies has indeed stimulated competition in telecommunications, it also resulted in the weakening of one of this nation's greatest intellectual assets, the Bell Laboratories. Furthermore, anyone who has suffered through the cattle car experience of hub-spoke air travel can question whether the deregulation of commercial aviation has been worth it. And, although the rate of increase in the cost of health care has been slowed very significantly by the competition unleashed in a restructured marketplace, there are increasing concerns about the quality and convenience of health care delivery in our intensely competitive—and many would maintain chaotic—deregulated health care marketplace.

The broadcasting and publication industries suggest that commercial concerns can lead to mediocrity, an intellectual wasteland in which the lowest common denominator of quality dominates. One can imagine a future in which the escalating costs of a residential, campus-based college education could price this form of higher learning beyond the range of all but the affluent, relegating much if not most of the population to low-cost (and perhaps low-quality) education via shopping mall learning centers or computer-mediated distance learning. In this dark, market-driven future the residential college campus could well become the gated community of the higher education enterprise, available only to the rich and privileged.

There is an important lesson here. Without a broader recognition of the growing learning needs of society, an exploration of more radical learning paradigms, and an overarching national strategy that acknowledges the public purpose of higher education and the important values of the academy, higher education will be driven to mediocrity. Many of the pressures on public universities are similar to those that have contributed so heavily to the current plight of K-12 education. Education has been viewed as an industry, demanding higher productivity according to poorly designed performance measures. The political forces associated with mass education have intruded on school management in general and governing boards in particular. Faculty members have no recourse but to circle the wagons, to accept a labor-management relationship, and to cease to regard their vocation as a calling rather than a job.

The primary concern here is that unbridled market forces could distract public colleges and universities from acting in the public interest and instead lead them to become, in their activities and their philosophies, indistinguishable from the for-profit sector. Quality could sink to a lowest common denominator provided by commodity products in the mass marketplace. The academy could lose control of content to commercial providers, particularly of e-learning products.

Balancing Market Forces with Public Purpose

Will this restructuring of the higher education enterprise really happen? If there is any doubt about it, just consider the health care industry. While Washington debated federal programs to control health care costs, the marketplace took over with new paradigms such as managed care and for-profit health centers. In less than a decade the health care industry was totally changed and continues to change rapidly today. Today higher education is a $225 billion per year enterprise, a significant part of the $665 billion per year spent in the United States on education. In many ways the education industry represents the last of the economic sectors dominated by public control and yet at risk because of quality, cost-effectiveness, and changing demands.

Regardless of who or what drives change, the higher education enterprise is likely to be dramatically transformed over the next decade.[14] It could happen from within, in an effort to respond to growing societal needs and limited resources. But it is more likely to be transformed by new markets, new technologies, and new competition. In this rapidly evolving knowledge business the institutions most at risk will not be of any particular type or size but, rather, those most constrained by tradition, culture, or governance.

Both public and private universities alike will be faced with the intense competition of the marketplace, driven by growing demands for advanced education, unleashed by emerging technology, and intensified by the entry of new competitors. All institutions will be seriously challenged to respond. Yet public institutions will have considerably greater difficulty in coping with these market pressures.

In this regard it is important to recall once again that the American public university was the result of public policy and public investment by way of both federal and state governments.[15] It was the federal government's commitment to extend the benefits of higher education to a broad segment of society which stimulated a range of policy actions, from the land grant acts to the GI Bill to the Higher Education Acts, coupled with the support of higher education by state governments which led to a public education enterprise that leads the world both in the quality of education and scholarship and in the opportunities it provides to citizens. These policies, programs, and commitments were driven by strong social values and a sense of national and regional priorities.

Yet today public leaders are increasingly discarding public policy in favor of market forces to determine priorities for social investment. The shift toward high-tuition/high-aid funding models, from grants to loans to tax benefits as the mechanism for student financial aid, from state-supported to state-assisted public higher education, all reinforce the sense that higher education today is seen increasingly as an individual benefit rather than a social good. Public higher education can no longer assume that public policies and investment will shield it from market competition.

Nevertheless, even as state and federal governments place increasing faith in the marketplace, they sometimes also hinder the capacity of public higher education to respond. In part the capacity of public universities to respond and compete is complicated by their size, inertia, and awkward governance structure. But even more significant is the reactive nature of public expectations and other, more overt political forces such as university governing boards. Efforts by public universities to respond to the marketplace will threaten both internal and external constituencies—the contented sacred cows who feed off of the status quo—thereby triggering political forces that will destabilize their governing boards.

Public universities hear time and time again from both elected public officials and governing board members that they desire a more market-focused, cost-effective, and competitive paradigm for the university. Yet these are also the first people to hold up their hand to halt the changes necessary to respond to the marketplace. If this ambivalence toward the marketplace arose from a recognition of the civic purpose of the public university, then perhaps it would be not only understandable but also acceptable. Clearly, market forces do not respond to many important needs of society and would not favor the broader purposes of higher education. The marketplace cares little about underserved elements of society or the role of the university as a social critic.

Yet, more likely, the conflicting pressures on the public university to compete in the marketplace while being constrained by political pressures is probably due as much to the nature of contemporary policies as to any public recognition of broader social purpose. Politics tends to be reactive rather than strategic and visionary. It tends to defend the status quo rather than embracing change. It is driven by image rather than by issue, preoccupied with the here and now rather than concerned about the future.

Hence, we may be unable to protect the civic purpose of the public university—which, of course, might be best served by changing the public university into a more learner-centered and society-serving institution. Instead, the reactive and constraining nature of political forces and public perceptions may thwart those very efforts to preserve and protect the capacity of these institutions to serve a changing society.

In facing the prospects of a deregulated and restructured marketplace for higher education, it is essential for academic leaders and policy makers to develop policies that protect the public interest. They need to protect both the core values of the universities and the broader character of the public university as a public good rather than simply a source of market products.

Organizations and industries that produce and distribute information and knowledge are entering a stage of convergence redefining entire value chains in many industries. As it emerges, the mega-industry created by the union of computers, communications, entertainment, media, and publishing will deliver education and learning in new ways and in such vast amounts that it will parallel, rival, and in some instances even displace schools as the major deliverer of learning.

The real danger will not be to any particular class of institutions but, rather, to universities that lack a strategy or focus and the willingness to change and improve. Institutions that choose to ignore the realities of the emerging marketplace either because of complacency or simply because of the glacial pace of their governance are at considerable risk.[16]

The market forces driven by increasing demand for higher education and unleashed by technology are very powerful. Yet, if they are allowed to dominate and reshape the higher education enterprise, we could well find ourselves facing a brave, new world in which some of the most important values and traditions of the university fall by the wayside. As we assess these market-driven emerging learning structures, we must bear in mind the importance of preserving the ability of the university to serve a broader public purpose.

CHAPTER SIX

Financing the Public University

The financing of the university—structuring its internal costs, pricing its educational services, and acquiring the resources necessary to support its activities—has become the center of a national debate. The rising costs of higher education during a period of stagnant or declining public support and the consequent increases in tuition have triggered great concern about both the access to and quality of higher education. Nowhere is this debate more intense than in public universities, where most of the nation's college students are currently educated.

The ever-increasing costs of the university should not be surprising in view of the exponential increase in knowledge and the growing educational needs of society. The demands upon public colleges and universities continue to increase, with the population of college-age students growing once again, while the needs of adult learners are expanding rapidly. States expect public universities to provide the basic and applied research so important to economic growth in a technology-dependent economy. The needs for professional services in areas such as health care, technology transfer, and economic development all continue to grow. Yet state governments are less inclined to provide the funding increases necessary to allow public universities to respond to the growing needs of a knowledge-driven society in the face of other social priorities such as crime prevention, health care, and K-12 education.

The acquisition, allocation, and management of financial resources are particular challenges to the public research university, both because of its scale and breadth of activities. With budgets in the hundreds of millions to billions of dollars, enrollments and employees numbering in the tens of thousands, and activities spanning the range from instruction to research to health care to economic development, financial issues are highly complex and consequential, particularly in the harsh light of public accountability. Both because of these complexities and our own backgrounds, we will focus primarily on the financial challenges to public research universities, including their changing resource base and the array of options available to cope with these changes. In particular we will stress the importance of new financial models that strive to build more diversified funding portfolios, less dependent upon state appropriations, which enable public universities not only to increase the resources available for academic program support but, moreover, to provide resilience against the inevitable ebb and flow of state support. Of particular importance here is the need to build an adequate reserve capacity, both in the budgets of operating units and through endowment accounts. How to allocate and manage resources, contain costs, and adopt efficiency measures common from business, such as systems reengineering and total quality management, are also relevant to the discussion.

But perhaps most significant is an entirely new approach to financial management, responsibility, and accountability which would enable the public research university to thrive during a period of constrained public support. We will make the case that these public institutions must break free from traditions and practices that depend heavily upon generous state support and instead manage their financial affairs much as private universities. They must become more entrepreneurial and proactive, seeking both the resources and the autonomy to allow them to thrive in spite of the vicissitudes of public funding. In a sense they must become increasingly privately financed and privately managed public universities, even as they maintain their public commitments.

The Challenge of Financial Constraints

Throughout most of their history, public universities have relied heavily upon state appropriations to support their activities. But there has always been an ebb and flow in public support of higher education, dependent upon the fortunes of state economies. The sustained growth in appropriations during the 1960s and 1970s, associated with a strong economy and the growing needs of the baby boom population, was followed by recession and deep cuts in state appropriations in the early 1980s and 1990s. More recently, the unusual prosperity of the late 1990s stimulated not only a growth in state and federal expenditures for higher education, but it also created a bull market sustaining growth in private giving and endowments. Yet, once again, boom has been followed by bust, as state appropriations and investment incomes have begun to decline with a weakening national and global economy in the early years of the twenty-first century.

Sometimes university leaders and governing boards seem to forget this cyclic nature of the financial resources available to public universities. They relax in the warm glow of a prosperous economy, typically committing to longer-term recurring expenditures associated with staff growth or new capital facilities, and lose much of the discipline necessary for containing costs and prioritizing expenditures. Then, when the inevitable downturn occurs, they awake to a series of financial crises demanding program retrenchment or even elimination. Although there is sufficient experience to suggest that such cycles of prosperity and austerity are a regular occurrence in public higher education, with a periodicity typically ranging from five to ten years, few institutions are prepared—or perhaps able—to take the actions during good times such as sustaining adequate growth in tuition or cost containment which would prepare them for the inevitable economic downturn.

Beyond these economic cycles, however, there are longer-term trends in the public funding of higher education which suggest that bolder strategies are necessary. During the boom years following World War II higher education accounted for a very significant portion of all appropriations from state tax dollars. Growth in state support of higher education began to slow in the late 1970s and early 1980s, however, as the states faced a host of competing demands for their limited resources. The public's demand for stiffer penalties for criminals called for huge outlays for prison construction and ongoing commitments for prison operations. The alarming deterioration in the quality of K-12 education boosted it ahead of higher education as a public priority. Unfunded federal mandates such as Medicaid placed ever greater burdens on limited state resources. Over a longer period of several decades there has been decided erosion in state support for public colleges and universities.

From a broader perspective public higher education, like many other so-cial services, has experienced a sea change in the nature of public support. Throughout the 1980s and early 1990s public colleges and universities faced the consequences of the structural flaws appearing in the budgets of federal and state governments, which were experiencing a growing imbalance between tax revenues and public expenditures. This imbalance undermined support for higher education and other essential public services as governments struggled to meet short-term demands at the expense of long-term investment.[1] Between 1978 and 1998 direct state appropriations as a proportion of the total revenue of public colleges and universities declined by nearly 25 percent, despite a con-tinued growth in college enrollments.[2] During the same period the net tuition revenues per full-time student in public institutions increased by over 60 percent. The booming economy of the late 1990s allowed some restoration of state support, but appropriations turned down once again as yet another economic recession greeted the new century.

Even in the face of declining public support, there was a continued expan-sion in the demand for higher education and a consequent expansion of the higher education enterprise. Strong local interests drove both growth in the number of regional institutions and the evolution of established institutions. It was the aspiration of community colleges to become four-year institutions, four-year colleges to start graduate programs and become universities, and regional universities to become national research universities. This trend was sustained by willing and energetic political constituencies. In the face of more limited public support this overexpansion of the enterprise raised serious concerns about eroding quality.

The costs of providing education, research, and service per unit of activity have increased at an even faster rate, since these university activities are depen-dent upon a highly skilled, professional workforce (faculty and staff) whose members require expensive new facilities and equipment and are driven by an ever-expanding knowledge base. Higher education has yet to take the bold steps to constrain cost increases which have been required in other sectors of society such as business and industry, in part because of the way colleges and universities are organized, managed, and governed. But, even if universities should acquire both the capacity and the determination to restructure costs more radically, it is debatable whether those actions adopted from the experi-ence of the business community in containing cost and enhancing productiv-ity could have the same impact in education. The current paradigm of higher education is simply too people- and knowledge-intensive. Furthermore, the organization of the contemporary university (i.e., semiautonomous academic and professional disciplines) and its governance and management style (i.e., shared governance and limited authority for line officers) make cost containment and productivity enhancement very difficult.

Public colleges and universities have been faced with the daunting task of maintaining quality within severely restricted revenues from traditional sources such as state appropriations. The better institutions have tried to compensate for declining appropriations by increasing tuition and launching private fund-raising campaigns. But, as the cost of attending college began to rise at rates outstripping the consumer price index (CPI), both students and parents raised objections. Although most public institutions have been able to keep the tuition levels considerably below those charged at private schools, their rate of increase also has outstripped the CPI, alarming students, parents, the public, politicians, and eventually governing boards.

Today it is clear that the strategy of increasing tuition to compensate for eroding public support cannot continue indefinitely. Although the competitive marketplace alone would certainly tolerate such price increases in public universities, in which tuition is still at a very nominal level, public resistance, as manifested through political pressures at the federal, state, and governing board level, simply will not allow institutions to continue to balance their books through tuition increases. Tuition levels stabilized in the mid- to late 1990s with strong state appropriations and even stronger political pressure. But, as state economies weakened at the end of the decade, tuition levels at public colleges and universities once again began to rise and are likely to continue to do so.

The reason is simple. The underlying structural factors leading to an imbalance between the costs of public university activities and the resources available from traditional sources such as state appropriation remain. Higher education has done little or nothing to address the inadequacy of its fundamental cost structure. Increased productivity based upon changing methods of teaching and research has not occurred. Faculties still behave in all material respects as they always have. Costs have continued to increase on a per–unit of activity basis, technology is employed in uneven ways and seldom integral to the learning process, and the shifting of blame has become a fine art. In fact, we continue to benchmark instructional costs in terms of old-fashioned parameters such as students per faculty or instructional contact hours, thereby implicitly assuming that pedagogy has not changed for decades (which it has not in most institutions).

Perhaps more troubling and undermining to reform has been mission creep. During the past two decades auxiliary services such as hospitals, intercollegiate athletics, and technology transfer have grown in number and breadth. On many campuses the amount spent on academic programs is less than half of the total university budget. These peripheral businesses are only tangentially related to the fundamental purposes of the university, but they consume disproportionate amounts of time, energy, and financial resources.

Everywhere there are signs that even the best public universities are at risk. As costs have risen, many able students have sought less expensive options such as community colleges for at least a portion of their education. A few business schools have capitalized on executive education programs, and those that have done so have prospered handsomely. But even these schools with significant successes are often looked upon by their arts and science colleagues as not being really serious members of the academy. The most prestigious public institutions have failed to appreciate the economic as well as the scholarly value of lifelong learning.

For the most part faculties have been both uninterested in and detached from the financial challenges faced by the university—unless, of course, it has had direct impact on faculty compensation. Professors have been insulated by their administrations from the realities of the marketplace—indeed, many are even unaware of the existence of a marketplace for higher education. Many believe that the sheltered life they live will continue and that fundamental systemic change is unnecessary and damaging to high-quality educational programs. Competition for the higher education dollar does not even appear on their radar screen.

The basic structure of the academy, its reward system, and its selection of faculty members all contribute to a condition that cannot long survive in its present form. Technological change and opportunity have made alternative options for learning not only possible but in many ways preferable. The cloistered environment in which scholars separated students from the distractions of broader society in order to prepare them to become productive and contributing members of that society becomes increasingly irrelevant in a connected global economy. The higher education enterprise in America must change dramatically if it is to restore a balance between the costs and availability of educational services needed by society and the resources available to support these services.

Diversifying the Resource Base of the Public University

Many public colleges and universities are almost entirely dependent upon state appropriations. They exist from one legislative session to the next, experiencing good times or hard times determined by the generosity of higher education appropriation committees. They endure periods of boom and bust, first expanding programs and capacity during times of prosperity and generous state support and then cutting programs and enduring financial hardship when their state's economy goes into the tank.

Little wonder, then, that many leaders of public universities have tried to break the cycle and reduce their dependence upon state appropriations by developing alternative sources of funding. They see a more diverse resource portfolio as not only essential to building and sustaining the quality of their institution but also as essential to providing the flexibility to ride out the inevitable downturns in state support. Closely related to this is a strategy to build reserve funds, both through cost controls generating budget savings that could be carried over into reserve accounts and through private gifts and additional revenues from auxiliary activities such as university health centers which could be invested in funds functioning as endowments. Such reserves provide an important hedge against downtimes, allowing more stability in institutional planning and operation. Furthermore, by enhancing the financial strength of the university, they frequently lead to higher Wall Street credit ratings and, hence, lower interest rates for debt financing major capital facility needs.

Although most public colleges and universities are heavily dependent upon state appropriations, they have access to other resources:

— Federal support for research and student financial aid
— State appropriations
— Tuition and fees paid by students
— Gifts and endowment income
— Auxiliary activities (such as hospitals, residence halls, and athletics)
— Technology transfer licensing and equity investments in spin-offs

The availability and attractiveness of each of these options varies greatly and depends upon the nature of the institution and its political environment.

For many public institutions that are heavily dependent upon state appropriations, a reasonable strategy might be to build the political influence necessary to protect or enhance state support. Small private institutions with modest endowments depend heavily upon tuition and fees, and issues such as enrollments and tuition pricing play a key role in financial strategies. Highly focused research universities such as the Massachusetts Institute of Technology (MIT) and Stanford University are heavily dependent upon federal research support and seek to influence federal research policies.

Although all dollars may be green, their utility for supporting the operations of the university varies greatly. Most resources have strings attached which restrict their use. For example, the funds provided by research grants and contracts are usually restricted to quite specific research activities. Most private support is given for particular purposes, such as supporting student financial aid or a specific building project. Tuition income and state appropriations generally have more flexibility, but here, too, there may be many constraints—for example, restrictions to the support of particular academic programs or the support of students who are state residents.

To understand better some of the issues involved in financing public higher education, it is useful to consider briefly each of these revenue and expenditure elements. Federal support of higher education occurs through direct programs such as research grants from federal agencies, student financial aid, and program support in critical areas such as health care. It also occurs through indirect mechanisms such as favorable tax treatment of private gifts and endowment appreciation. Although federal support grew rapidly during the postwar years, it began to level off in the 1980s, as other national priorities moved ahead of higher education and efforts were launched to limit federal spending.[3] More specifically, research funding has stayed roughly constant since the 1980s, although the number of universities and faculty seeking federal research support has grown. Although there has been some modest growth in recent years, it has been heavily biased toward biomedical research, which primarily benefits universities with large medical centers. Federal programs aimed at funding specific academic programs to sustain social priorities such as public health and education have largely disappeared.

Although the federal support of student financial aid has remained relatively stable, its shifting nature from need-based grants to more broadly available loans to tax benefits has redirected funding from those with needs to those with political power. The Taxpayer Relief Act of 1997 was good news for the middle class, with almost $40 billion of tax assistance for college expenses. But this government support will flow to students and families, not necessarily to higher education. Furthermore, this budget-balancing strategy is only a stop-gap measure. Without a major restructuring in federal entitlement programs or a dramatic increase in national productivity, the imbalance between federal commitments and revenues is likely to become even more serious over the next two decades, as the baby boomers move into retirement. It is also likely that the trend toward increasing federal regulation will continue (in areas such as health, safety, conflict of interest, scientific misconduct, foreign involvement), and the costs associated with compliance will continue to rise.

It is in the states that the public role in supporting higher education has changed most dramatically over the past decade.[4] As late as 1980, the states contributed 45 percent of all higher education revenues. By 1993 that share had fallen to 35 percent. Although there was a mild recovery with the economic prosperity of the late 1990s, most public universities enter the new century barely back to where they were in the 1970s, although they once again are facing growing enrollments with declining appropriations as the economy weakens again. For public institutions the contribution of state and local government spending has reached its lowest level since World War II, con-stituting roughly 53 percent of the support base. Cost shifting from the fed-eral government through unfunded mandates, such as Medicare, Medicaid, the Americans with Disabilities Act (ADA), and the Occupational Safety and Health Administration (OSHA), has destabilized state budgets. Many states have made massive investments in prisons and commitments to funding K-12 education through earmarks off the top of the state budget. These expenses have undermined their capacity to support higher education. In fact, in many states today the appropriations for prisons have now surpassed the funding for higher education and show no signs of slowing.

There is a growing consensus that, unlike the need for retrenchment experi-enced in the 1980s, the erosion in state support for higher education in the early 1990s and then once again a decade later is part of a more permanent shift in funding priorities. Generous public support of higher education is unlikely to be sustained in most states over the longer term, even though the echo of the baby boom will lead to a significant growth in college-age students in many parts of the country over the next decade. Ironically, even as states throttle back public support of higher education in the face of other competing social priorities and demand increasing accountability, they are also demanding that public universities serve the ever-expanding needs of the growing population of college-age students and the research and service needs of an increasingly knowledge-driven economy.

Whether public or private, most colleges and universities draw the majority of their revenues from operations—tuition from instruction, rentals from housing, clinical income from health care, and so on. In many states even appropriations are indexed to instructional activity. An increasingly significant revenue source for many public universities is tuition, the price charged to students for their college education. Yet, as we discussed in chapter 3, the relationship between revenue and pricing in higher education is very complex. In both public and private colleges and universities the true costs of a college education are heavily subsidized with public and private funds. Often tuition is discounted still further through financial aid programs. This is certainly an important consideration from the point of view of the student, but it is also important from the perspective of financial operations, since financial aid is a direct write-off against tuition revenue in many institutions, particularly at the margin. Some institutions have found that the incremental cost of financial aid programs necessary to protect their student applicant pool actually exceeds the additional revenue from tuition increases.

Determining tuition rates involves a complex set of considerations, including the actual costs of instruction at the institution, the availability of other revenue sources that can be used to subsidize instructional costs (e.g., tax support, private giving, and income from endowment), competition with other institutions for students, and an array of other political factors. These factors can be woven together in several ways to determine tuition levels. Private universities relying on high-tuition/high-financial aid strategies are much more constrained by market concerns. Institutions of comparable reputation generally have comparable tuition levels.

For most public colleges and universities determining pricing tends to be influenced more by political pressures than by considerations of educational costs, financial needs, or market sensitivity. As we have noted, tuition levels in public universities were held at very nominal levels, amounting to only a small fraction of actual costs, until the 1980s. As institutions attempted to compensate for eroding state appropriations by increasing tuition in the late 1980s and early 1990s, they triggered first public concern and then political reactions.

As a consequence, today many state legislatures and public university governing boards have learned that strong opposition to tuition increases makes eminently good politics, even during times when state appropriations are dropping. Although they sometimes rationalize this behavior by suggesting that universities will become more efficient if they have less money to spend, it is also clear that concerns about quality in higher education do not carry as much political weight as concerns about prices. In some states public institutions have also found that there is a direct link between tuition and state appropriation; increasing one decreases the other. For most institutions either market forces or political pressures strongly constrain tuition increases and revenues.

Clearly, public agencies such as state legislatures and university governing bodies need to understand better the interplay between market pressures and the impact of public subsidization. While it may be tempting to respond to the public demand for low-cost higher education by simply mandating low tuition levels, this move would conflict with an educational marketplace in which pricing will be increasingly set by private institutions and proprietary providers. If the state constrains the tuition levels of public institutions below this natural market price, then it must either provide adequate public appropriations to offset the difference or accept the inevitable deterioration in quality which will occur among public institutions.

In the face of inadequate appropriations and constrained tuitions many institutions have no choice but to sacrifice quality. Yet some universities do have the reputation and capability to restructure themselves to emphasize activities with income-generating potential which are less regulated. For example, professional education, applied research, technology transfer, and professional services are examples of relatively unregulated and sometimes profitable activities. Here too, however, there is a public concern, since shifting institutional focus from state appropriation–starved, tuition-constrained academic programs such as undergraduate education to profitable professional education may not respond to the highest public priorities.

For many universities private fund raising provides the most immediate opportunity for enhancing support.[5] For private colleges and universities private fund raising, particularly that aimed at building endowments, has long been a critical priority. But, increasingly, even for public universities, private fund raising may represent a more realistic option in the face of strong political opposition to tuition increases. Most colleges and universities are making major investments in their fund-raising activities, increasing development staff and developing new public relations efforts. Yet, while they find there are generally near-term payoffs to these efforts, they also find themselves competing with other institutions for private gifts from the same sources.

People give to universities for many reasons. Some contribute to say thanks, to pay institutions back for the educational opportunities they enjoyed. Others support higher education as a way to have an impact on the future. Some people wish to achieve immortality through contributions to a perpetual or endowment fund. Still others want monuments and thus fund campus construction. Yet all too often donors prefer to give to wealthy universities, to see their names associated with buildings or endowed chairs at elite institutions (what some refer to as the "edifice complex"). The old maxim seems to apply in higher education as elsewhere: the rich get richer, and the poor fall further and further behind.

The revenue generated by auxiliary units of the universities—particularly, their academic medical centers—has been the fastest-growing component of the resource base of many large public universities over the past two decades. Yet it is also the most uncertain element of a university's resource base because it depends upon rapidly changing markets and shifting public policies. With the rapid evolution of managed care and capitation and the entry of for-profit health care providers, the academic medical center has become an endangered species. Most other auxiliary units, such as intercollegiate athletics, generate revenue barely sufficient to cover their own operating expenses. But there are occasional opportunities elsewhere. For example, continuing education presents an excellent opportunity to produce additional revenue. The executive education programs conducted by many business schools provide examples of the degree to which high-quality programs, aggressively marketed, can generate resources that directly benefit academic units while aligning well with the teaching mission of the institution. Technology transfer activities, through royalty licenses and equity interest in business startups, have provided revenue streams for some research universities.

The diverse and ever-changing nature of the portfolio of resources available to finance higher education has stimulated and been tapped by marketlike or entrepreneurial behavior of universities and their faculties. For both major private and public research universities most of the resources necessary to support academic activities are generated through the entrepreneurial activities of the institutions—for example, by attracting sufficient enrollment to generate the necessary tuition revenue, competing for federal research grants, and seeking private gifts. As a result, faculty members became quite skillful at generating the resources necessary to support their activities.[6]

While creating highly resilient institutions capable of weathering financial storms, such a market-driven, entrepreneurial culture has also had less beneficial consequences. Many contemporary universities resemble shopping malls, with programs and activities determined largely by available resources rather than student needs. Programs such as business, medicine, and engineering, with strong resource opportunities, are usually winners; others such as the arts and the humanities, with fewer opportunities for external support, can become impoverished backwaters. Furthermore, with the ebb and flow of various elements of the university's resource portfolio, both its missions and programs would shift in order to adapt. Put another way, shifting revenue streams and obsolete cost structures suggest that the very nature of the enterprise is changing. For the longer term we cannot depend upon simply substituting one revenue stream for another or cutting costs at the margin. We must consider changing the entire mix of activities to respond to the changing needs of those whom public higher education serves.[7]

Yet here public universities will face the challenge of relating to the ever-broadening constituencies associated with a diversified resource portfolio. As tuitions rise, students and parents will demand more in the way of educational quality and campus experiences. Donors, whether individuals, foundations, or corporations, will expect more attention to their interests and needs as their contributions to public universities rise. The resources provided by state and federal government programs such as sponsored research and medical training generally have strings attached which require both accountability and adherence to complex rules and regulations. And, as public universities become more actively involved in the commercial marketplace, with revenue-generating activities such as technology licensing, distance learning, and equity interest in spin-off companies, they will be subject to the same market forces that press upon for-profit companies.

Public universities may have a particularly difficult time responding to the diversity of patron expectations and needs because of the politics and public pressures that swirl about their activities. It seems obvious that universities must take care in deciding what efforts they are willing to make in order to secure additional resources. Yet this may prove difficult for public colleges and universities long accustomed to attempting to satisfy all of the needs of their many constituencies. Furthermore, as the share of university support provided by state appropriations declines, the other patrons of the public university may demand more attention to their needs, this in the face of political and public pressure to do even more to respond to state needs despite more limited public funding.

The Importance of Reserves

Many public colleges and universities have been forced to operate in a hand-to-mouth mode, totally dependent on state largesse from appropriation cycle to appropriation cycle, with little funding capacity to respond to unusual challenges or opportunities. Some public institutions have even been required to return unexpended appropriations to the state treasury at the end of each fiscal year.

Yet the obligations of the public university are much too significant to leave to the whims of the legislative appropriation process, at least for the short term. Students must be educated. Patients must be treated. There are federal obligations for research grants and contracts to be fulfilled. And the university must respond to a host of other important services to both the public and private sector. Moreover, while costs structures are generally both relatively fixed and straightforward to estimate, the revenues associated with many activities such as patient care in hospitals or television income for athletic events can be quite unpredictable. For this reason prudent management would suggest the wisdom of building significant reserves in accounts associated with key activities.

For example, at the University of Michigan, where we had sufficient autonomy from state government to allow us to manage our own financial affairs, we made it a very high priority to accumulate sufficient reserves to protect both the university and its programs and employees in the event of a serious downturn in state support. We had learned a hard lesson from the difficult days of the late 1970s and 1980s, when a serious recession reduced state appropriations by roughly 30 percent, necessitating traumatic budget cuts, program reductions, and staff downsizing. To this end we used expenditure control to build reserves in both operating and capital accounts at both the central and department level. Furthermore, we used excess revenues during prosperous years to build reserves in the accounts of volatile auxiliary activities to levels such that the interest earned by investing these reserves would cover any conceivable shortfall in revenues. For example, in intercollegiate athletics we tried to carry reserves of at least $25 million to $30 million, while for our university hospitals we built reserves to over $1 billion. In both cases the reserves were roughly comparable to one year of total revenue.

While such reserves had an important impact on our capacity to manage the university effectively in the face of the inevitable and unpredictable challenges and opportunities, they also had a second important benefit. They allowed us to make the case for higher credit ratings from Wall Street agencies, raising the university's ratings to the highest Aaa level in 1997 (along with the University of Texas, a first for a public university) and allowing us to issue debt through bonds and other instruments at minimal interest rates.

Of comparable importance to the financial strength of public universities are endowment funds. Endowments are contributed funds, held and invested by the university in perpetuity, whose proceeds are dedicated for a particular purpose, such as supporting a distinguished faculty member (e.g., establishing an endowed professorial chair), a student (e.g., creating an endowed scholarship or fellowship), or perhaps an academic program. Frequently, the benefactor's name is associated with the endowed activity.

Since the management of endowments is intended to honor the original intent of the donor in perpetuity, only a fraction of the income is distributed for the designated purpose of the fund. The rest is reinvested to maintain the purchasing power of the fund in the face of inflation. For example, although an endowment fund might earn a 10 percent return, only 4 percent might be distributed, while 6 percent would be reinvested, thereby allowing the endowment to appreciate.

Yet, even during the 1990s, when endowment investment returns frequently were in the 15 to 20 percent range, many of the wealthier institutions set distributions at 3 percent or less, thereby allowing the funds to appreciate to enormous magnitudes (e.g., in 2001 Harvard currently had an endowment of $19.2 billion; Yale, $10.1 billion; Texas, $10 billion; and Michigan, $3.5 billion).[8] The soaring magnitude of some endowment funds has raised concerns both about the appropriateness of such a low distribution rate, which invests in future opportunity rather than meeting current needs, and the staggering magnitude of certain endowment funds. In fact, it has been suggested that some universities, from a financial perspective, look more like banks than educational institutions, since their most significant economic activity involves managing their endowment investments.

Yet it must also be stressed that in 2002 only forty universities in America had endowments over $1 billion. In fact, only 10 percent of the nation's thirty-six hundred colleges and universities had endowments above $50 million, with the vast majority having endowments well under $10 million. Hence, while endowment income is important to a small number of elite institutions, it remains inconsequential to most of higher education in America.[9]

The Allocation and Management of Resources

The operation of a university, like other enterprises in society, requires the acquisition, allocation, and management of adequate resources to cover the costs of activities. This is a somewhat more complex task for academic institutions because of the great diversity of the constituencies they serve, the wide array of their activities, and the cross-subsidies that flow among these activities.

The not-for-profit culture of the university, whether public or private, leads to a somewhat different approach to the development of a business plan than one would find in the private sector. Universities usually begin with the assumption that all of their current activities are both worthwhile and necessary. They first seek to identify the resources that can fund these activities. Beyond that, since there is always an array of meritorious proposals for expanding ongoing activities or launching new activities, the university always seeks additional resources. It has only been in recent years that the possibility of re-allocating resources away from ongoing activities to fund new endeavors has been seriously considered.

Financial Budgeting and Management

Over the past decade it has become increasingly clear that universities must develop more effective financial management systems, capable of sustaining their core missions—teaching, research, and service—in the face of the rapid changes occurring in their resource base. Good managers will make good (cost-effective) decisions when they are provided with the necessary information and proper incentives. The first challenge for a university is to select good managers and to provide training for them. The second challenge is to identify the appropriate level at which decision-making authority should lie with respect to each type of decision. If it is at too high a level, there may not be an understanding of the primary impact on the unit or individuals (e.g., if the president were to assign faculty to courses). If it is at too low a level, there may not be an understanding of the secondary impact on related units or individuals (e.g., if each faculty member were to choose his or her own courses).

Many universities, particularly public universities, have relied for decades on a system of resource allocation best described as "incremental budgeting," based on a fund-accounting system.[10] In this system a unit begins each fiscal year with the same base level of support it had received the previous year, raised by some incremental amount reflecting inflation, a unit's additional needs and aspirations, and the university's capacity to provide additional funds. These resources are partitioned into specific funds, more determined by historic traditions than strategic management—for example, the General and Education Fund, Restricted Fund, Restricted Expendable Fund, Auxiliary Fund, and Capital Fund. Beyond simply serving as an accounting tool, firewalls are constructed between these funds to limit transfers.

This system worked well enough during the three decades following World War II, when the increases in public support outpaced inflation. Universities had the additional dollars each year to launch many new initiatives, to do many important new things, without disturbing the resource stream to ongoing activities. But, with the erosion in public support—particularly state support—which began to occur in the late 1970s and has continued through today, it has become apparent that such incremental budgeting and fund accounting approaches are increasingly incapable of meeting new challenges and opportunities. Indeed, in the face of a more limited resource base they eventually lead to the slow starvation of all university activities.

The more constrained resource base facing higher education during the 1990s and beyond will force many institutions to abandon incremental budgeting if they are to preserve their core values, mission, and character. Universities must retain the capacity to set priorities and allocate resources to achieving them. There are many ways to do this. One can continue to implement targeted resource reallocation based upon decisions made by the central administration, assisted by faculty advisory groups. But in most universities today not only are most costs incurred at the unit level, but this is also where most of the institution's revenues are generated. Hence, centralized resource management schemes are increasingly incompatible with the realities of highly decentralized resource generation and expenditure.

An alternative is to decentralize resource management entirely, that is, to institute an "every tub on its own bottom" (ETOB) strategy, similar to that used at several private institutions. Each unit has full authority and responsibility for its financial operation. A serious drawback is that it is difficult to address university-wide values or objectives with such a highly decentralized approach.

Many private universities and a few public universities have chosen an intermediate route to decentralize resource management through a system known as "responsibility center management" as an alternative to the more commonly used incremental fund accounting system.[11] In its simplest form this system allows units to keep the resources they generate. It holds them responsible for meeting the costs they incur. It then levies a tax on all expenditures to provide a central pool of resources necessary to support central operations (such as the university library) while providing the additional support needed by academic units unable to generate sufficient resources to support their activities.

Although the appropriate degree of decentralization in resource control and responsibility will depend on institutional character, culture, and tradition, it is clear that the highly centralized, incremental budgeting accompanied by fund accounting systems may no longer suffice in the rapidly changing resource environment of the contemporary university. Moving from crisis to crisis or subjecting institutions to gradual starvation through across-the-board cuts simply are not adequate long-term strategies.

Another necessary change will be in the way universities plan. The changing financial environment demands that planning exercises be conducted with significantly tightened and restrictive revenue assumptions. No longer will it be feasible, or even acceptable, to develop expenditure budgets first and then to close the gap between expenditure plans and revenue projections by a price increase (e.g., tuition). There will have to be much more care in setting priorities, along with a painful acknowledgment that in order to do something new one generally will have to eliminate something old. Innovation by substitution, not growth by incremental resources, will have to become the operative management philosophy. For instance, an academic unit that wishes to embrace a new subfield of its basic discipline may be required to phase out some other activity in order to make room for the new endeavor.

The necessity for cost containment need not be placed in a negative context. It is an opportunity to restore credibility with the various clients and stakeholders of the university. It is also an opportunity to demonstrate to potential private supporters of the university that its top administrators are serious about cost-effectiveness and institutional efficiency. They need to know that their future support will be used wisely in the delivery of instructional, research, and public service programs.

Underlying nearly all of these comments is the fundamental premise that universities simply cannot afford to engage in planning that is always "cost-plus" in nature. One cannot always start by allocating existing resources to sustain ongoing activities and then depend on additional resources to undertake a new or innovative activity. It will be necessary to consider eliminating, reducing, or otherwise changing a current activity to make budgetary room for the new activity that we believe to be important.

Reducing costs, improving productivity, and enhancing quality in order to generate flexible operating funds do not sound like easy tasks. They will not be easy. But they have been done in other environments and can be done in the university.

Cost Drivers

Most institutions now realize that they need to focus on the other side of the ledger, on costs. Not only do they need to reduce costs and increase productivity, but they also need to consider reducing the number of activities so that they can better focus their limited resources to sustain and enhance quality. All universities have a capacity to become more efficient or productive. Some will be able to achieve a sufficient gain in productivity to retain or enhance their existing portfolio of programs and activities while achieving their desired levels of quality. For most of them the dominant strategy will involve the painful process of focusing resources to achieve quality by shedding a number of missions and activities.

Several factors drive the costs of a college education: salaries paid to faculty and staff; costs of building and maintaining instructional facilities; infrastructure costs, such as libraries, computer centers, and laboratories; and costs of various support and administrative services. As one attempts to understand the nature of cost increases in higher education, it is tempting to place the blame for the increasing costs of a college education on external forces. These outside forces might include the need to compete for high-quality faculty, staff, and students; the external imposition of new rules and regulations; or the increasing litigiousness of society. While they clearly influence a university's costs, they are only part of the picture. Just as important are the costs universities impose on themselves by operating inefficiently, for example, continuing to depend upon systems and processes that allow or even encourage waste, duplication, and rework. Wasting resources, because of inefficient operations, occurs more often that universities care to admit.

Market-driven external forces that greatly influence costs are in large part the result of institutional objectives, such as comprehensiveness and quality. Such objectives require that institutions of the same caliber compete with one another for both faculty and students. They must meet market rates for faculty salaries, workloads, and other resources and must compete effectively for the best undergraduate and graduate students. Faculty needs for computing services, library resources, laboratory facilities, support staff, and associated expenses such as travel are also competitively driven. It is clear that different choices related to comprehensiveness or excellence lead to different markets and potentially lower-cost resources.

There also exist many costly external forces that are not market driven. These consist of rules, regulations, and social forces. In addition, the university is asked to provide public service as well as time and talent to local, state, national, and international organizations for a wide variety of important activities and concerns.

Certain cultural factors sustain the current cost structures of higher education. Most institutions tend to focus on inputs rather than outputs. We tend to recruit faculty with the best reputations and students with the highest scores on standardized tests. We measure the success of leaders of higher education by how many private gifts they procure or the size of the university endowment they create. Rarely do we focus on more traditional measures of productivity and value added: the learning of students and the impact of scholarship. In part this arises from the priority given to institutional reputation, or prestige, in management decisions. Most colleges and universities are driven by the competitive marketplace to increase their financial capacity continually in order to hire better faculty, attract more talented students, and enhance the reputation of their academic programs. During the 1990s the exceptional growth in the equity markets and consequent surge in private giving and endowments, coupled with substantial tuition increases and subsidized in part by favorable federal financial aid policies, allowed private colleges and universities to become ever more competitive in the prestige race. Although public universities have attempted to keep pace, political constraints on tuition levels and state appropriations have eroded the competitive position of public higher education for the top faculty and best students.

Even during periods of relative prosperity such as the late 1990s, states appeared reluctant to increase appropriations for the purpose of enhancing faculty salaries or establishing new programs. As long as the market is being driven by institutions that believe that high expenditures correlate with national prestige, these fiscal trends will disadvantage public universities, which are increasingly being monitored and evaluated for greater efficiency.

Financial Restructuring

The fiscal pressures resulting from reduced revenue streams and uncontrolled cost drivers can be substantial. These pressures can lead to negative results within the normal university environment, with a long tradition of incremental budgeting. How can such pressures be made positive, and how can the funds that will be needed for new ideas and continuing improvement be found?

Cost Containment and Productivity

Higher education has been slow to focus creative attention on a careful understanding of quality and how quality relates to costs. As we face an era in which incremental resources become scarcer for the university, learning how to achieve higher quality while containing costs will be absolutely vital. During the past two decades people in many organizations, in business, government, and health care, learned that to improve quality and overall institutional performance they needed—often for the first time—to identify their customers carefully, to learn more about their needs and expectations, and then to strive to improve their performance based upon what they learned. Although some faculty members bristle at the term in this context, in truth the university does indeed have customers. The most obvious ones are external to the institution, such as prospective students and faculty. But customers may also be internal— that is, one university unit may be the customer of another. Attention to defining a unit's customers and to understanding their needs and expectations is key to quality improvement and a step toward understanding and eliminating unnecessary costs.

A second major insight from industry's experiences in the 1980s is that the pursuit of certain dimensions of quality clearly increases costs (e.g., hiring "star" faculty members, increasing the specialized programs available to undergraduates, or adding staff to improve the quality of support for any activity). But the pursuit of some dimensions of quality can actually lead to cost reductions. This is a major change from the traditional thinking that quality (always) costs more. For example, by providing students and faculty with direct access to university services through the Internet, an institution can not only improve the timeliness and effectiveness of service activities but also eliminate the costs associated with layers of unnecessary management and bureaucracy.

Restructuring and Reengineering

Beyond the continual efforts to contain costs, increase productivity, and innovate through substitution rather than growth, universities need to follow industry's lead by asking more fundamental questions. They need to shift from asking "Are we doing things right?" to "Are we doing the right things?" They need to grapple with the difficult challenge of restructuring and reengineering the most fundamental activities of the institution.[12]

Most institutions have considered the redesign of administrative processes, such as managing financial operations, student services, and research administration. But, because the core activity of the university involves academic processes, this too will eventually need fundamental reexamination. Here institutions face more serious challenges. First among them is the faculty culture that strongly resists business methods. But there are other fundamental obstacles as well.

For decades universities have defined academic quality in terms of inputs— for example, the caliber of students and faculty, resources, and facilities— rather than outputs such as student performance. Rethinking the core academic functions of the university requires a shift in perspective from resources to results. This turns the institutional focus from faculty productivity to student productivity, from faculty disciplinary interests to what students need to learn, and from faculty teaching styles to student learning styles. It reconceptualizes the university as learner centered rather than faculty centered. It grapples with the most fundamental processes, such as the way decisions are made, how information is shared, how students are taught, how students learn, how faculty work, how research is conducted, and how auxiliary enterprises are managed.

Nonetheless, there are constraints on the internal actions an institution can take to control costs. The impact of tenure or collective bargaining agreements limits the institution's capacity to reduce faculty size. Political pressures can influence the maintenance of enrollment levels and program breadth. And, as a matter of fact, many institutions are already operating at the margin in terms of cost reduction, at least within the current higher education paradigms. Ironically, the only unconstrained variable that many institutions can adjust is quality. Efforts to reduce costs to stay within a given budget can sometimes only be achieved by accepting lower-quality standards. In sharp contrast to the business sector, revenue-driven models of higher education could well lead to a significant erosion in program quality.

Even for those universities that accept the challenge of restructuring academic processes, there can be disappointments.[13] The pattern of retrenchment, reorganization, restructuring, and reengineering may not yield substantial productivity gains. Something more may be needed—namely, a fundamental transformation of both the university and the higher education enterprise, a topic for the later chapters of this book.

Financial Management, Responsibility, and Accountability

Despite the fact that in many ways the public university has become one of the most complex institutions in modern society—considerably more complex, for example, than most corporations or governments—its management and governance could best be described as amateurish. That is, although competent professionals have usually been sought to manage key administrative areas such as investments, finances, and accounting, the general leadership, management, and governance of the university has been the responsibility of either academics or lay board members. In fact, many public universities take great pride in the fact that they not only are led and managed by "true academics" with little professional experience but also are governed by lay boards with little business or educational experience.

Yet today the typical public university affects the lives not simply of thousands of students and faculty but also thousands more staff members and hundreds of thousands of community and state citizens who depend upon its critical services for such things as education, health care, and economic development. Furthermore, these institutions attract and expend billions of dollars of public and private funds. We can no longer pretend that the detached, amateurish academic leadership model is sufficient. Nor is it any longer sufficient to rely upon politically selected lay boards for their governance. Like other major institutions in society, we must demand new levels of accountability of the university for the integrity of its financial operations, the quality of its services, and the stewardship of its resources.

Although some universities still draw much of their leadership from academic ranks, more and more are recognizing that the vast scope, complexity, and impact of these institutions requires the presence of talented and qualified management professionals. Too much is at stake, both for the institution and the society it serves, to tolerate the limited experience and business acumen of the academy. In fact, there are increasing calls for more formal training in business and management for all of those in academic administration, from presidents to deans to department chairs. Too many people depend upon their decisions, too many dollars are involved, and too much legal liability is at stake to rely upon the limited management experience of most academics.

Yet, even with adequate training and experience, the administration of the public university faces many challenges. Most institutions lack serious financial planning—which is not surprising given that the academy resists any suggestion that academic units should develop a business plan. Universities are plagued by a serious incompatibility in the responsibility and authority assigned to those in administration. All too often those charged with the responsibility for various administrative activities simply are not provided with the authority to carry out these tasks. By the same token many with relatively little responsibility have great authority to prevent decisive action. Little wonder that the university administration is frequently unable and unwilling to tackle major issues such as the downsizing or elimination of obsolete programs in order to free up resources for new initiatives. Sacred cows such as intercollegiate athletics continue to graze on the core academic programs of the institution.

This mismatch between authority and responsibility can be attributed to many factors—for instance, a faculty culture that resists strong leadership or the relatively short tenure of most academic administrators. But ultimately all of these factors can be traced to the political nature and the limited experience of the governing boards at most public institutions. In a legal sense the governing board of a public university is responsible for its integrity. It has a fiduciary responsibility for its financial operations as well as a legal responsibility for its welfare. Yet this responsibility exists largely in theory and not practice, since board members are rarely held personally accountable for their decisions or actions. Indeed, governing boards as bodies are rarely evaluated with respect to their competence and actions in financial matters.

A Broader Perspective

The current trends in both the funding and costs of higher education suggest that we may be headed toward a crisis in the years ahead. The dilemma has been described earlier: if colleges and universities continue to increase tuition to compensate for the imbalance between societal demand for higher education and rising costs, on one hand, and stagnant public support, on the other, millions of Americans will find a college education priced beyond their means. While cost containment and renewed public investment are clearly needed, it could well be that entirely new paradigms for providing and financing higher education are required for the longer term.

It will become even more important to use increasingly limited public dollars for higher education wisely. We have noted that recent experience has demonstrated that raising prices for middle- and upper-income students in public higher education does not discourage enrollments. In a similar sense using federal dollars to subsidize the lending costs of middle- and upper-income students does little to create new opportunities for college enrollment.

In fact, some go still further and suggest that the very principle of low tuition levels at public universities is, in reality, a highly regressive social policy that subsidizes the rich at the expense of the poor. Few families will ever pay sufficient state taxes to cover the educational costs of their children at a public university. Low tuition levels subsidize many middle- and upper-income families that could afford to send their students to more expensive institutions. This subsidy is being provided through the tax dollars paid by many lower-income families whose children may never have the opportunity to benefit from a college education at four-year institutions, public or private, because of inadequate availability of financial aid.[14]

This issue becomes even more serious when it is recognized that public higher education has increasingly become the choice of higher-income students. In 1994, 38 percent of students from families earning more than $200,000 were enrolled in public institutions, compared to 31 percent in 1980.[15] Parents and students from wealthy backgrounds are increasingly asking why they should attend the elite private colleges when they can get nearly as good an education for one-third the price. In fact, in several states the average income of students enrolling in public universities is now higher than that of private colleges. Clearly, this raises a public policy issue, since these wealthier students, who could afford to attend more expensive private institutions, are displacing students from less fortunate economic circumstances in public higher education. Although holding tuition to nominal levels in public higher education may be good politics, it is questionable social policy. In effect we ask those who cannot afford a college education to pay taxes to subsidize those who can—welfare for the rich at the expense of the poor. For this reason many believe that a high-tuition, high–financial aid policy would be more socially progressive, since it would mean that rich students pay at or near full fare, while a public subsidy is provided to low-income students.

To be sure, some of the stronger public universities do have the capacity to compensate for the loss of state funding with other sources such as tuition revenue, private gifts, and sponsored research. Some, like the University of Michigan, have already been forced to move quite far down the road to becoming a privately financed state university, with state support declining to roughly 10 percent of its revenue base.

Equally troubling is the academic culture itself. In most colleges and universities the professorate expects others to generate the resources necessary to support their teaching, research, and professional activities. Although faculty entrepreneurs are essential in generating the resources needed for quality education and scholarship, in many institutions these individuals are held in low regard by the rank and file. The awards of the academy most often go to those who behave in traditional roles, depending upon others for their existence and not seeing themselves as having a responsibility to bring resources to the institution. Yet it may very well be that the most vibrant universities of the future will be institutions with faculties who are deeply engaged in the economics of education. The most productive scholars would be rewarded for that effort, and those rewards would encourage other able colleagues to follow.

This direct engagement by the academy in financing public higher education is important, as suggested by a comparison with the plight of K-12 education in the United States. In many ways the great challenges faced by primary and secondary education today arose because of the loss of control of public financing by the public school systems. The property tax simply did not have the elasticity to sustain an educational system operating under demands made by legislators, Congress, parents, and students. The fundamental mission of the public schools was enlarged to take on a whole host of society's wishes, but they were not expected to take away from the primary mission. When that failed, criticism increased. Property owners revolted. Legislatures and governors enacted programs that were reactions rather than prescriptions. Because the schools were at the sufferance of the local taxpayer, they could not make the changes required to become efficient. Special interest candidates were elected to local school boards in the name of accountability, and the curriculum became the domain of the dominant constituency. Teachers were powerless. Had they been able to become more entrepreneurial with prices set according to demand, they would have been players in the debate, as suggested by the recent trend toward charter schools.

Higher education, with high costs, embedded inefficiencies, and disparate missions, faces a similar and no less daunting task. As stewards of the public trust, academic leaders and governing boards share with federal and state leaders the responsibility to find a better way to deliver educational and financial resources to the people who need them. We must not allow public colleges and universities to follow the path taken by K-12 education during the twentieth century.

The system of higher education in the United States is regarded as the best in the world. But having high-quality universities means little if our own people cannot attend them or if the quality of life that a college education promises, for the individual and for the nation, becomes unattainable. It is in our national interest to provide educational opportunities to everyone who has the desire and the ability to learn. Many people believe that it is time to halt the erosion in public support of higher education and once again reaffirm the national commitment one generation makes to the next. Yet it is unlikely that the fiscal constraints faced by local, state, and federal governments will lessen in the years ahead, since there continues to be strong public resistance against additional taxation.

The Privatization of Public Higher Education in America

Today, in the face of limited resources and more pressing social priorities, the century-long expansion of public support of higher education has slowed. While the needs of society for advanced education can only intensify as we evolve into a knowledge-driven world culture, it is not evident that these needs will be met by further growth of the existing system of public universities.

The terms of the social contract that led to these institutions are changing rapidly. The principle of general tax support for public higher education as a public good and the partnership between the federal government and the universities for conducting research are both at risk. These changes are being driven in part by increasingly limited tax resources and the declining priority given to higher education in the face of competing social needs.[16]

We now have at least two decades of experience that would suggest that the states are simply not able, or willing, to provide the resources needed to sustain growth in public higher education, at least at the rate experienced in the decades following World War II. In many parts of the nation states will be hard-pressed even to sustain the present capacity and quality of their institutions. Little wonder that public university leaders are increasingly reluctant to cede control of their activities to state governments. Some institutions are even bargaining for more autonomy from state control as an alternative to growth in state support, arguing that, if they are granted more control over their own destiny, they can better protect their capacity to serve the public.

Most pessimistically, one might even conclude that America's great experiment of building world-class public universities supported primarily by tax dollars has come to an end. The concept of a world-class, comprehensive state university might not be viable over the longer term, at least in terms of having an institution heavily dependent upon state appropriations. It simply may not be possible to justify the level of tax support necessary to sustain the quality of these institutions in the face of other public priorities, such as health care, K-12 education, and public infrastructure needs—particularly during a time of slowly rising or stagnant economic activity.

One obvious consequence of declining state support is that several of the leading public universities may increasingly resemble private universities in the way they are financed and managed.[17] They will move toward higher tuition–high financial aid strategies. They will use their reputations, developed and sustained during earlier times of more generous state support, to attract the resources they need from federal and private sources to replace declining state appropriations. Many will embrace a strategy of being increasingly privately financed, even as they strive to retain their public character.

In such "privately financed, public universities" only a small fraction of operating or capital support will come from state appropriations. Like private universities, these hybrid institutions will depend primarily upon the revenue they generate directly from their activities—tuition, federal grants and contracts, private gifts, and revenue from auxiliary services such as health care—rather than upon direct appropriations. They will manage these resources much as private universities do, moving toward more decentralized "tub-on-its-own-bottom" budgeting philosophies in which their academic units have both the responsibilities and incentives for generating resources and containing costs.

State universities choosing—or forced—to undergo this privatization transition in financing must appeal to a broad array of constituencies at the national and global level while continuing to exhibit a strong mission focused on state needs. In the same way as private universities, they must earn the majority of their support in the competitive marketplace—that is, via tuition, research grants, and gifts—and this will sometimes require actions that come into conflict with state priorities. Hence, the autonomy of the public university will become one of its most critical assets, perhaps even more critical than state support for some institutions.

Several public universities, such as the University of Michigan and the University of Virginia, are well on their way down this road. Several other leading public research universities are likely to follow, as state appropriations continue to decline as a fraction of their revenue base. Both within higher education and state government there are ongoing discussions about new institutional forms, such as public corporations similar to the U.S. Postal Service, in which control and accountability are assigned to independent boards of directors even though assets remain owned by the state. Another possible approach is the charter college or university, in which independent institutions gain state support in exchange for long-term commitment to detailed performance goals. The extreme point in the evolution toward increasing privatization is represented by voucher systems in which public funds flow primarily to students who are then free to procure educational services from a competitive marketplace of colleges and universities, public, private, and even for-profit.

Such steps toward the privatization of financing mechanisms and management philosophy may allow some of the leading public universities to maintain their quality during a time of constrained or declining public support. However, these options will not be available to most public colleges and universities that face more limited resource opportunities and tighter political constraints. Furthermore, such a privatization strategy raises a number of very important issues about the very nature of a public university. For example, how does one preserve the public character of a privately financed institution even when it has a public charter? Clearly, as a public university becomes more independent of the purse strings from state appropriations, it becomes less inclined to follow the dictates of state government, particularly if it possesses constitutional or statutory autonomy. No longer is its public simply the taxpayer; rather, it becomes an array of stakeholders including parents and students, federal agencies, donors, and business and industry. Such privately supported public universities face a particular challenge in balancing their traditional public purpose with the pressures of the marketplace.

CHAPTER SEVEN

University Leadership

Like other social institutions, the public university requires capable leadership during today's time of great change, challenge, and opportunity. Clearly, universities that are capable of attracting and supporting strong, decisive, and visionary leaders will not only survive with their quality intact but will likely flourish during times of change. Yet many public universities seem to drift and to seek leaders who will preserve the status quo and not rock the boat.

Stated simply, the current environment on many public campuses today neither tolerates nor supports strong, visionary leadership. The governing boards of public institutions are much too political, with members too focused on personal agendas or chained to special interest groups and too threatened by anyone who would challenge the status quo. The faculty is highly fragmented, their members operating within their own narrow disciplinary worlds and largely resistant to changes that threaten to upset their comfortable niche, even those that would clearly benefit the university. Scattered throughout our institutions is a large herd of sacred cows—obsolete programs, outdated practices, and archaic policies—grazing on the seed corn of the future and defended by those determined to hang on to power and control, even at the expense of the institution. Public opinion is largely reactionary and, when manipulated by the media, can block even the most urgently needed change.

Although capable leaders are clearly important to universities, as in other organizations, they are generally not well accepted by several of the most important constituencies in a university: the faculty, the student body, and, most ironically, the governing board. Faculty members resist—indeed, deplore—the command-control style of leadership characterizing the traditional pyramid organizations of business and government. Many members of the faculty are offended by the suggestion that the university can be compared to other institutional forms such as corporations and governments. The academy takes great pride in functioning as a creative anarchy.

Yet faculty members also recognize the need for leadership, not in details of teaching and scholarship but in the abstract, in providing a vision for their university and stimulating a sense of optimism and excitement. They also seek protection from the forces of darkness which rage outside the university's ivy-covered walls: politics, greed, anti-intellectualism, and mediocrity, which threaten the most important academic values of the university.

The student body also generally tends to resist leadership. After all, challenging authority is an important part of growing up, and many university students are at that stage of their lives. Whether it is a residence hall supervisor, a classroom instructor, or even a president of the university, getting students to accept the authority necessary for effective leadership can be problematic.

One might expect that governing boards would seek and support strong leadership for their universities. After all, in the end they will be (or should be) held publicly accountable for the welfare of their institutions. Yet the political nature of the lay boards governing public universities leads them all too frequently to seek leaders chosen primarily for their willingness to accommodate the particular agendas, indeed, whims, of board members while avoiding those who might challenge the faculty, the alumni, or the status quo. Having leaders with energy, vision, and experience, which one would think of as desirable qualities, is not only undervalued but sometimes even viewed as a threat to the authority of the board.

All large, complex organizations require not only leadership at the helm but also effective management at each level where important decisions must be made. To be sure, organizations in business, industry, and government are finding it important to flatten administrative structures by removing layers of management. Yet, despite what the press, many politicians, and even a few trustees think, most universities already have rather thin and ineffective management organizations compared to corporations, inherited from earlier times when academic life was much simpler and institutions were considerably smaller.

There is a growing epidemic of presidential turnover which is both a consequence of these problems and a factor that contributes to them. The average tenure for the presidents of major public universities is about five years, too brief to provide the stability in leadership necessary for achieving effective change.[1] While some of these changes in university leadership are the result of natural processes such as retirement, others reflect the serious challenges and stresses faced by universities, which all too frequently destabilize their leadership. The contentious politics on college campuses, from students to faculty to governing boards, coupled with external pressures exerted by state and federal governments, alumni, sports fans, the media, and the public at large, all make the public university presidency a very hazardous profession these days. At a time when universities require courageous, and visionary, leadership the eroding tenure and deteriorating attractiveness of the public university presidency role pose a significant threat to the future of these institutions.[2]

The Issues

There is a seemingly endless array of decisions bubbling up, swirling through and about, the contemporary university. At the core are those *academic decisions* that most directly affect the academic process: Whom does the university select as students (admissions)? Who should teach them (faculty hiring, promotion, and tenure)? What should they be taught (curriculum and degree requirements)? How should they be taught (pedagogy)? There is a long-standing tradition that decisions most directly affecting the activities of teaching and scholarship are best left to the faculty itself. Yet in many institutions, particularly those that suffer from overly intrusive government controls or adversarial labor-management relationships between faculty and administration, this academic autonomy can be compromised.

Since most universities are large, complex organizations, enrolling tens of thousands of students, employing thousands of faculty and staff, and involving annual expenditures of hundreds of millions or even billions of dollars, there is also an array of important *administrative decisions* facing the university. Where will it get the funds necessary to support its programs, and how should they be spent (resource acquisition and allocation, budget development)? How will it build and maintain the campus environment necessary for quality teaching and research (capital facilities)? How does it honor its responsibilities and accountability to broader society (financial audits, compliance with state and federal regulations, and diversity)? How should it manage its relationships with the multiple stakeholders of the university (public relations, government relations, and development)?

In addition to the ongoing academic and administrative decisions necessary to keep the university moving ahead, there is always a host of unforeseen events—challenges or opportunities—which require immediate attention and rapid decision making. For example, when student activism explodes on the campus, an athletic violation is uncovered, or the university is attacked by politicians or the media, *crisis management* becomes critical. While the handling of such matters requires the time and attention of many senior university administrators, from deans to executive officers and governing boards, all too frequently crisis management becomes the responsibility of the university president. At any meeting of university presidents, frequent disruptions by pagers, faxes, or cell phone calls provide evidence of just how tightly contemporary university leaders are coupled to the issues of the day. A carefully developed strategy is necessary for handling such crises, both to prevent universities from lapsing into a reactive mode as well as to take full advantage of the occasional possibility of transforming a crisis into an opportunity.

More generally, universities need to develop a more strategic context for decision making during a period of rapid change. Yet *strategic planning* in higher education has had mixed success, particularly in institutions of the size, breadth, and complexity of the public university. Planning exercises are frequently attacked by faculty and staff alike as bureaucratic. In fact, many universities have traditionally focused planning efforts on gathering data for supporting the routine decision process rather than on providing a context for longer-term considerations. As a result, all too often universities tend to react to, or even resist, external pressures and opportunities rather than to take strong, decisive actions to determine and pursue their own goals. They frequently become preoccupied with process rather than objectives, with "how" rather than "what."

The final class of decisions consists of those involving more fundamental or even radical transformations of the university. The major paradigm shifts that will likely take place in higher education in the years ahead will require a more strategic approach to *institutional transformation* which is capable of staying the course until the desired changes have occurred. Many institutions already have embarked on transformation agendas similar to those adopted by organizations in the private sector.[3] Some even use similar language as they refer to their efforts to "transform," "restructure," or even "reinvent" their institutions. But herein lies one of the great challenges to universities, since their various missions and their diverse array of constituencies give them a complexity beyond that encountered in business or government. For universities the process of institutional transformation is necessarily more complex and possibly more hazardous. It must be approached strategically rather than reactively, with a deep understanding of the role and character of its institutions, their important traditions and values from the past, and a clear and compelling vision for their future.

The University Administration

Universities, like other institutions, depend increasingly on strong leadership and effective management to face the challenges and opportunities posed by a changing world. Yet in many universities the concept of management is held in very low regard, particularly by the faculty. To both students and faculty alike, the term *university administration* has a sinister connotation, in the same way that *federal government, bureaucracy,* and *corporate organization* do. In reality the university administration is simply a leadership network, primarily composed of members of the faculty themselves, sometimes on temporary assignment, which extends throughout the university. The academic programs of the university are organized into units that reflect the intellectual organization of the university. At the first level are schools and colleges organized along accepted disciplinary or professional lines, such as arts and sciences, medicine, engineering, and music. They are broken down into more manageable size through departments, such as philosophy and geology. At each level the administration consists of academic leaders, a dean or department chair, assisted by other academic and professional staff.

At the highest organizational level of the central administration are the president, provost, and various vice presidents with broad administrative responsibilities, which together constitute the "executive officers" of the university. For example, the provost or vice president for academic affairs is responsible for the various academic reporting lines of the academic units, including the deans, faculty appointments, budget allocations, and academic program evaluation. Other executive officers are responsible for particular functions of activities of the university, including research, student services, public relations, and business operations. As a general rule, executive officers who are responsible for academic programs and personnel (faculty and students) are generally selected from among the faculty and continue to have academic rank. Those responsible for various administrative, support, and business functions of the university such as finance, physical plant, and government relations generally have experience and training in these areas. Like other complex organizations in business or government the university requires a high level of professional management and administration in areas such as finance, physical plant maintenance, and information technology. Yet all presidents, provosts, and deans have heard the suggestion on occasion— usually from one of the more outspoken members of the faculty senate—that any one on the faculty, chosen at random, could be an adequate administrator. After all, if one is a strong teacher and scholar, these skills should be easily transferable to other areas, such as administration. Yet, in reality, talent in management is probably as rare a human attribute as the ability to contribute original scholarship. And there is little reason to suspect that talent in one characteristic implies the presence of talent in the other.

One of the great myths concerning higher education in America, and one that is particularly appealing to faculty members and trustees alike, is that university administrations are bloated and excessive. To be sure, organizations in business, industry, and government are finding it important to flatten administrative structures by removing layers of management. Yet most universities have rather lean management organizations, inherited from earlier times when academic life was much simpler and institutions were far smaller, particularly when compared to the increasing complexity and accountability of these institutions.

The Role of the University President

The American university presidency is both distinctive and complex. In Europe and Asia the role of institutional leadership—a rector, vice chancellor, or president—is frequently a temporary assignment held by a faculty member, sometimes elected, and generally without true executive authority. In these cases the institution's leader serves as a representative of collegial faculty views, while government officials or civil servants actually administer the university. In contrast, the American presidency has more of the character of a chief executive officer, with ultimate executive authority for all decisions made within the institution. Although today's university presidents are less visible and authoritative than in earlier times, they are clearly of great importance to higher education in America. Yet, while their leadership can be essential, particularly during times of change, most university presidents do not currently have the authority commensurate with the responsibilities of their positions.[4] As one colleague put it, we may have shared governance, but nobody wants to share power with the president.

American university presidents are expected to develop, articulate, and implement visions for their institutions which sustain and enhance their quality. This includes a broad array of intellectual, social, financial, human, and capital facilities and political issues that envelope the university. Through their roles as the chief executive officers of their institutions, they also have significant management responsibilities for a diverse collection of activities, ranging from education to health care to public entertainment (e.g., intercollegiate athletics). Since these roles generally require the expertise and experience of talented professionals, the president is the university's leading recruiter, identifying talented people, recruiting them into key university positions, and directing and supporting their activities. Unlike most corporate CEOs, however, the president is expected to play an active role in generating the resources needed by the university, whether by lobbying state and federal governments, seeking gifts and bequests from alumni and friends, or employing clever entrepreneurial efforts. There is an implicit expectation on most campuses that the president's job is to raise money for the provost and deans to spend, while the chief financial officer and administrative staff watch over their shoulders to make certain it is done wisely and prudently.

The university president also has a broad range of important responsibilities that might best be termed *symbolic leadership*. As head of the university, the president is responsible for the complex array of relationships with both internal and external constituencies, including students, faculty, and staff on the campus. The myriad external constituencies include alumni and parents; local, state, and federal government; business and labor; foundations; the higher education community; the media; and the public at large. The president has become a defender of the university and its fundamental qualities of knowledge and wisdom, truth and freedom, academic excellence and public service. Needless to say, the diverse perspectives and often conflicting needs and expectations of the various groups make managing relationships an extremely complex and time-consuming task.

Of course, there is an important and obvious fact of life here, which is that no single individual can possibly fulfill all the dimensions of the president's role. Hence, one must first determine which aspects of the role best utilize his or her talents. Then a team of executive officers and senior staff must be assembled which can extend and complement the activities of the president to deal with the full spectrum of the university leadership role. In this sense, then, a most important skill of presidential leadership lies in exercising "good taste" in identifying talented leaders and then persuading them to join the presidential leadership team. Just as in college sports, recruiting is as important as coaching.

The presidency of a major public university is an unusual leadership position from another perspective. Although the responsibility for everything involving the university usually floats up to the president's desk, direct authority for university activities almost invariably rests elsewhere. There is a mismatch between responsibility and authority which is unparalleled in other social institutions. As a result, there are many people, including university presidents, who have become convinced that the contemporary public university is basically unmanageable and unleadable.

There are numerous approaches to university leadership. Some presidents adopt a fatalistic approach, taking to heart the idea that the university is basically unmanageable. They instead focus their attention on a small set of issues, usually tactical in nature, and let the institution essentially drift undirected in other areas. This laissez-faire approach assumes that the university will do fine on its own; indeed, most institutions can drift along for a time without strategic direction, although they will eventually find themselves mired in a swamp of commitments that are largely reactive rather than strategic.

Other university leaders view themselves as change agents, setting bold visions for their institution and launching efforts to move toward these visions. Like generals who lead their troops into battle rather than sending orders from behind the front lines, these leaders recognize that winning the war sometimes requires personal sacrifice. The risks associated with proposing bold visions and leading change are high, and the tenure of such leaders is short—at least in public universities.

The Presidential Search

Despite the stress and rigor of the position, many people view a university presidency as the top rung in the academic ladder. The university presidency can be—or, at least, should be—a valued position, if only because of the importance of this remarkable social institution. It is therefore logical to expect that the selection of a university president ought to be a careful, thoughtful, and rational process. In reality, however, the search for a university president is a complex, time-consuming task conducted by the governing board of the university using a Byzantine process more akin to the selection of a pope than a corporate CEO. In public universities choosing a new president is more like a political campaign than a careful search for an academic leader.

The search process usually begins rationally enough. Typically, a group of distinguished faculty is asked to serve as a screening committee, with the assignment of sifting through the hundreds of nominations of candidates to determine a small group for consideration by the governing board. This task seems straightforward enough, yet it can be difficult in public universities because of the impact of sunshine laws, which require public meetings of governing bodies and allow the press access to written materials via freedom of information laws. So too, faculty members on the search committee are lobbied hard by their colleagues, by neighbors, and even occasionally by trustees to make certain that the right people appear on the short list of candidates they finally submit to the governing board.

In an effort both to expedite and to protect the faculty search process, there is an increasing trend at major universities to use executive search firms to assist in the presidential search process. These search consultants are useful in helping the faculty search committees to keep the process on track, gathering background information, developing realistic timetables, and even identifying key candidates. Furthermore, particularly for public institutions subject to sunshine laws, search consultants can provide a secure, confidential mechanism to communicate with potential candidates without public exposure, at least during the early stages of the search.

There are sometimes downsides to the use of search consultants. Some of them tend to take on too many assignments at a time and thus do an inferior job. There have been many occasions in which consultants have failed to check background references thoroughly. More seriously, there have been instances in which search consultants have actually attempted to influence the search process by promoting a preferred candidate. Yet most consultants act in a highly professional way and view their role as one of facilitating rather than influencing the search.

While the early stage of a presidential search is generally steered in a thoughtful way by the faculty screening committee, the final selection phase often involves a bizarre interplay of politics and personalities. The sunshine laws of some states not only require the final slate of candidates to be made public but, moreover, require these candidates to be interviewed and even compared and selected in public by the governing board. These public beauty pageants can be extremely disruptive to the integrity of the search process as well as to the reputation of the candidates. A great many attractive candidates will simply not participate in such a public circus because of the high risk this exposure presents to their current jobs. Universities subject to sunshine laws generally find their candidate pools restricted to those who really have nothing to lose by public exposure—for example, those in lower positions such as provosts or deans or leaders of second-rank institutions or perhaps even politicians. For these candidates public exposure poses little risk with the potential for significant gain.

Furthermore, the interview process, whether public or private, is simply not a very effective way to assess the credentials of candidates. As former University of Texas president Peter Flawn has noted, many governing boards have been burned by a "charmer," a candidate for the president who is charming and engaging, eloquent about "the academy," politically astute, yet who, once on the job, will turn the management over to vice presidents, enjoy the emoluments, entertaining, and social interactions for a few years, and then move on, leaving the institution as good as the vice presidents can make it.[5] Flawn observes that only in extraordinary situations does the charisma last for more than a few years.

Trustees are lobbied hard both by internal constituencies (faculty, students, and administrators) and by external constituencies (alumni, key donors, politicians, and the press). Since the governing board making the selection is usually rather small, strong personalities among governing board members can have a powerful influence over the outcome. The politics of presidential selection becomes particularly intense for public universities, since their governing boards are themselves selected by a partisan political process—gubernatorial appointment or election. The open nature of these searches, dictated by sunshine laws, allows the media to have unusual influence not only in evaluating candidates but also in putting political pressure on governing board members to support particular individuals.

Many public university presidential searches are "wired" from the beginning, with powerful board members manipulating the process to favor preferred internal or external candidates. Sometimes political groups sabotage the candidacy of individuals during the public phase by misrepresenting the background of a candidate or leaking false information to the media. Many individuals who have participated in good faith in public university searches have been seriously compromised.

What characteristics, then, should one look for in a president? What checklist should the governing board give the faculty search committee and the search consultant? The specific wish list will depend on the institution, its challenges and its opportunities, but there are also a number of generic qualifications for the leader of a public university.

First, there are matters of character, which are difficult to measure but obviously of great importance. These include attributes such as integrity, courage, fair-mindedness, compassion, and a fundamental and profound understanding of academic culture. The leadership of an educational institution requires a certain degree of moral authority; hence, possessing a strong moral character and demonstrating exemplary behavior also become quite important.

Second, there are a number of characteristics from a candidate's track record:

— Academic credibility. The faculty will likely not take seriously a president who lacks strong credentials as a teacher and a scholar, and neither will peer institutions.

— Proven management skills. The comprehensive public university is one of the most complex institutions in society. In these days of increasing legal and financial accountability, universities appoint inexperienced candidates to senior campus leadership positions at their own risk.

— Strong leadership skills. Of course, leadership goes beyond management skills. Although public governing boards and faculty senates sometimes shy away from strong candidates, times of challenge and change require such leadership.

— Other measurable experience. A range of background experiences is useful, although not mandatory, in candidates for public university presidencies, including familiarity with state and federal relations, private fund raising, and, perhaps unfortunately, some understanding of the complex world of intercollegiate athletics.

Beyond these obvious criteria there is another set of qualifications which are harder to measure but of particular importance at this moment in the history of public higher education in America:

— The ability to work with the university community and its multiple constituencies to develop a shared vision of the future and to unite these communities in a common effort to pursue this vision.
— A strong commitment to excellence, including the ability to recognize excellence when it is present and to admit it when it is absent.
— A driving passion to achieve diversity and to achieve and defend equity for all members of the university community.
— An impeccable "taste" in the choice of people—that is, the ability to identify and attract the most outstanding talent to key leadership positions in the university, to shape them into teams, and to provide them with strong support and leadership.
— Physical stamina, energy, and very thick skin.

Many important characteristics should be easily discernible from the past record of candidates and not left simply to the vagaries of superficial impressions from interviews. In fact, candidates with the experience and achievement necessary to be considered as a public university president will likely have a track record a mile long and a mile wide. The typical career path to a university presidency is through a sequence of administrative assignments as department chair, dean, and provost. Examining a candidate's effectiveness in these roles provides search committees and governing boards with ample opportunities to assess the full qualifications of presidential candidates long before they are invited to the campus. Ironically, however, many search committees do not give adequate due diligence to assessing the background of candidates, with sometimes disastrous results.

The number of truly successful presidential searches at major public universities has been declining in recent years. Sometimes this situation is actually by design. Some public university governing boards avoid seeking strong, visionary leadership, fearful that their own authority will be challenged or their weaknesses exposed. The political, public nature of the searches and the manipulative nature of governing boards all too frequently lead to the selection of individuals who will serve as figureheads, unwilling to rock the boat but willing to pamper board members and support their personal agendas. Not surprisingly, more and more public university presidencies are being filled by politicians, either by profession or persuasion.

Occasionally, inexperienced or insecure governing boards will intentionally select amateur leaders, that is, individuals who clearly do not have the experience or level of previous achievement which would qualify them for a major university presidency. Such individuals are viewed as more controllable and nonthreatening to board members. But these presidents quickly become overwhelmed by the complexity of their roles and all too frequently follow the same pattern of insecurity by selecting subordinates even less qualified than they are. As a result, some universities have had to contend with a cascade of incompetence, kind of a sequential Peter Principle, in which inexperienced amateurs, in over their heads, populate most of the administrative positions in an institution.[6]

Of course, some might suggest that such amateur leadership might be preferable to a professional bureaucracy that characterizes many administrative organizations in business or government. And to be sure, in earlier and simpler times, inexperienced leadership by seasoned academics was sometimes acceptable. But in today's unforgiving political and financial climate inexperienced leadership often has disastrous consequences, putting faculty members, students, staff, and the institution itself at great risk.

Similarly, we would challenge the belief of some governing boards that, since the president of a public university must function in an intensely political environment, they should place political skills highest on the list of qualifications. Frequently, while such leaders may be effective in pleasing politically determined boards or politically elected state leaders, they may be totally lacking in the intellectual skills necessary to lead an academic institution or the executive skills necessary to manage the complexity of the contemporary university. While such leadership might be tolerated for the short term if paired with strong, experienced academic administrators in roles such as provosts and deans, when isolated from academic traditions and values, such political appointments can also spell disaster.

A final stereotype is provided by itinerant university presidents, those individuals who view their presidency as simply another step in a career path and move from one campus leadership role to another. Although some itinerant presidents can occasionally accomplish a good deal in the short time they remain at a particular institution, more frequently they simply take the easy course, appeasing trustees, faculty, and alumni and avoiding anything that might rock the boat.

When selection as a university president usually occurred late in one's career, typically at an age of fifty-five or sixty, it was common to serve in this role for several years and then retire from academe. The challenges of today's university, however, require great energy and stamina. It is a job for the young. Hence, we find the itinerant president model has become more the norm, with individuals serving in executive roles at several universities, jumping from institution to institution every five years or so, and leaving just before the honeymoon ends (or the ax falls).

The Challenges to Presidential Leadership

Public universities by their very nature can become caldrons of intense political controversy. From their governing boards, determined by the political process of either gubernatorial appointment or popular election, to the contentious nature of academic politics, student unrest, and strident attacks by the press, public university presidencies are subject to stresses more intense than in other arenas of higher education. As a result, public university presidents must develop not only an unusually thick skin but an acute instinct to sense danger as well.

As indicated earlier, the president is expected to be part chief executive officer, intellectual leader of the faculty, educational leader, parent of the students (occasionally), political lobbyist with both state and federal politicians, cheerleader for the university, representative to the media, fund-raiser extraordinary, entertainer par excellence, and servant to the governing board. And usually the performance in any particular one of these roles is considered as the singular basis for evaluating the president's performance by the corresponding affected constituency.

Perhaps one of the reasons for the great stresses upon university presidents has to do with the role they play in responding to crises. Of course, each president has a particular suite of skills and talents. Some are good at politics, some at fund raising; some are particularly skillful at pampering trustees. But, regardless of the particular strengths of presidents, all are expected to play key leadership roles during times of crisis. For example, when student activism explodes on campus or an athletic violation is uncovered or the university is attacked by politicians or the media, the president is expected to lead the response.

But public universities are also characterized by the more partisan politics of state government, federal government, and political governing boards. In fact, to many, including the press, the central administration of a university is viewed as an administration in Washington is. When an election changes the political stripes of the governing board, then the president may become a political casualty. All too often governing boards and entering presidents adopt the philosophy of a changing political administration, sweeping through the layers of leadership of the institution and replacing large numbers of long-serving, experienced, and dedicated administrators. While such administrative housecleaning is understandable in the political environment of government, sustained by an experienced and immovable civil service, it can lead to absolute disaster in universities that are heavily dependent upon loyal and experienced staff to balance the administrative inexperience and naïveté of academic administrators. So, too, it is important to achieve an appropriate balance between the appointment of internal and external candidates to key posts of academic or administrative leadership. The institution-hopping careers of many external candidates, some of whom are quite capable leaders, undermine both their ability to understand the culture and traditions of the university as well as their perceived loyalty to the new institution.

Yet universities are not governments. They are institutions based on long-standing traditions and practices. Forcing them to function as state or federal government would not only destroy any sense of continuity, but it would conflict with the most important values of an academic institution. For this reason universities have been provided with certain characteristics designed to protect them from the intrusion of partisan politics: academic freedom, tenure, and, at least in theory, institutional autonomy as manifested in independent governing boards.

The Environment for Leadership

The environment for leadership in the contemporary university is a challenging one. Beyond the complexity of the role, the sometimes bewildering array of issues, and the limited authority most university administrators possess to deal with their considerable responsibilities, the academic culture itself is not particularly tolerant of the leadership role. The rank-and-file faculty sees the world quite differently from campus administrators.[7] There are significant differences in perceptions and understandings of the rights and responsibility of the faculty and the challenges and opportunities facing the institution and higher education more broadly. Such a gap can lead to an erosion in trust and confidence on the part of the faculty toward university leaders and undercut the ability of universities to make difficult yet important decisions and to move ahead.

In part the widening gap between faculty and administration has to do with the changing nature of the university itself. The modern university is a large, complex, and multidimensional organization, engaged not only in the traditional roles of teaching and research but also in a host of other activities such as health care, economic development, and social change. At the same time, the intellectual demands of scholarship have focused faculty increasingly within their particular disciplines, with little opportunity for involvement in the broader array of activities characterizing their university. While they are— and should always remain—the cornerstone of the university's academic activities, they rarely have a deep understanding or responsibility for the many other missions of the university in modern society.

The increasing specialization of faculty, the pressure of the marketplace for their skills, and the degree to which the university has become simply a way station for faculty careers have destroyed the sense of institutional loyalty and stimulated more of a "what's-in-it-for-me" attitude on the part of many faculty members. So, too, has the university reward structure. The system for determining salary, promotion, and tenure is clearly a meritocracy in which there are clear "haves" and "have-nots." The former generally are too busy to become heavily involved in institutional issues. The latter are increasingly frustrated and vocal in their complaints. Yet often they are the squeaky wheels that drown out others and capture attention.

Finally, many large campuses have allowed the deterioration in the authority and attractiveness of mid-level leadership positions such as department chairs and project directors. This has arisen in part due to the increasing accountability demands on the management structure of the university and in part in deference to concerns of formal faculty governance bodies, which generally harbor deep suspicions of all administrative posts. As a result, many universities are characterized by an awkward and ineffective administrative structure, in which faculty leaders in posts such as department chair and deans simply do not have the authority to manage, much less lead, their units. Likewise, the lack of career paths and mechanisms for leadership development for junior faculty and staff has decimated much of the mid-level management. This mismatch between authority and responsibility propagates upward throughout the administrations of most public universities until it reaches its most extreme in the office of the president.

A 1996 report of the National Commission on the Academic Presidency, sponsored by the Association of Governing Boards, reinforced these views about the limited capacity of the modern university presidency to provide leadership.[8] The commission stressed its belief that the governance structure at most colleges and universities is inadequate. At a time when higher education should be alert and nimble, they believed that most institutions were slow and cautious instead, hindered by traditions and mechanisms of governing which did not allow the responsiveness and decisiveness the times required. At the heart of this situation is the weakness of the academic presidency. The commission found that the authority of university presidents is being undercut by all of its partners—trustees, faculty members, and political leaders—and at times by the presidents' own lack of assertiveness and willingness to take risks for change.

As a result, the commission concluded that most university presidents are currently unable to lead their institutions effectively. They operate from one of the most anemic power bases in any of the major institutions in American society, lacking the clear lines of authority they need to act effectively, and forever compelled to discuss, negotiate, and seek consensus. And all too often, when controversy develops, presidents find that their major partner—their governing board—does not back them up.

With trustees and faculty immersed in a broad range of everyday decision-making processes, presidents are bogged down by demands for excessive consultation, a burdensome requirement for consensus, and a fear of change. *Consultation* has become a code word for consent or capitulation. In practice either of the two groups—governing boards or faculty—can effectively veto proposals for action, either through endless consultation or public opposition.

Of course, there are some who believe that the president of a university should be simply an employee of its governing board. Some argue that in the case of public universities the president and other senior officers are essentially senior civil servants. As such, they are obligated to carry out with total dedication, and silence, all decisions and edicts of their boards, whether they agree with them or not. In this sense presidents are seen primarily as administrators carrying out governing board policies rather than as leaders of an institution.

Yet governance in higher education is more complex, particularly in a world in which various constituencies, including both faculty bodies and governing boards, may occasionally drift away from the best interests of the university. As the National Commission on the Academic Presidency put it, "The current practice of shared governance leads to gridlock. Whether the problem is with presidents who lack the courage to lead an agenda for change, trustees who ignore institutional goals in favor of the football team, or faculty members who are loath to surrender the status quo, the fact is that each is an obstacle to progress."[9]

The environment for presidential leadership is particularly challenging in public universities. These institutions have increasingly become political tempests in which all the contentious political issues swirling about society churn together—for example, civil rights versus racial preference or social responsibility versus market-driven cost-effectiveness. Little wonder that the public university president is frequently caught in a crossfire of opposing political viewpoints. Little wonder, too, that the presidency of a major public university is both less attractive and considerably more difficult than it once was. And, as the all too frequent departures of public university presidents suggest, the job is substantially less attractive than a corresponding position within a private university.

The presidencies of most major public universities now tend to turn over every few years. Increasingly, these changes in presidential leadership reflect not only the wear and tear of the myriad pressures on public universities and their leadership but also the tensions and confusion that exist between the governing boards and the presidents about the roles of each. Frequently, politically appointed or elected governing boards have taken an activist stance that demands that university presidents carry out the policies of a particular political philosophy or constituency without regard for the concerns of the faculty, the student body, or even the president's personal vision for the future of the institution. It is hardly surprising that university leaders are becoming more timid, passive, and bureaucratic. And it is also not surprising that they often jump ship to private institutions that offer greater opportunities for true leadership, with supportive governing boards, and which are free from the public glare and political accountability.[10]

This instability in the public university presidency has significantly weakened the office and will harm public higher education over the long run. Unless the presidents of public universities can be provided with more security, more authority, and more capacity for leadership, the public university will be at significant risk during a period of rapid social change.

Leadership for a Time of Change

The presidency of a public university may indeed be one of the more challenging roles in society because of the imbalance between responsibility and authority. Yet it is nevertheless a position of great importance. While one style of leadership may be appropriate for a given institution at a particular time, the general leadership attributes outlined in this chapter are of universal importance.[11]

Governing boards, faculty, students, alumni, and the press tend to judge a university president according to the issue of the day. Their true impact on the institution is usually not apparent for many years after their tenure. Decisions and actions must always be taken within the perspective of the long-standing history and traditions of the university and for the benefit not only of those currently served by the institution but also on behalf of future generations.

Frequently, particularly in public universities, the environment simply does not tolerate strong leadership. All too often university presidents and other academic leaders take the easy way out, deferring to the whims of outspoken faculty members or the political agendas of governing boards. Why rock the boat when one's tenure is only a few brief years? Little wonder that weak leadership characterizes much of public higher education. Generally speaking, the other partners in the academic tradition of shared governance—the faculty and the governing board—would not have it any other way.

Yet public universities will need strong leadership in the years ahead as academia faces more fundamental questioning. Politicians, pundits, and the public increasingly challenge university leaders at the same time that social, economic, and technological change steadily drives them. They must address myriad questions, including: What is the institution's purpose? What should the faculty teach, and how are they to teach it? Who teaches and under what terms? Who measures quality, and who decides what measures to apply? Who pays for education and research? Who benefits? Who governs and how? What and how much public service is part of a university's mission? What are appropriate alliances, partnerships, and sponsorships? To face these challenges, to respond effectively, the public university requires strong, visionary, and courageous leadership. This, in turn, requires a governing board, a faculty, and a public understanding that not only tolerates but also demands strong leadership.

CHAPTER EIGHT

Governance

The public university is one of the most complex social institutions of our times. The importance of this institution to society, its myriad activities and stakeholders, and the changing nature of the society it serves all suggest the importance of having experienced, responsible, and enlightened university leadership, management, and governance. Here perhaps we should distinguish between leadership and management at the institution or academic unit level, as exercised by administrative officers such as presidents, deans, and chairs, and governance of the institution itself as exercised by governing boards, statewide coordinating bodies, and state and federal government. The governance of public universities is particularly complex, involving the participation and interaction of many organizations with responsibilities not only for the welfare of the institution but also for the funding and the regulation of its activities and its accountability to the public. Beyond the creation of specific governing bodies, such as appointed or elected lay boards of regents or trustees, both state and federal government have also developed and implemented a broad array of public policies and regulations that shape and guide public higher education.

American universities have long embraced the concept of "shared governance" involving public oversight and trusteeship, collegial faculty governance, and experienced but generally short-term and usually amateur administrative leadership. While this system of shared governance engages a variety of stakeholders in the decisions concerning the university, it does so with an awkwardness that can inhibit change and responsiveness.

Furthermore, while this collegial style of governance has a long history both in this country and abroad, the extraordinary expansion of the roles and mission of the university over the past century has resulted in a contemporary institution with only the faintest resemblance to those in which shared governance first evolved. Despite dramatic changes in the nature of scholarship, pedagogy, and service to society, the university today is organized, managed, and governed in a manner little different from the far simpler colleges of the early twentieth century. This is particularly true, and particularly inappropriate, for the contemporary public university.

University governing boards already face a serious challenge in their attempts to understand and govern the increasingly complex nature of the university and its relationships to broader society because of their lay character. This is made even more difficult by the politics swirling about and within governing boards, particularly in public universities, which not only distract boards from their important responsibilities and stewardship but also discourage many of our most experienced, talented, and dedicated citizens from serving on these bodies. The increasing intrusion of state and federal government in the affairs of the university, in the name of performance and public accountability but frequently driven by political opportunism, can trample upon academic values and micromanage institutions into mediocrity. Furthermore, while the public expects its institutions to be managed effectively and efficiently, it weaves a web of constraints through public laws that make this difficult. Sunshine laws demand that even the most sensitive business of the university must be conducted in the public arena, including the search for a president. State and federal laws entangle all aspects of the university in rules and regulations, from student admissions to financial accounting to environmental impact.

Efforts to include the faculty in shared governance also encounter obstacles. While faculty governance continues to be both effective and essential for academic matters such as faculty hiring and tenure evaluation, it is increasingly difficult to achieve true faculty participation in broader university matters such as finance, capital facilities, or external relations. When faculty members do become involved in university governance and decision making, often they tend to become preoccupied with peripheral matters such as parking or intercollegiate athletics rather than strategic issues such as academic programs or undergraduate education. The faculty traditions of debate and consensus building, along with the highly compartmentalized organization of academic departments and disciplines, seem incompatible with the breadth and rapid pace required to keep up with today's high-momentum, high-risk decision-making environment.

The university presidency is frequently caught between these opposing forces, between external pressures and internal campus politics, between governing boards and faculty governance, between a rock and a hard place. Today there is an increasing sense that neither the lay governing board nor elected faculty governance has either the expertise or the discipline, not to mention the accountability, necessary to cope with the powerful social, economic, and technological forces driving change in society and its institutions. The glacial pace of university decision making and academic change simply may not be sufficiently responsive or strategic enough to allow the university to control its own destiny. In this chapter we will explore governance and decision making in the public university—the issues, the players, the process, and the many compelling challenges and necessary changes.

The Players

Governance in a university involves a diverse array of internal and external constituencies that depend on the university in one way or another, just as educational institutions depend upon each of them in turn. Internally, the key players include students, faculty, staff, and governing boards. Externally, the stakeholders include parents, the public and their elected leaders in government, business and labor, industry and foundations, the press and other media, and the full range of other public and private institutions in society. The management of the complex roles and relationships between the university and its many constituencies is one of the most important challenges facing higher education, particularly when these relationships are changing rapidly.

The Internal Stakeholders

Power in a university is broadly dispersed and in many cases difficult to perceive. Although the views and roles of each of the players in shared university governance are highly diverse, most groups share one common perspective: they all believe they need and deserve more power than they currently have.

Of course, the key stakeholders in the university should be its students. These are its principal clients, customers, and, increasingly, consumers of its educational services. Although students pressed in the 1960s for more direct involvement in university decisions, ranging from student life to presidential selection, today's students seem more detached. Their primary concerns appear to be the cost of their education and their employability following graduation, not in participating directly in the myriad decisions affecting their education and their university.

Probably the most important internal constituency of a university is its faculty, since the quality and achievements of this body, more than any other factor, determine the quality of the institution. From the perspective of the academy any great university should be "run by the faculty for the faculty" (a statement that would likely be contested by students or elements of broader society). Involving faculty in the governance of the modern university in a meaningful and effective fashion is both an important goal and a major challenge. While the faculty plays the key role in the academic matters of most universities, particularly at the level of the academic department, its ability to become directly involved in the broader management of the institution has long since disappeared, as issues have become more complex and the time scale of the decision process has contracted. Faculty members frequently feel powerless and thwarted by bureaucracy at every turn.

Historically, there has been relatively little faculty involvement in the strategic evolution of higher education in America. Although some public universities such as Michigan began as faculty-governed institutions, faculty governance was rapidly replaced by lay boards and state coordinating bodies. And, although there were also some efforts made to assert faculty power at different points during the twentieth century, they were frequently overwhelmed by more powerful social trends—the war effort, the Depression, the great expansion of higher education following World War II, and the social protests of the 1960s.

The operation of a university requires a large, professional, and dedicated staff. From accountants to receptionists, investment officers to janitors, computer programmers to nurses, the contemporary university would rapidly grind to a halt without the efforts of thousands of staff members who perform critical services in support of its academic mission. Although staff members make many of the routine decisions affecting academic life, from admissions to counseling to financial aid, they frequently view themselves as only a small cog in a gigantic machine, working long and hard for an institution that sometimes does not even appear to recognize or appreciate their service.

American higher education is unique in its use of lay boards to govern its colleges and universities. Here it is important to recognize that, by law or charter, essentially all of the legal powers of the university are held by its governing board, although they are generally delegated to the administration and the faculty, particularly in academic matters. In the case of private institutions governing boards are typically elected by alumni of the institution or self-perpetuated by the board itself. In public institutions board members are generally either appointed by governors or elected in public elections that are often highly politically charged. While the primary responsibility of such lay boards is at the policy level, they frequently find themselves drawn into detailed management decisions. Boards are expected first and foremost to act as trustees, responsible for the welfare of their institution. But in many public institutions politically selected board members tend to view themselves more as governors or legislators rather than trustees, responsible to particular political constituencies rather than simply to the welfare of the institution they serve. Instead of buffering the university from various political forces, they sometimes bring their politics into the boardroom and focus it on the activities of the institution.[1]

The External Constituencies

The university's external constituencies are broad and complex and include clients of its services such as the patients at its hospitals and spectators at its athletic events; federal, state, and local governments; business and industry; the public and the media. The university is not only accountable to this vast base of present stakeholders, however, but it also must accept a stewardship to the past and a responsibility for future stakeholders. In many ways the increasing complexity and diversity of the modern university and its many missions reflect the character of American and global society. Compared to its counterpart in other nations, American higher education has been relatively free from government interference. Yet, although we have never had a national ministry of education, the impact of federal, state, and local government on higher education in America has been substantial. But so too have the resources provided to higher education by each of these entities.

The federal government channels most of its support of higher education through individuals—financial aid grants and loans to students, research grants and contracts to faculty members. With this federal support, amounting to almost $70 billion in direct grants and considerably more in tax benefits in 2002, has also come federal intrusion. Universities have been forced to build large administrative bureaucracies to manage their interactions with those in Washington. From occupational safety to controlling hazardous substances to health care regulations to accounting requirements to campus crime reporting, federal regulations reach into every part of the university. Furthermore, universities tend to be whipsawed by the unpredictable changes in Washington's policies with regard to regulation, taxation, and funding, shifting with the political winds each election cycle.

Despite this strong federal regulatory role, it has been left to the states and the private sector to provide the majority of the resources necessary to support and sustain the contemporary university. The relationship between public universities and state government is a particularly complex one, and it varies significantly from state to state. Increasingly, state governments have moved to regulate public higher education, thereby lessening the institutional autonomy of universities. In many states public universities are caught in a tight web of state government rules, regulations, and bureaucracy. Statewide systems and coordinating bodies exercise greater power than ever over public institutions. An example is the rise of performance funding, in which state appropriations are based on institutional performance as measured by a set of quantitative outcome indicators such as student credit hours, faculty contact hours, and graduation rates.[2] These metrics are often specified by the state legislature and rarely related to a program's quality.

While recognizing the opportunism inherent in state politics, however, we also should not underestimate the growing and legitimate frustration on the part of many state leaders about what they perceive as higher education's lack of accountability and its unwillingness to consider the implications of the changes taking place in other parts of society. This erosion in political support is becoming more serious in many states. Certainly, the state should have some role in higher education beyond simply providing adequate funding. Public policies are necessary not only to protect universities but also to ensure they are responsive to the public interest. Yet states can, and do, sometimes intrude too far into the operation of their universities, threatening their efforts to achieve quality and serve society.

The relationship between a university and its surrounding community is also a complex one, particularly in cities dominated by major universities. For these communities the plus side is the fact that the university provides the community with an extraordinary quality of life and economic stability. It stimulates strong primary and secondary schools, provides rich cultural opportunities, and generates an exciting and cosmopolitan community. But there are also drawbacks, since the presence of such large, nonprofit institutions takes a great amount of property off the tax rolls. The impact of these universities, whether it is through parking, crowds, or student behavior, can create inevitable tensions between town and gown. These issues become particularly important to public universities, since they can trigger powerful political forces. For example, most universities have governing board members living in the community who can serve as lightning rods for community concerns. So, too, a community's state representatives can exert legislative pressure on the university to conform to local agendas.

Public opinion surveys reveal that at the most general level the public strongly supports high-quality education in U.S. colleges and universities.[3] But, when we probe public attitudes more deeply, we find many concerns about cost, improper student behavior (e.g., alcohol and drug use and violent political activism), and intercollegiate athletics. Perhaps more significantly, the priority that the public places on higher education relative to other social needs has eroded. This is particularly true on the part of elected officials, who generally rank health care, welfare, K-12 education, and even prison systems higher on the funding priority list than higher education. This parallels a growing spirit of cynicism toward higher education and its efforts to achieve excellence. Ironically, the growing criticism of higher education has come at a time when taxpayers have become ever smaller contributors to the support of public colleges and universities.

Universities are clearly accountable to many constituents. They have an obligation to communicate with the people who support them, to be open and accessible. For much of its history the public university was not the object of much public or media interest, aside from intercollegiate athletics. Many institutions essentially ignored the need to develop strong relationships with the media. Communications efforts were frequently combined with public relations and focused on supporting fund raising or presidential ambition rather than media relations.

But things are different now. People want to know what public universities are doing and where they are going, and they have an obligation to be forthcoming. But here they face several major challenges. First, they have to be honest in admitting that communication with the public, especially via the media, does not always come easily to academics. We are not always comfortable when we try to reach a broader audience. We speak a highly specialized and more exacting language among ourselves, and it can be difficult to explain ourselves to others. But we need to communicate to the public to explain our mission, to convey the findings of our research, and to share our learning.

In earlier times the relationship between the university and the press was one of mutual trust and respect. Since there were many values common to both the professions of journalism and the academy, journalists, faculty, and academic leaders related quite well to one another. The press understood the importance of the university, accepted its need for some degree of autonomy similar to its own freedoms, and frequently worked to build public understanding and support for higher education.

More recently, all societal institutions have come under attack by the press, and universities prove to be no exception. Partly, this is due to an increasingly adversarial approach taken by journalists toward all of society, embracing a certain distrust of everything and everyone as a necessary component of investigative journalism. Partly to blame is the arrogance of many members of the academy, university leaders among them, in assuming that the university is somehow less accountable to society than other social institutions. Yet in the long run, without an interested, informed, and responsible press, the public understanding necessary for the support of public colleges and universities is at risk.

The issue of sunshine laws is a particular concern for public institutions. Although laws requiring open meetings and freedom of information were created to ensure the accountability of government, they have been extended and broadened to apply to most public institutions through court decisions. Ironically, the only public organizations typically exempted are the very legislative bodies responsible for drafting the laws and the judicial bodies that have extended them. Today public universities increasingly find that these sunshine laws seriously constrain their operations. Open meetings laws prevent governing boards from discussing sensitive policy matters in private. Freedom of information laws allow the press to go on fishing expeditions through all manners of university documents. They have also been used to hamstring searches for senior leadership, especially university presidents.

Most of America's colleges and universities have more than once suffered the consequences of ill-informed efforts by politicians to influence everything from what subjects can be taught to who is fit to teach and who should be allowed to study. As universities have grown in importance and influence, more political groups are tempted to use them to achieve some purpose in broader society. To some degree the changing political environment of the university reflects a more fundamental shift from issue-oriented to image-dominated politics at all levels—federal, state, and local. Public opinion drives political contributions, and vice versa, which in turn determine successful candidates and eventually legislation. The development of public policy is largely an aftermath exercise, since the agenda is really set by polling and political contributions. Issues, strategy, and "the vision thing" (in the words of a former U.S. president) are largely left on the sidelines. And, given that higher education has never been particularly influential either in determining public policy or in making campaign contributions, the university is frequently left with only the option of reacting as best it can to an agenda set by others.

Higher education in the early twenty-first century faces greater pressure than ever to establish its relevance to various stakeholders in society. The diversity—indeed, incompatibility—of values, needs, and expectations of the various constituencies served by higher education poses one of its most serious challenges. The future of U.S. colleges and universities will be determined in many cases by their success in linking the many concerns and values of diverse groups, even as their relationships with these constituencies continue to change.

The Process

Throughout its long history the American university has been granted special governance status because of the unique character of the academic process. The university has been able to sustain a public acceptance that its activities of teaching and scholarship could best be judged and guided by the academy itself rather than by the external bodies such as governments or the public opinion which govern other social institutions. Key in this effort was the evolution of a tradition of shared governance involving several key constituencies: a governing board of lay trustees or regents as both stewards for the institution and protectors of the broader public interest, the faculty as those most knowledgeable about teaching and scholarship, and the university administration as leaders and managers of the institution.

Institutional Autonomy

The relationship between the university and the broader public is a particularly delicate one, because the university has a role not only as a servant to society but as a critic as well. It serves not merely to create and disseminate knowledge but also to remain independent and to question accepted judgments and values. To facilitate this role as critic, universities have been allowed a certain autonomy as a part of a social contract between the university and society. To this end universities have enjoyed three important traditions: academic freedom, faculty tenure, and institutional autonomy.[4] Although there is a considerable degree of diversity in practice—as well as a good deal of myth—there is general agreement about the importance of these traditions. In practice government, through its legislative, executive, and judicial activities, can easily intrude on university matters.[5] The autonomy of the university depends both on the attitudes of the public and the degree to which it serves a civic purpose. If the public or its voices in the media lose confidence in the university—in its accountability, its costs, or its quality—it will begin to ask whether that autonomy has been earned and at what price. In the long run institutional autonomy rests primarily on the amount of trust that exists between state government and institutions of higher education.

The Influence of Governments

The federal government plays a significant role in shaping the nature and agenda of higher education in the United States. We have discussed earlier examples, such as the federal land grant acts of the nineteenth century creating public colleges and universities and the GI Bill following World War II, which rapidly expanded the campuses to provide the opportunities for a college education to a significant portion of the American population. Federal funding for campus-based research in support of national security and health care shaped the evolution of the contemporary research university. Federal investments in key professional programs such as medicine, public health, and engineering have shaped the curriculum. Federal financial aid programs involving grants, loans, and work-study have provided the opportunity for a college education to millions of students from lower- and middle-class families. And federal tax policies have not only granted colleges and universities tax-exempt status, but they have also provided strong incentives for private giving.

For the most part the federal government's influence on higher education has been channeled through programs aimed at individuals rather than institutions. The GI Bill and federal financial aid programs provide grants and loans to individual students. Federal support of academic health centers flows through programs such as Medicare and Medicaid which provide funds to reimburse the costs of treating individual patients. Research grants and contracts fund the activities of individual faculty investigators and small teams of researchers. Even federal tax benefits are most clearly seen in the tax deductibility of gifts to universities, which are treated as charitable donations in the tax code. Although such federal programs may have been stimulated by public policies designed to influence the higher education enterprise, they generally work through the activities of individuals—that is, in effect, through the marketplace.

The federal government has a more direct impact on higher education through the labyrinth of rules and regulations it applies to colleges and universities. Since all academic institutions receive some degree of federal support, even if only indirectly through mechanisms such as student financial aid or Medicare reimbursement, all are subject to an array of regulations in areas such as equal opportunity, occupational health and safety, and environmental impact. Furthermore, the wide-ranging activities of the contemporary universities in areas such as research, technology transfer, and student housing come under additional layers of rules. Finally, the financial activities of the university are subject to a degree of accounting scrutiny from the Internal Revenue Service and various federal agencies similar to that of business corporations.

Yet, despite these broad federal roles and powers, state governments have historically been assigned the primary role for supporting and governing public higher education in the United States. At the most basic level the principles embodied in the Constitution make matters of education an explicit state assignment. Public colleges and universities are largely creatures of the state. Through both constitution and statute the states have distributed the responsibility and authority for the governance of public universities through a hierarchy of governing bodies, including the legislature, state executive branch agencies or coordinating boards, institutional governing boards, and institutional executive administrations. In recent years there has been a trend toward expanding the role of state governments in shaping the course of higher education, thereby diminishing the institutional autonomy of universities. Few outside of this hierarchy are brought into the formal decision-making process, although many constituencies such as students, patients of university health clinics, and corporate clients may have strong interests at stake.

As state entities, public universities must usually comply with the rules and regulations governing other state agencies, which vary widely, from contracting to personnel requirements to purchasing to setting limits on out-of-state travel. Although regulation is probably the most ubiquitous of the policy tools employed by state government to influence institutional behavior, policies governing the allocation and use of state funds are probably ultimately the most powerful, and these decisions are generally controlled by governors and legislatures.

Statewide Systems and Coordinating Boards

In response to the growing complexity of higher education needs and resources, coupled with an increasing call for public accountability and responsiveness, most states have created statewide higher education systems and/or coordinating or governance boards at the state level. In the United States forty-five states have such statewide structures aimed at allocating public funding for higher education among institutions, preventing unnecessary duplication of programs, and ensuring that state educational needs are met. Today almost 80 percent of all students enrolled in higher education in the United States today attend an institution that is part of a statewide system.

Although such statewide governance structures can be useful in coordinating the delivery of educational services from a diverse system of public colleges and universities, they can pose a challenge to public research universities with more complex missions. Statewide coordinating boards can, for instance, make it difficult for flagship state universities to make the case for the differential appropriations necessary for professional and graduate programs. They sometimes constrain faculty compensation and support per student to the lowest common denominator of institutions. In general, they are frequently more focused on quantity than quality. And in some cases their coordinating role has even evolved into a regulatory function, similar to other government agencies.

Governing Boards

The lay board has been the distinctive American device for "public" authority in connection with universities.[6] The function of the lay board in U.S. higher education is simple, at least in theory: the governing board has final authority for key policy decisions and accepts both fiduciary and legal responsibility for the welfare of the institution. But, because of its very limited expertise, it is expected to delegate the responsibility for policy development, academic programs, and administration to professionals with the necessary training and experience. For example, essentially all governing boards share their authority over academic matters with the faculty, generally acceding to the academy the control of academic programs. Furthermore, the day-to-day management of the university is delegated to the president and university administrators, who provide the necessary experience in academic, financial, and legal matters.

Faculty Governance

The premise that faculty members should govern themselves in academic matters, making decisions about what should be taught and who should be hired, has long been accepted. There are in fact two levels of faculty governance in the contemporary university. The key to governing the academic mission of the university effectively rests not at the level of the governing board or the administration but, rather, at the level of the academic unit, typically a department or school. At this level the faculty generally has a very significant role in most of the key decisions concerning who gets hired, who gets promoted, what gets taught, how funds are allocated and spent, and so on. The mechanism for faculty governance at this level usually involves committee structures—for example, promotion committees, curriculum committees, and executive committees. Although the administrative leader, a department chair or dean, may have considerable authority, he or she is generally tolerated and sustained only with the support of the faculty leaders within the unit.

The second level of faculty governance occurs at the university level and usually involves an elected body of faculty representatives, such as an academic senate, which serves to debate institution-wide issues and advise the university administration. Faculties have long cherished and defended the tradition of being consulted in other institutional matters, of "sharing governance" with the governing board and university officers. In sharp contrast to faculty governance at the unit level, which has considerable power and influence, the university-wide faculty governance bodies are generally advisory on most issues, without true power. Although they may be consulted on important university matters, they rarely have any executive role. Most key decisions are made by the university administration or governing board.

Actually, there is a third level of informal faculty power and control in the contemporary research university, since an increasing share of institutional resources flow directly to faculty entrepreneurs as research grants and contracts from the federal government, corporations, and private foundations. These research programs act as quasi-independent revenue centers with considerable influence, frequently at odds with more formal faculty governance structures such as faculty senates.

The Challenges to Effective Governance

While public universities have been both remarkably resilient during times of change and responsive to the needs of society, the same willingness and ability to adapt can make effective decision making and enlightened governance challenging indeed.

The Complexity of the University

The modern university is composed of many activities, some nonprofit, some publicly regulated, and some operating in intensely competitive marketplaces. It teaches students; it conducts research for various clients; it provides health care; it engages in economic development; it stimulates social change; and it provides mass entertainment (e.g., athletics). The organization of the contemporary university compares in both scale and complexity with many major global corporations. Yet, at the same time, the intellectual demands of scholarship have focused faculty increasingly within their particular disciplines, with little opportunity for involvement in the broader array of activities characterizing their university. While faculty members are—and should always remain—the cornerstone of the university's academic activities, they rarely have deep understanding or accept the accountability necessary for the many other missions of the university in modern society.

Faculties have been quite influential and effective within the narrow domain of their academic programs. The very complexity of their institutions, however, has made substantive involvement in the broader governance of the university problematic. The current disciplinary-driven governance structure makes it very difficult to deal with broader, strategic issues. Since universities are highly fragmented and decentralized, one frequently finds a chimney organization structure, with little coordination or even concern about university-wide needs or priorities. The broader concerns of the university are always someone else's problem. Ironically, the same can be said for many governing boards, usually consisting of lay volunteers with limited understanding of academic activities or cultures and, in the case of many public universities, more experience in political patronage than experience in managing organizations on the vast scale of the contemporary university.

Bureaucracy

The increased complexity, financial pressures, and accountability of universities demanded by government, the media, and the public at large has required stronger management than in the past.[7] Recent furors over issues such as federal research policy, labor relations, financial aid and tuition agreements, and state funding models all involve complex policy, financial, and political issues. While perhaps long ago universities were treated by society, and its various government bodies, as largely well-intentioned and benign stewards of education and learning, today we find the university facing the same demands for accountability as any other billion-dollar public corporation. Yet, as universities have developed the administrative staffs, policies, and procedures to handle such issues, they have also created a thicket of paperwork and bureaucracy which has eroded the authority and attractiveness of academic leadership.

Part of the challenge is to clear the administrative underbrush cluttering the contemporary university. Both decision making and leadership are hampered by bureaucratic policies, procedures, and practices, along with the anarchic style of committee and consensus decision making. Many outstanding members of the faculty feel quite constrained by the university, their colleagues, the "administration," and bureaucracy. Universities need to devise a system that releases the creativity of faculty members while strengthening the authority of responsible leaders.

The Quality of Governing Boards

Across the nation public university presidents are united in, although understandably discreet in stating, their belief that one of the greatest challenges they face is protecting their institutions from their own governing boards. The burdens boards place on their presidents is particularly severe: the amount of time required to accommodate the special interests of board members, the abuse presidents receive from board members with strong personal or political agendas, the increasing tentativeness presidents exhibit because they never know whether their boards will support or attack them. At an international conference on university governance held in 2000, Harold Williams, former regent of the University of California and president of the Getty Foundation, summarized the current situation well: "While the principle of lay boards instead of government control is still of value, the public board system is in trouble, suffering from a poor process for selecting, educating, and evaluating board membership."[8]

Traditionally, the governing boards of public universities have served as advocates for higher education to the public and the body politic as well as defenders to protect academic programs from political intervention. In recent years, however, there has been a pronounced shift in board roles from advocacy to a greater emphasis on oversight and public accountability. As the politics of board selection have become more contentious, board members have increasingly advocated strong political agendas—for example, to restructure the curriculum to stress a specific ideology, reduce costs even at the expense of quality, or even oust a particular university president (usually because he or she was not adequately accommodating to the whims of particular board members). In a sense governing boards have become conduits for many of the political issues swirling beyond the campus. Political factors are more important than expertise or institutional commitment in determining who will serve on the board. Once appointed or elected, board members generally serve for long terms, typically six to ten years, subject only to a recall action taken by the electorate or removal by the courts for malfeasance. There is ample evidence to suggest that, for all practical purposes, board members are effectively isolated from accountability for even the most blatant incompetence or grievous misbehavior.[9] Political accountability falls far short of true fiduciary accountability.

Williams' comment was also bolstered by a 1996 study commissioned by the Association of Governing Boards, which highlighted many of the weaknesses of public boards.[10] The report notes that too many trustees of public university boards lack a basic understanding of higher education or a significant commitment to it. Many trustees understand neither the concept of service on a board as a public trust nor their responsibilities to the entire institution. Public boards tend to spend too much of their time concentrating on administrative matters rather than the urgent questions of educational policy. Inexperienced boards all too often become captivated by the illusion of the quick and easy fix, believing that, if only the right strategic plan is developed or the right personnel change is made, then everything will be fine, their responsibilities will be met, and their personal influence over the university will be visible. Finally, most public governing boards are quite small (from eight to twelve members) compared to private governing boards (with thirty to fifty members). Their relatively small size makes it difficult for public governing boards to span the broad range of institutional interests and needs of the contemporary university. Furthermore, a small board can be held hostage by the special interests, narrow perspectives, or personality of a single member.

There is little doubt that the deteriorating quality of governing boards, the confusion concerning their roles, and the increasingly political nature of their activities have damaged many public universities and threaten others. While perhaps superficially reassuring government leaders, the media, and the public that greater oversight and accountability is being exercised, the quality of leadership, faculty, and academic programs of many public universities is frequently at risk because of the political agendas of their board. There used to be an old saying that no institution can be better than its governing board. Today, however, the counterpoint seems to apply to public universities: a governing board is rarely as good as the institution it serves.

Shared Governance or Shared Anarchy?

Although shared governance is viewed by many, at least among the faculty, as a cornerstone of higher education, history suggests that the faculty has had relatively little influence over the evolution of the university in America, especially when balanced against transformative pressures brought to bear upon the university by the society it serves, by government policy, and by market forces. Furthermore, the contemporary university has many activities, many responsibilities, and many constituencies, resulting in many overlapping lines of authority which tend to mitigate any direct power faculty might exert. To some degree shared governance is an ever-changing balance of forces involving faculty, trustees, staff, and administration.

True faculty participation in university governance and leadership is problematic for many reasons. First, as we have noted, the contemporary university is too complex and fragmented to allow for substantive faculty involvement in the broader governance of the university. On most campuses faculty suffer from a chronic shortage of information—and hence understanding—about how the university really works. In part this arises because university administrations have attempted to shield the faculty and the academic programs from the forces of economic, social, and technology change raging beyond the campus. But there are deeper issues. The faculty culture typically holds values that are not necessary well aligned with those required to manage a complex institution. For example, faculty members value academic freedom and independence, while the management of the institution requires responsibility and accountability. Faculty members tend to be individualists, highly entrepreneurial lone rangers, rather than the team players required for management. Faculty members tend to resist strong, visionary leadership and vigorously defend their personal status quo. It is frequently difficult to get faculty commitment to, or even interest in, broad institutional goals that are not necessarily congruent with their personal goals. There is yet another factor mitigating against faculty governance. As we have seen, the fragmentation of the faculty into academic disciplines and professional schools, coupled with the strong market pressures on faculty in many areas, has created an academic culture in which faculty loyalties are generally first to their scholarly discipline, then to their academic unit, and only last to their institution. Many faculty members move from institution to institution, swept along by market pressures and opportunities, unlike most nonacademic staff, who often remain at a single university throughout their careers. Although faculty members decry the increased influence of administrative staff, it is their own academic culture, their preference for disciplinary loyalty rather than institutional loyalty, coupled with the complexity of the contemporary university, which has led to this situation.

The academic practice of tenure also presents a challenge. Although intended in theory as a protection of academic freedom, in reality the tenure system has evolved into a mechanism for lifetime employment security, regardless of one's competence or effort. As such, it has also become a powerful force thwarting change and protecting the status quo.

It is ironic that many of those elected to faculty governance seem more interested in asserting power and influence on matters outside the traditional concerns of the faculty—for example, reviewing budgets, overseeing athletic departments, and setting policies in peripheral areas such as parking. Unfortunately, it has been difficult to get faculty governance to focus on issues about which they are uniquely competent such as the curriculum, student learning, and academic values and ethics.

Beyond the fact that it is frequently difficult to get faculty members committed to or even interested in broad institutional goals that are not necessarily compatible with their personal goals, there is an even more important element that prevents true faculty governance at the institution level. Responsibility and accountability should always accompany authority: deans and presidents can be fired. Yet the faculty, through important academic traditions such as academic freedom and tenure, are largely insulated from the consequences of their debates and recommendations. It would be difficult if not impossible, either legally or operationally, to ascribe to faculty bodies the requisite level of accountability which would necessarily accompany executive authority.

Little wonder that shared governance, as it exists today, is largely dysfunctional, failing to serve either the institution or its stakeholders. The lines of authority and responsibility are intentionally blurred. Shared governance tends to protect the status quo—or perhaps even a nostalgic view of some idyllic past—thereby preventing a serious discussion about the future. Furthermore, to the extent that the increasing marketplace mobility of faculty erodes any sense of institutional loyalty, how can we expect faculty members to participate constructively in making decisions that are in the best long-term interests of the institution? It is thus hardly surprising that parking concerns dominate curriculum debates in the agenda of most faculty governance.

Many universities follow the spirit of shared governance by selecting their senior leadership—deans, directors, and executive officers—from the faculty ranks. These academic administrators can be held accountable for their decisions and their actions, although, even if they should be removed from their administrative assignments, their positions on the faculty are still protected. Faculty members in these positions often face harsh criticism from their own colleagues about their participation in university governance, and many of the criticisms of shared governance as an institution come from the faculty themselves. In a sense faculty are governing more and enjoying it less, at least if the reluctance of many faculty members to become involved in the tedious committees and commissions involved in shared governance is any measure.

Turf Problems

In theory shared governance delegates academic decisions (e.g., student admissions, faculty hiring and promotion, curriculum development, and awarding degrees) to the faculty and administrative decisions (e.g., acquiring resources and planning expenditures, designing, building, and operating facilities) to the administration, leaving the governing board to focus on public policy and accountability (e.g., compliance with federal, state, and local laws;

fiduciary responsibilities; and selecting key leadership such as the president). Put another way, shared governance allocates the tasks of leading and managing the institution to the administration, academic matters to the faculty, and public accountability and stewardship to the governing board.

Yet turf problems abound. Frequently, governing boards become involved in management details, ranging from meddling with highly visible activities such as intercollegiate athletics to tampering with the academic process (e.g., challenging tenure at the University of Minnesota or specifying curriculum at the State University of New York). Although faculty governance can work well in academic matters at the level of departments or schools, faculty members often attempt to extend their influence to broader issues beyond their responsibility or expertise. Of particular concern here is the tendency of faculty governing bodies to focus on the "*P* issues"—parking, pay, and the plant department but rarely productivity.

In contrast to the tendency of boards to trample on academic turf or faculty governance to become preoccupied with administrative trivia, there remains a wide range of important institutional issues that sometimes fall through the cracks. Examples include crisis management, long-term strategic planning, and institutional transformation. One of the key challenges to effective university governance is to make certain that all of the constituencies of shared governance—governing boards, administrations, and faculty—clearly understand their roles and responsibilities.

The Complex Relationship with State Government

The relationship between public universities and state government adds yet another complexity, although the precise relationship varies significantly from state to state. The most frequent cause of tension between the university and the state has to do with the multiple missions of the contemporary university. This diversity of missions corresponds to a complex array of constituencies and engenders a particularly complex set of political considerations. For example, as universities strive to serve underrepresented segments of society, they encounter the political wars over affirmative action and "racial preference" raging across America. In their efforts to stimulate economic development they run afoul of private sector concerns about unfair competition from tax-exempt university activities, whether these are local commercial enterprises or equity interest in high-tech spin-offs. Public institutions with selective admissions policies frequently face pressure from elected public officials responding on behalf of constituents who are disappointed when their children are not admitted.

A related issue in many states involves achieving an appropriate division of missions among state colleges and universities. Although most states have flagship state universities, they also have many other public colleges and universities that aspire to the full array of missions characterizing the comprehensive public research university. Community colleges seek to become four-year institutions, undergraduate colleges seek to add graduate degree programs, and comprehensive universities seek to become research universities. Since all colleges and universities generally have regional political representation, if not statewide influence, they can frequently build strong political support for their ambitions to expand missions. Even in states characterized by "master plans" such as California, there is evidence of politically driven mission creep, leading to the unnecessary growth of institutions and wasteful overlap of programs.

The 1950s and 1960s were a time of extraordinary expansion of public higher education, as returning veterans, then baby boomers, and finally the growing research and service needs of the nation spurred rapid growth. State leaders were not prepared to deal with such dramatic growth, nor were they able to sustain the claim that higher education was making on scarce state tax dollars. To assist in managing the growth of their public colleges and universities and to determine resource priorities, many states created statewide systems of higher education under a governing or coordinating board. It was expected that professionals would staff these boards and commissions and that they would understand the needs of the institution and could make recommendations to the legislatures which would ensure the most effective uses of limited resources. Many states established policies for determining the role and scope for their colleges and universities. In most cases the state's flagship university was intended to remain at the top of the pyramid of the statewide higher education system, and state policies often referred to the need for that institution to be more competitive with its counterparts in other states.

Unfortunately, but perhaps naturally, the results have not come close to meeting these grand expectations. The battleground for funds shifted from the halls of the legislature to the offices of the bureaucrats who came to staff the state coordinating bodies. Instead of attracting highly qualified individuals with an understanding of higher education and its peculiar ways, more often than not the people who filled these positions were little more than administrative functionaries or state bureaucrats. Very often their response was to make the universities look more like state agencies than to make their differences understandable to the legislators. They created adversarial relationships and became immersed in the numbers game just as the legislators had done before them.

The most damaging result to the more prestigious institutions came through the homogenizing process that these boards and commissions occasionally established as the basis for funding recommendations—English was English in their view, and the cost of its instruction should be the same everywhere. The proposition seemed so logical that even universities that knew it was based on flawed logic seldom challenged it. Research universities are inherently more expensive to run than others. They perform all sorts of academic and scholarly activities that contribute to the enhanced quality of a course, say, in English, and those rich and liberating activities always cause their instructional activities to be more expensive. State bureaucracies simply cannot deal with such evaluations; they can defend numbers but not quality. As a result, many flagship universities have now been homogenized to such a degree that they have become little more than second- or third-tier state universities.

Further exacerbating the dilemma for the flagship university has been the deluge of rules and regulations spewing forth from state agencies and board staffs. These rules and regulations are often made in response to single examples of misuse rather than to endemic, general problems and rarely take into consideration the cost-to-benefits ratio of the newly minted regulations. Entire administrative layers have been created at universities to respond to them. Such state agencies generally add no value, contributing only to bureaucracy, red tape, and additional expense.

By forcing flagship institutions to become a part of a general standardized system of colleges and universities, despite the fact that public colleges and universities have vastly different missions and academic standards, the quality of many of the nation's leading public universities has been threatened. In many states the public university system office is really nothing more than a state agency masquerading as an academic organization, and all too often the leadership of statewide systems is chosen in much the same way as that of other state agencies, with a greater concern for political savvy and influence than solid academic credentials. As a result, flagship universities that have been welded onto such systems find themselves with the additional challenge of circumventing the inevitable tendency of the system office to ignore the unique nature of their graduate- and research-intensive programs and instead to lower their academic quality to the level of other institutions in the system in the name of equity.

Some Prescriptions for Change

As we have noted, the contemporary university is buffeted by powerful and frequently opposing forces. The marketplace demands cost-effective services. Governments and the public demand accountability for the expenditure of public funds. The faculty demands (or at least should demand) adherence to long-standing academic values and traditions such as academic freedom and rigorous inquiry. Yet the long-standing tradition of shared governance, in which power is distributed more or less equally among all potential decision makers, is cumbersome and awkward at best and ineffective and indecisive at worst.

Some Fundamental Principles

In considering ways to improve the ways in which public universities are governed, it is useful to begin with several key principles. University leadership and governance should always reflect the fundamental values of the academy—particularly freedom of inquiry, an openness to new ideas, a commitment to rigorous study, and a love of learning. Yet these processes should also be willing to consider and be capable of implementing institutional changes when necessary to respond to the evolving needs of society.

Luc Weber, former rector at the University of Geneva, suggests that higher education would do well to draw its attention to the economic theory of federalism, which was developed to address the challenges faced by the European Economic Community.[11] First, one should stress the importance of externalities in all decisions, that is, that the benefits or costs of a decision accrue not only to the members of the community that makes it but also to the broader community it serves. In the United States we would recognize this as a "customer-oriented" strategy, focusing on those who will be served. Second, a principle of subsidiarity should characterize governance in which all decisions ought to be made at the lowest possible level. Efforts to decentralize budget authority in order to provide strong incentives for cost containment and entrepreneurial behavior represent this philosophy. Finally, we should remember that the voluntary culture (some would say anarchy) of the university responds better to a process of consultation, communication, and collaboration than to the command-control-communication process familiar from business and industry.

Traditional planning and decision-making processes are frequently found to be inadequate during times of rapid or even discontinuous change.[12] Tactical efforts such as total quality management, process reengineering, and planning techniques such as preparing mission and vision statements, although important for refining status quo operations, may actually distract an institution from more substantive issues during volatile periods. Furthermore, incremental change based on traditional, well-understood paradigms may be the most dangerous course of all, because those paradigms may simply not be adequate to adapt to a future of change. If maintaining the status quo is no longer an option, if the existing paradigms are no longer viable, then more radical transformation becomes the wisest course. It is sometimes necessary to launch actions associated with a preliminary strategy long before it is carefully thought through and completely developed. In the course of such rapid decision making, management can come under criticism for a "fire, ready, aim" style of leadership. It is a challenge to help others recognize that traditional planning and decision making are simply ineffective during times of great change.[13]

Structural Issues

The modern university functions as a loosely coupled adaptive system, evolving in a highly reactive fashion to its changing environment through the individual or small group efforts of faculty entrepreneurs. Although this approach has allowed the university to adapt quite successfully to its changing environment, it has also created an institution of growing size and complexity. The ever-growing, myriad activities of the university can sometimes distract from or even conflict with its core mission of learning.

Although it is perhaps impolitic to be so blunt, the simple fact is that the contemporary university is a public corporation that must be governed, led, and managed with competence and accountability in order to benefit its stakeholders. The academic tradition of extensive consultation, debate, and consensus building before any substantive decision can be made or action taken poses a particular challenge, since this process is simply incapable of keeping pace with the profound changes facing effective governance of the public university. Not everything is improved by making it more democratic. A quick look at the remarkable pace of change required in the private sector—usually measured in months, not years—suggests that universities must develop a greater capacity to act rapidly. Doing so will require a willingness by leaders throughout the university to make difficult decisions and to take strong action without the traditional consensus-building process.

The leadership of the university should be provided with authority commensurate with its responsibilities. The president and other executive officers should have the same degree of authority to take actions, to select leadership, and to take risks and move with deliberate speed that their counterparts in business and government possess. The challenges and pace of change faced by the modern university no longer allow the luxury of "consensus" leadership, at least to the degree that *building consensus* means seeking the approval of all concerned communities before any action is taken. Nor do they allow the reactive nature of special interest politics to moor the university to an obsolete status quo, thwarting efforts to provide strategic leadership and direction.

Yet a third controversial observation is that, although academic administrations generally can be drawn as conventional hierarchical trees, in reality the connecting lines of authority are extremely weak. In fact, one of the reasons for cost escalation is the presence of a deeply ingrained academic culture in which leaders are expected to "purchase the cooperation" of subordinates, that is, to provide them with positive incentives to carry out decisions. Deans, for example, expect the provost to offer additional resources in order to gain their cooperation on various institution-wide efforts. Needless to say, this "bribery culture" is quite incompatible with the trend toward increasing decentralization of resources. As the central administration relinquishes greater control of resource and cost accountability to the units, it will lose the pool of resources which in the past was used to provide incentives to deans, directors, and other leaders to cooperate and support university-wide goals.

Hence, it is logical to expect that both the leadership and management of universities will need increasingly to rely on lines of true authority, just as their corporate counterparts do. That is, presidents, executive officers, and deans will almost certainly have to become comfortable with issuing clear directives from time to time. So, too, throughout the organization subordinates will need to recognize that the failure to execute these directives will likely have significant consequences, including possible removal from their positions. Here we are not suggesting that universities adopt a top-down corporate model inconsistent with faculty responsibility for academic programs and academic freedom. While collegiality will continue to be valued and honored, the modern university simply must accept a more realistic balance between responsibility and authority.

Clearly, an effort should be made to rebuild leadership strength at middle levels within the university, both by redesigning such positions to improve the balance between authority and responsibility and by providing leadership development programs. This effort may involve some degree of restructuring the organization of the university to respond more effectively to its responsibilities, challenges, and opportunities. In this regard there should be a greater effort made to identify the "administration" as a broader body than simply the executive officers of the university, including deans, chairs, and directors. It is also critical to get members of this broader group to be perceived, and to perceive themselves, as representing the university's objectives.

Restructuring Governing Boards

Needless to say, such accountability starts at the top, at the level of the university's governing board. Such bodies should always act in the interests of the long-term welfare of the institution and the multiple constituencies it serves. Yet, as long as the governing boards of public universities continue to be selected through political mechanisms and are allowed to pursue political or personal agendas without concern for the welfare of their institution or its service to broader society, it is unlikely that a new culture of responsiveness and accountability can take hold within the public university.

As the contemporary university becomes more complex and accountable, perhaps we should look more toward the model of corporate governance. Perhaps we should shift from lay boards, with their strongly political character, to true boards of directors similar to those in the private sector. Ideally, corporate board members are selected for their particular expertise and experience. They are in theory held accountable to the shareholders for the performance of the corporation. Their performance is reviewed at regular intervals, both within the board itself and through more external measures such as the company's financial performance. Clearly, directors can be removed either through action of the board or shareholder vote. Furthermore, they can be held legally and financially liable for the quality of their decisions—a far cry from the limited accountability of the members of most governing boards of public universities.

It is our belief that university governing boards should function with a structure and a process that reflects the best practices of corporate boards.

Board members should be held clearly accountable—indeed, liable—for their actions and decisions. Just as corporate boards must act in the interests of shareholders or risk litigation, governing board members should always serve the interests of the welfare of the university and the stakeholders it serves or be removed promptly from the board. There should be a clear process for removing a member from a board should the situation merit this step.

The Association of Governing Boards took an important first step toward addressing this issue in 1995 through a series of recommendations. It recommended that the size of public boards be increased to fifteen or more members to minimize the vulnerability of small boards to the behavior of maverick members. The boards should include a majority of carefully selected members who have demonstrated experience with large organizations, their financing, and their complex social and political contexts. Some experience with and interest in higher education was also considered a desirable criterion.

As the association demonstrates in its report, there is little positive evidence to support the partisan election of governing boards. But, because total reliance on gubernatorial appointment also has problems, the wisest course might be to use a variety of mechanisms to determine the composition of a given board. For example, one might imagine a board composed of twenty-four members: eight members nominated by the governor and approved by the legislature, eight members elected at large on a nonpartisan basis, and eight representing certain constituencies such as alumni, students, business, and labor. With overlapping terms such a board would be highly representative and yet stable enough to offset the influence of any political or special interest group.

Although it is important to provide board members with sufficient tenure to develop an understanding of the university, it is also important to avoid excessively long tenures. It is probably wise to limit public university board service to a single term, since this would prevent members from "campaigning" during their tenure for future appointment or election to additional terms. To this end selection for a single eight- to ten-year term would be optimal.

Again drawing on the experience of corporate boards, we recommend the more radical suggestion that university presidents in public universities should have some influence over the selection of board members, just as their colleagues in private universities and CEOs in the corporate sector do. Here we are not proposing that university presidents actually nominate or select board members. But consideration should be given to their right to evaluate and possibly veto a proposed board member if the individual is perceived as unduly political, hostile, or simply inexperienced or incompetent.

We also believe that all university governing boards, both public and private, would benefit greatly from the presence of either active or retired university presidents or senior administrators (e.g., provosts and chief financial officers) or distinguished faculty members from other institutions among their membership. Since the experience of most lay board members is so far removed from the academy, it seems logical to suggest that boards would benefit from the experience such seasoned academics could bring. After all, most corporate boards find it important to have experienced business executives and chief financial officers, either active or retired, among their membership. University boards might do the same.

An equally controversial variation on this theme would be to provide faculty with a stronger voice in true university governance by appointing faculty representatives as members of the governing board. This would be similar, in a sense, to the practice of some corporate boards of providing a seat for a representative from organized labor. There would need to be a clear sense of accountability and liability in such an appointment, however, so that the faculty board members would not simply become advocates for the faculty position but would be responsible to the entire institution.

Every effort should be made to convince leaders of state government that politics and patronage have no place in the selection of university governing boards or efforts to determine their administrative leadership. Quality universities require quality leadership. Of course, there may be some states or public institutions in which either public statute or state constitution makes it simply impossible to avoid excessively political and inexperienced boards. In these cases one might consider a holding company structure, in which a politically determined lay board responsible for the public aspects and policies of the university would be assisted by a number of interlocking appointed boards that would in turn handle various specialized functions of the university, such as the academic medical center, business and finance, fund raising, and educational issues. In this way the specialized boards could be served by individuals who bring both experience and expertise to these areas, while the public board could be more responsive to the body politic. Note that in this model the formal governing board and the leadership of the institution would become a small, lean organization, responsible for broad policy development but kept rather distant from management and academic details.

Ironically, while public university governing boards have become increasingly political and thus more sensitive to special interests, they have also become increasingly isolated from accountability with respect to their quality and effectiveness. Not only should all boards be subject to regular and public review, but the quality and effectiveness of governing boards should also be an important aspect of institutional accreditation.

Governing in the Public Interest

Many universities find that the most formidable forces controlling their destinies are political in nature—from governments, governing boards, faculty senates, and perhaps even public opinion. Unfortunately, these bodies are not only usually highly reactive in nature, but they frequently either constrain the institution or drive it away from strategic objectives that would better serve society as a whole. Many university presidents, particularly those associated with public universities, believe that the greatest barrier to change within their institutions lies in the manner in which they are governed, both from within and from without. Universities have a style of governance which is more adept at protecting the past than preparing for the future.

The 1996 report of the National Commission on the Academic Presidency reinforced these concerns when it declared that the governance structure at most colleges and universities is inadequate. "At a time when higher education should be alert and nimble," it concluded, "it is slow and cautious instead, hindered by traditions and mechanisms of governing that do not allow the responsiveness and decisiveness the times require." The commission went on to note its belief that university presidents were currently unable to lead their institutions effectively, since they were forced to operate from "one of the most anemic power bases of any of the major institutions in American society."[14]

This view was also voiced in a study performed by the RAND Corporation, which noted: "The main reason why institutions have not taken more effective action [to increase productivity] is their outmoded governance structure—i.e., the decision-making units, policies, and practices that control resource allocation have remained largely unchanged since the structure's establishment in the 19th century. Designed for an era of growth, the current structure is cumbersome and even dysfunctional in an environment of scarce resources."[15]

In this chapter we have raised a number of concerns about the administration, management, and governance of public universities. Governing boards have become overly politicized, focusing more on oversight and accountability than on protecting and enhancing the capacity of their university to serve the changing and growing educational needs of society. Faculty governance, at least at the university level, is largely unworkable, in many cases even irrelevant, to either the nature or pace of the issues facing the contemporary university. University leadership, whether at the level of chairs, deans, or presidents, has insufficient authority to meet the considerable responsibilities engendered by powerful forces of change in higher education. And nowhere, either within the academy, at the level of governing boards, or in government policy, is there a serious discussion of the fundamental values so vital to the nature and role of the public university.

It seems clear that the public university of the twenty-first century will require new forms of governance and leadership capable of responding to the changing needs and emerging challenges of society and its educational institutions. The contemporary university has many activities, responsibilities, constituencies, and overlapping lines of authority. From this perspective shared governance models still have much to recommend them: a tradition of public oversight and trusteeship, shared collegial internal governance of academic matters, and, experienced administrative leadership.

Yet shared governance is, in reality, an ever-changing balance of forces involving faculty, trustees, staff, and administration.[16] The increasing politicization of public governing boards; the ability of faculty senates to use their powers to promote special interests, delay action, and prevent reforms; and weak, ineffectual, and usually short-term administrative leadership all pose risks to the university. Clearly, it is time to take a fresh look at the governance of the nation's public institutions.

Governing board members should be selected for their expertise and commitment and then held accountable for their performance and the welfare of their institutions. Governing boards should be challenged to focus more on policy development rather than management issues. Their role is to provide the strategic, supportive, and critical stewardship for their institution. Faculty governance should become a true participant in the academic decision-making process rather than simply being a watchdog of the administration or defenders of the status quo. Faculty governance should focus on issues that most directly concern academic programs, and faculty members should be held accountable for their decisions. Faculties also need to accept and acknowledge that strong leadership is important if their institution is to flourish during a time of significant change. Our institutions must not only develop a tolerance for strong leadership; they must demand it.

It is simply unrealistic to expect that the governance mechanisms developed decades or even centuries ago still fit the needs of the contemporary public university or the society it serves. To assign the fate of these important institutions to inexperienced, political lay governing boards or charge-resistant faculty senates isolated from accountability is simply not in the public interest. Furthermore, during times of dramatic change those responsible for the administration of public institutions simply must cut through the Gordian knot of shared governance, of indecision and inaction, to allow public universities to better serve society. To remain blind to these realities is to perpetuate a disservice to those they seek to benefit, both present and future generations.

CHAPTER NINE

University Transformation

A rapidly evolving world has demanded profound and permanent change in most, if not all, social institutions. Corporations have undergone restructuring and reengineering. Governments and other public bodies are being overhauled, streamlined, and made more responsive. Even the relevance of the nation-state is being questioned and reexamined. Certainly, most U.S. colleges and universities also are attempting to respond to the challenges and opportunities presented by a changing world. They are evolving to serve a new age. Yet most of them are evolving within the traditional paradigms, according to the time-honored processes of considered reflection and consensus which have long characterized the academy. Change in the university has proceeded in slow, linear, incremental steps—improving, expanding, contracting, and reforming without altering its fundamental institutional mission, approach, or structure.

While most colleges and universities have grappled with change at the pragmatic level, few have contemplated the more fundamental transformations in mission and character which may be required by a changing world. Most institutions continue to approach change by reacting to the needs and opportunities of the moment rather than adopting a more strategic approach to their future.

Furthermore, change in the university is rarely driven from within. After all, one of the missions of the university is to preserve time-honored values and traditions. So, too, tenured faculty appointments tend to protect the status quo, and the process of shared governance provides the faculty with a mechanism to slow or even block change. Most campus administrators tend to be cautious, rarely rocking the boat in the stormy seas driven by politics either on campus or beyond. Governing boards are frequently distracted from strategic issues in favor of personal interests or political agendas.

Although the university as a social institution has survived largely intact for over a millennium, it has done so in part because of its extraordinary ability to change and adapt. The remarkable diversity we see today among institutions— from small liberal arts colleges to gigantic university systems, from storefront proprietary colleges to global "cyberspace" universities—demonstrates both the survival and evolution of the species and how rapidly change can occur.

Earlier examples of change in American higher education, such as the evolution of the land grant university, the growth of higher education following World War II, and the evolution of the research university, represented reactions to major forces and policies at the national level. Examples of major institutional transformation driven by internal strategic decisions and plans from within are relatively rare. Change is a particular challenge to the public university, surrounded as it is by powerful political forces and public pressures that tend to be conservative and reactionary.

Yet, if it is even to maintain its traditional public mission, the university must continue to ask two questions: "Whom do we serve?" and "How can we serve better?" What will students need in the twenty-first century? What will citizens of the new world require? How can university leaders forge new missions to serve a changing society even as they hold firmly to the deep and common values that have guided the American university over two centuries of evolution?

Transformation

The capacity for change, for renewal, has become an important objective in other sectors of society. We frequently hear about companies "restructuring" or "reengineering" themselves to respond to rapidly changing markets. Government is also challenged to transform itself to be more responsive and accountable to the society that supports it. Yet transformation for the university is necessarily more challenging, since its various missions and diverse array of constituencies give it a complexity beyond that encountered in business or government.

How, then, might we approach the transformation of an institution as complex as the modern public university? Historically, universities have accomplished change by using a variety of mechanisms. In earlier times of growing budgets they were able to buy change with additional resources. When the pace of change was slower, they had more time to build the consensus necessary for grassroots support. Occasionally, a key personnel change was necessary to bring in new leadership. Of course, universities did not always have the luxury of additional resources or even adequate time to effect change and would resort to less direct methods, such as disguising or finessing change or even accomplishing change by stealth. In fact, sometimes the pace of change required leaders to take a "Just do it!" approach, making top-down decisions followed by rapid execution.

As we have argued, these past approaches may not be adequate to address the major paradigm shifts that will likely take place in higher education in the years ahead. From the experience of other organizations in both the private and public sector, we can identify several features of the transformation processes that also apply to the university. It is essential to recognize that the real challenge lies in transforming the culture of an institution. Financial or political difficulties can be overcome if the organization can let go of rigid habits of thought, organization, and practice which are incapable of responding rapidly or radically enough. To this end those most directly involved in the core activities of the university, teaching and research, must be involved in the design and implementation of the transformation process. Clearly, in the case of a university this means that the faculty must play a key role.

Yet sometimes in order to drive change one needs assistance from outside. In the past government policies and programs have served as an impetus. Increasingly, however, as society experiences a rapid transformation, many people believe that the pressures from the marketplace will play this role. Beyond these forces it is usually necessary to involve external groups both to provide credibility to the process and to assist in putting controversial issues on the table (e.g., tenure reform).

Traditional planning exercises tend to focus on the development of an institutional vision. But transformation requires something beyond this, the development of a strategic intent. A strategic intent for an organization provides a "stretch vision" that cannot be achieved with current capabilities and resources.[1] It forces an organization to be inventive and to make the best use of all available resources if it is to move toward this goal. The traditional view of strategy focuses on the fit between existing resources and current opportunities; strategic intent creates an extreme misfit between resources and ambitions. In this way an institution is challenged to close the gap by building new capabilities.

Finally, experience in other sectors has shown the critical importance of leadership. Major institutional transformation does not occur by having someone far from the front lines and issuing orders. Rather, university leaders must pick up the flag and lead the institution into battle. Granted, this usually entails risk.

Of course, transforming an institution as complex as the university is neither linear nor predictable. Transformation is an iterative process; as an institution proceeds, experience leads to learning that can modify the transformation process.[2] Furthermore a university must generally launch a broad array of initiatives in a variety of areas such as institutional culture, mission, finance, organization and governance, academic programs, and external relations, all of which interact with one another. It is instructive to consider some of the issues that arise in each of these areas.[3]

Mission

The most fundamental transformation issues involve the changing character and mission of universities. To understand better the issues involved in this transformation of mission, we might begin by asking why these institutions have been so successful in the past. What has been their unique role, their mission? What has been the key to their longevity?

In this context it is clear that the role of public universities is to serve the societies that have created, supported, and depended upon them—in a sense, to implement the Jeffersonian model of an educational institution created by the people to serve the people. The institutional mission to provide education, and later research and service, to broader elements of society has always been a key to their character. *Opportunity through access* and *service to society* continue to be operative phrases, and they have been achieved through the traditional triad mission of teaching, research, and service.

The Kellogg Commission on the Future of Land-Grant Universities proposes a new agenda for the public university which better addresses the needs of a changing society: learning, discovery, and engagement. *Learning* characterizes a more active paradigm of education in which the university becomes a learning community of students, faculty, and staff. *Discovery* similarly extends the concept of research to encompass the process of adding to the knowledge base of scholarship. *Engagement* is defined by the commission as a redesign of the various activities of the university to become even more sympathetically and productively involved with their communities.

In the past the capacity of the public universities to play these roles was provided through strong public investment. But, as state support has become a declining component of the resource base, the traditional role of these institutions to serve primarily their state has also changed. In many ways a large number of state universities have evolved, effectively, into national or even global universities.

There is a certain dilemma here. Many people, including most state political leaders, members of the media, and numerous private citizens, still see the state university's primary mission as providing low-cost and, if possible, quality education and service to the state itself. Yet today it is clear that there are now many institutions capable of providing low-cost education of moderate quality. Few, however, can provide the high-quality, high-reputation education, research, and service characterizing the flagship state research universities. And, judging from the marketplace and particularly those constituents that provide an increasing share of university resources, this latter role, which emphasizes quality rather than cost, is the most appropriate mission for many public universities.

Resources

The issues involved in the financial restructuring of the university go beyond traditional revenue and expenditure considerations, which typically dominate university concerns. As we noted in chapter 6, most universities still rely on incremental budgeting, in which they accept the continuation of the status quo and concentrate on making small changes to it—primarily through small increases allocated on a selective basis. Clearly, more sophisticated and flexible budgeting and resource allocation schemes need to be implemented.

One of the most critical issues facing the university involves the level of funding needed for investing in new opportunities. Clearly, universities will need significant resources to fuel the transformation process, probably at the level of 5 to 10 percent of the total university budget. During a period of limited new funding it will take considerable creativity (and courage) to generate these resources. As we noted earlier in our consideration of financial issues, the only sources of funding at the levels required for such major transformation are tuition, private support, and auxiliary activity revenues. Universities must recapture a capacity to generate such "venture capital" funds, even if this requires substantial internal reallocation.

Beyond resource allocation there are many other issues that must be addressed in any financial restructuring plan. To address near-term budgetary needs, for example, most universities have very limited options for generating additional revenue. They can raise prices, that is, increase tuition, albeit with possible market or political implications. And they can sometimes generate additional resources from auxiliary activities such as health care or licensing. Of course, over the longer term there are other opportunities, such as increasing private giving, endowment growth, new types of "profit-generating" academic programs such as distance education, intellectual property licensing, and equity positions in spin-off companies. But these measures require a dedicated effort for many years before they produce substantial and reliable resource streams.

It is also important to consider other resource allocation and control mechanisms. Perhaps public universities should wean from state appropriation those units capable of generating sufficient alternative resources (e.g., schools of business, medicine, and law) to enable them to better focus their limited resources on undergraduate education and core support services, such as central libraries. Clearly, universities need to provide units with longer-range financial control and planning capability, even if it means that commitments of central resources are necessarily more conservative. For example, the administration might require rolling five-year financial plans for each unit.

As universities move toward providing units with more control of resources, they should consider "recentralizing" other controls. For example, they may need to institute policies retaining tight central control of faculty positions similar to those of many private institutions so that they can maintain institutional balance and control growth. Universities need to develop alternative funding models and policies for degree-granting academic programs (in which faculty tenure resides) and for interdisciplinary centers and institutes. While the premise is usually that academic programs will be sustained unless there is sufficient cause for discontinuing them, sunset provisions should probably be placed on many centers and institutes, which would make it easier to terminate programs that have outlived their relevance or deteriorated in quality.

Characteristics

We have noted that achieving institutional goals requires a careful optimization of the interrelated features of quality, size, and comprehensiveness. It also requires excellence and innovation in selected areas. A university's unique combination of these characteristics both is determined by and evolves from past circumstances, which can constrain and, to a degree, affect future options. The size of many comprehensive universities, for example, demands particular organizational structures that will rule out many of the transformation options taken by smaller private institutions. On the other hand, the richness and diversity provided by a larger scale will also better position the university to take risks that might be unacceptable for smaller institutions.

There are many issues associated with transforming the characteristics of a university. Campus size is an important issue. While major enrollment changes are difficult for many reasons—tuition revenue and political reaction, for example—it is also important to reassess the optimum size of an institution and its various units from a variety of perspectives, including available resources and academic vitality.

Much of the emphasis of institutional planning during the 1980s and 1990s has been on focusing resources, on becoming smaller but better. But, in an age of knowledge in which educated people and ideas have become the wealth of nations, higher education is, in fact, a strong growth enterprise. Therefore, it seems clear that the university should explore a broader range of options, including possible growth in selected areas. Universities should develop the capacity to consider, more strategically, differential growth among units, including the creation and disappearance of academic programs.

This effort should include a consideration of new market strategies. Perhaps higher education needs to stress new kinds of degrees such as graduate certificates. Universities could distinguish, for example, among on-campus residential instruction, commuter instruction, and distance learning, since these activities represent quite different educational experiences ("products") and probably should have quite different pricing. Many academic units, such as the executive management education programs run by business schools, are already heavily involved in nondegree education.

Organization and Governance

The current organization of the university into departments, schools and colleges, and various administrative units is largely historical rather than strategic in nature. To some degree it represents a by-product of an incremental style of resource allocation, in which the presumption is made that units and activities continue indefinitely. Rarely does it result from a conscious strategy or rational intellectual organization. As universities approach a period in which significant rapid transformation will be the order of the day, they must assess whether such existing organizational structures are capable of making such transformations. Most evidence suggests that, although traditional academic units are capable of modest internal change, they are generally threatened by broader institutional change and will strongly resist it.

Of particular concern is the well-entrenched department structure of the university, which organizes schools and colleges along disciplinary lines. While such department structures serve important roles in meeting instructional loads and maintaining broadly accepted standards, they also pose a major impediment to change. They maintain a disciplinary focus that is increasingly orthogonal to the rapid pace of intellectual change and proves particularly frustrating to faculty, students, and sponsors. They also perpetuate practices of selecting, evaluating, and rewarding people which hinder the development of a more cohesive university community capable of serving a rapidly changing world. Finally, they make strategic resource allocation very difficult, as evidenced by the cumbersome, frustrating nature of efforts to reduce or eliminate weak academic programs.

Clearly, we need to develop a greater ability to reorganize and restructure academic units. Program discontinuance policies are frequently so cumbersome as to be essentially unworkable. We need to make more use of novel organizational structures such as interdisciplinary centers and institutes which reach across disciplinary boundaries and are intentionally designed with sunset provisions. Yet we need to go farther than this. We might well consider building alternative "virtual" structures that draw together students, faculty, and staff. So, too, we might try to establish affinity clusters that draw together basic disciplines and key professional schools—for instance, a cluster of biological and clinical sciences.

A number of important organizational issues should be addressed in discussions of university-wide transformation. Most large organizations continue to be based upon a command-communication-control hierarchy, largely inherited from military organizations of past centuries, in which layer upon layer of middle management is used to channel and control information flow from the top to the bottom, or *vice versa*, in the organization. Such hierarchical organizations, however, are largely obsolete in an information-rich environment facilitated by modern information technology that enables direct, robust communication among all points in the organization.

The structures of many academic units are sustained by external constituencies, such as accrediting bodies. Many of the proliferating department structures in medicine and engineering are driven, for example, by professional licensing requirements. And schools of pharmacy, public health, education, and social work often exist as separate entities, largely because of accreditation pressures. Universities need to understand better just how restrictive these accreditation requirements are and, if they are found to be too constraining, work with peer institutions to modify them.

It seems clear that many university personnel policies and practices are antiquated and make it difficult to reorganize rapidly and reduce unnecessary bureaucracy. Beyond restructuring policies, universities might learn some lessons in human resource management from the corporate sector. They might strongly encourage administrative staff to be rotated to new positions at regular intervals, particularly at senior levels, as a part of their career development. This action would not only loosen up the organization, but it would also provide a mechanism to deal with the casualties of the Peter Principle (in which employees rise through the ranks until they are finally trapped in positions where they can no longer succeed and advance).

Intellectual Change

Many of the most important, and also most difficult, transformations will concern intellectual areas such as teaching and scholarship. These issues range from the structure of undergraduate and graduate programs to the organization of research and even the merit of degree programs generally.

It has become more and more apparent that undergraduate education is likely to change significantly in the years ahead. While a number of universities have launched major efforts to improve the quality of the undergraduate experience, most of them remain within the traditional paradigm of four-year degree programs in specialized majors designed for high school graduates and approached through solitary (and often passive) pedagogical methods. Yet society is demanding more radical changes.

Graduates now enter a world in which they will be required to change careers many times during their lives. Thus, a highly specialized undergraduate education may be inappropriate. Instead, more emphasis should be placed on breadth of knowledge and the acquisition of skills for further learning—that is, on a truly liberal education. In a sense an undergraduate education should prepare a student for a lifetime of further learning. Are we ready to face up to the fact that we have too many majors and offer too many courses? Can we create a truly coherent undergraduate learning experience as long as we allow the disciplines to dominate the academic undergraduate curriculum? How do we address the fact that most of graduates are "quantitatively illiterate," being inadequately prepared in intellectual disciplines that will shape their lives such as science, mathematics, and technology? The same could be said for their broader knowledge of history and culture.

Perhaps it is time that universities attempt to develop a rigorous under-graduate degree program that will prepare outstanding students for the full range of further educational opportunities, from professions such as medicine, law, business, engineering, and teaching to further graduate studies across a broad range of disciplines from English to mathematics. Far from being a Renaissance degree, this "Bachelor of Liberal Learning" would be more akin to the type of education universities tried to provide decades ago, before the deification of academic disciplines and of specialized scholarship and teaching which took over these institutions and their curricula.

Much of the research university's instructional activity is at the advanced level, within graduate and professional programs. In general most professional degree programs have been quite responsive to the changes in society and have adapted well. Examples include the new practice-focused curricula introduced in many schools of medicine and business administration. In contrast, despite great efforts to shorten the time-to-degree, Ph.D. programs remain largely mired in the past, frequently attempting to clone graduate students in the mold of their faculty mentors. As doctoral programs have become more spe-cialized and the time-to-degree has lengthened, these programs have become less and less attractive to the most outstanding undergraduates. In contrast to professional degrees such as law and business, which are viewed as creating further opportunities for graduates, the Ph.D. degree is viewed today as a highly specialized degree that actually narrows one's options. Perhaps the degree itself is obsolete, and what is needed is a "liberal-learning" advanced degree that would prepare graduates for broader roles than simply specialized academic scholarship.

One might go beyond undergraduate and graduate degree programs and ask the more provocative question of whether degrees even make sense in a society that requires a lifetime commitment to learning. More and more faculty effort is directed toward nondegree learning through programs such as continuing education activities in professional schools, short courses, and special seminars. Perhaps universities should consider in a more strategic fashion the provision of the "just-in-time" learning opportunities sought by people when they actually need the knowledge, rather than requiring them to go through the rigors of a formal degree program while they are young.

Cultural Issues

As we noted at the outset, the most important and most difficult transformations of all will be those required within the culture of the university. Actually, there are many cultures characterizing the contemporary university: academic, student, administrative, athletic, social, and so forth. While one generally thinks first of changing the faculty culture—and, to be sure, this will be one of the greatest challenges to the university—major changes will be required in the multiple cultures of staff and students.

Clearly, the culture that determines how faculty members are selected, promoted, tenured, and rewarded must evolve as the responsibilities of the university change. Universities have a rather one-dimensional reward system in which achievement is usually measured narrowly and simplistically in terms of the quantity of scholarship and rewarded through salary and promotion. It does not reflect the great diversity in faculty roles or the ways in which these roles change during a faculty member's career.

One of the most critical issues facing the modern university is the limited degree to which faculty members accept responsibility and accountability for their obligations to society. After all, society expects a great deal in return for providing faculty members with the perquisites of academic life—tenure, academic freedom, generous compensation, and prestige. So, too, faculty members have significant responsibilities to the university, although they are often regarded as secondary to responsibilities to their discipline or profession.

There is great diversity—and inequity—in the effort expected of the faculty across the university. In some areas faculty members are not only expected to be actively engaged in teaching and research, but they also must be actively involved in delivering professional services (e.g., clinical care in medicine or consulting services in engineering). Many faculty members are also expected to be entrepreneurs, attracting the resources necessary for their activities through competitive grants or clinical income. While this diversity in faculty roles and effort has long been an important characteristic of research universities, it is frequently not well understood by either those inside or outside these institutions.

In many ways the traditional mechanisms used for evaluating faculty performance, for making promotion and tenure decisions, tend to discourage risk taking and venturesome activities. Young faculty members who tackle challenging problems or devote considerable effort to developing new pedagogy put themselves at risk. Universities must create more of a "fault-tolerant" culture in which their most talented people are encouraged to take on tough challenges. They must keep in mind the old saying that, if one does not fail on occasion, it is probably because his or her goals are not being set high enough.

Perhaps universities should approach the challenge of changing the faculty culture as an effort to "free the faculty" from traditional arrangements and mind-sets that discourage creativity and innovation. They should encourage faculty members to broaden their activities and become citizens of the university rather than simply members of a department or a school.

Key players in any transformation process will be department chairs and unit managers. The current management culture of the university makes achieving major change at this lowest level of academic or administrative leadership very difficult and encourages conservative leadership and resistance to efforts to change from higher levels of management. Universities must change this culture by providing strong incentives for department chairs and managers to participate in the institution-wide transformation process as well as strong disincentives to stonewalling decisions. Here the use of change agents among faculty and staff will be critical if universities are to break through the bureaucracy and stimulate grassroots pressures for change.

Further Observations

For change to occur, a delicate balance needs to be achieved between the forces that make change inevitable (whether they be threats or opportunities) and a certain sense of confidence and stability which allows people to take risks. How do universities establish sufficient confidence in the long-term support and vitality of the institution, even as they make a compelling case for the importance of the transformation process?

Large organizations resist change. They try to wear change agents down or wait them out. Leaders throughout the institution should be given every opportunity to consider carefully the issues compelling change, with strong encouragement to climb on board the transformation train. But, if they are unable or unwilling to support it, then personnel changes may be necessary.

One of the objectives of a university transformation process is to empower the best among the faculty and staff to exert the influence on the intellectual directions of the university which will sustain its leadership. Here, however, universities must address two difficulties. First, there is the obvious challenge that large, complex hierarchically organized institutions become extremely bureaucratic and conservative and tend to discourage risk taking and stifle innovation and creativity. Second, the faculty has so encumbered itself with rules and regulations, committees and academic units, and ineffective faculty governance that the best faculty are frequently disenfranchised, outshouted by their less productive colleagues, who have the time and inclination to engage in campus politics. It will require determination and resourcefulness to break this stranglehold of process and free the very best minds.

From a more abstract viewpoint major change involves taking a system from one stable state to another. The transition itself, however, involves first forcing the system into instability, which will present certain risks. It is important to minimize the duration of such instability, since the longer it lasts, the more likely the system will move off in an unintended direction or sustain permanent damage.

Many people resist change, but others relish it and support bold initiatives if a convincing case can be made. An institution must develop an effective internal marketing strategy for themes of transformation, conveying a sense of confidence that it has the will and the capacity to follow through and that in the end the university will emerge stronger than ever.

The Capacity for Change and Adaptation

Although both public and private colleges and universities face the challenge of change, there is a significant difference in their capacity to adapt and serve a changing world. Private universities are generally more nimble, both because of their smaller size and the limited number of constituencies they have to consult, and convince, before change can occur. Whether driven by market pressures, resource constraints, or intellectual opportunity, private universities usually need to convince only trustees, campus communities (faculty, students, and staff) and perhaps alumni before moving ahead with a change agenda. Certainly this can be a formidable task, but it is a far cry from having to appease the broader political constituencies associated with public universities.

The public university must always function in an intensely political environment. Their governing boards are generally political in nature, frequently viewing their primary responsibilities as being to various political constituencies rather than to the university itself. Any changes that might threaten these constituencies are generally resisted, even if they might enable the institution to better serve broader society. The public university also must operate within a complex array of government regulations and relationships at the local, state, and federal level, most of which tend to be highly reactive and supportive of the status quo. Furthermore, the press itself is generally more intrusive in the affairs of public universities, viewing itself as the guardian of the public interest and using powerful tools such as sunshine laws to hold public universities accountable.

As a result, actions that would be straightforward for private universities, such as enrollment adjustments, tuition increases, or program reductions, can be formidable for public institutions. Actions taken by many public universities to adjust to eroding state support through tuition increases or program restructuring, for example, have triggered major political upheavals that threaten to constrain further efforts to balance activities with resources.[4] Sometimes the reactive nature of the political forces swirling about and within the institution is not apparent until an action is undertaken. Many a public university administration has been undermined by an about-face by its governing board, when political pressure forces board members to switch from support to opposition on a controversial issue.

Little wonder that administrators sometimes conclude that the only way to get anything accomplished within the political environment of the public university is by heeding the old adage: "It is simpler to ask forgiveness than to seek permission!" Yet even this hazardous approach may not be effective for the long term. It could well be that public universities will simply not be able to respond adequately during periods of great change in society.

The public research university faces a particular set of challenges. Recall that only a relatively small number of public universities—roughly one hundred out of twenty-two hundred—are classified as research and graduate intensive. Yet these institutions serve as a primary source of basic research for the nation and the source of the next generation of scholars and professionals. The changing market forces and social policies reshaping the broader higher education enterprise raise a number of important questions concerning the future of the public research university: What will be the impact on these institutions of the profound restructuring now under way in the broader postsecondary learning marketplace? Will they be able to maintain their traditional roles of research, graduate education, and professional training? Will they be able to protect their important academic traditions and values? Will they continue to play a leadership role in society?

Throughout much of the history of higher education in the United States, public research universities have been leaders for the broader college and university enterprise. They have provided the faculty, the pedagogy, the textbooks and scholarly materials, and the standards for all of higher education. They have maintained a strong relationship and relevance to the rest of the enterprise, even though they were set apart in role and mission. While the unique roles, prestige, and prosperity of the public research university might allow it to defend the status quo for a time, this stance too will pose certain dangers. As the rest of the enterprise changes, there is a risk that, if the public research university becomes too reactionary and tenacious in its defense of the status quo, it could well find itself increasingly withdrawn from and perhaps even irrelevant to the rest of higher education in America and throughout the world.

Recognizing the unique mission and value of the public research university even as we seek to preserve its relevance to the rest of higher education raises several possibilities. Some elite private research universities may adopt a strategy of relying on their prestige and prosperity to isolate themselves from change, to continue to do just what they have done in the past, and to be comfortable with their roles as niche players in the higher education enterprise. But for public universities the activities of graduate education and basic research are simply too expensive to sustain without paying attention to the marketplace. Besides, their public charter mandates a broader mission.

Perhaps a more constructive approach would be to apply the extraordinary intellectual resources of the public research university to assist the broader higher education enterprise in its evolution into forms better capable of serving the changing educational needs of a knowledge-driven society. Although research- and graduate-intensive universities might not be the most appropriate for direct involvement in mass or universal education, for example, they certainly are capable of providing the templates, the paradigms, which others can use. They have done this before in other areas such as health care, national defense, and the Internet. To play this role the public university must be prepared to participate in experiments in creating possible futures for higher education.

Extending this role somewhat, flagship public research universities might enter into alliances with other types of educational institutions, regional universities, liberal arts colleges, community colleges, or even newly emerging forms such as for-profit or cyberspace universities. This would allow them to respond to the changing needs of societies while remaining focused on their unique missions as research universities. One could also imagine forming alliances with organizations outside of higher education such as information technology, telecommunications, entertainment companies, information services providers, and government agencies.

Some Lessons Learned

Values

It is important to begin any transformation process with the basics, to launch a careful reconsideration of the key roles and values that should be protected and preserved during a period of transformation. How would an institution prioritize among its roles, including educating the young (e.g., undergraduate education), preserving and transmitting the national culture (e.g., libraries, visual and performing arts), basic research and scholarship, and serving as a responsible critic of society? Similarly, what are the most important values to protect? Clearly, academic freedom, being open to new ideas, a commitment to rigorous study, and aspiring to excellence would be on the list for most institutions. But what about values and practices such as shared governance and tenure—should they be preserved? At what expense?

More generally, there are deeper values that define what the university stands for and what it professes. The Kellogg Commission on the Future of the Land-Grant University suggests that these values correspond to fundamental commitments that define the character of the public university: to access, diversity, and the global nature of the university; to expanding the boundaries of knowledge through basic and applied research that is useful in people's lives; to academic excellence and rigorous standards; to honest inquiry, the discovery of truth, and academic freedom; and to service to family, community, the nation, and the world.[5]

Engaging the Stakeholders

As a social institution, the public university should endeavor to listen carefully to members of society, learning about and understanding their varied and ever-changing needs, expectations, and perceptions of higher education. Not that responding to all of them would be desirable or even appropriate for the public university. But it is important to focus more attention on those whom universities were created to serve.

Public universities also must engage internal stakeholders. After all, the university is characterized first and foremost by its people, acting as a learning community. Although the most important constituency must always be the students, the one that is most significant to institutional quality and progress is the faculty.

Alliances

Public universities should place greater emphasis on building alliances with other institutions which will allow them to focus on core competencies while relying on alliances to address the broader and diverse needs of society. For example, flagship public universities in some states will be under great pressure to expand enrollments to address the expanding populations of college-age students, possibly at the expense of their research and service missions. It might be more constructive for these institutions to form close alliances with regional universities and community colleges to meet the growing demands for educational opportunity.

Here alliances should be considered not only among institutions of higher education (e.g., partnering research universities with liberal arts colleges and community colleges) but also between higher education and the private sector (e.g., information technology and entertainment companies). Differentiation among institutions should be encouraged, while relying upon market forces rather than regulations to discourage duplication.

Experimentation

It is important to recognize the profound nature of the rapidly changing world faced by higher education. Many of the forces driving change are disruptive in nature, leading to quite unpredictable futures and requiring a somewhat different approach to the transformation effort.

During the 1990s we led an effort at the University of Michigan to transform the institution, to reinvent it so that it better served a rapidly changing world. We created a campus culture in which both excellence and innovation were the highest priorities. We restructured finances so that Michigan became, in effect, a privately supported public university. We dramatically increased the diversity of the campus community. We launched major efforts to build a modern environment for teaching and research using the powerful tools of information technology.

Yet with each transformation step we took, with every project we launched, with each objective we achieved, we became increasingly uneasy. The forces driving change in society and its institution were stronger and more profound than we had first thought. Change was occurring more rapidly that we had anticipated. The future was becoming less certain as the range of possibilities expanded to include more radical options. We came to the conclusion that in a world of such rapid and profound change, as we faced an uncertain future, the most realistic near-term approach was to explore possible futures of the university through experimentation and discovery. That is, rather than continue to contemplate possibilities for the future through abstract study and debate, it seemed more productive to build several prototypes of future learning institutions as working experiments. In this way we could actively explore possible paths to the future.

We explored the possible future of becoming a privately supported but publicly committed university by completely restructuring the university's financing, raising over $1.4 billion in a major campaign, increasing tuition levels to market levels, and dramatically increasing sponsored research support (to the point, in fact, where the university led the nation in research expenditures). Ironically, the more state support declined as a component of the revenue base (dropping to roughly 10 percent), the higher the university's Wall Street credit rating, finally achieving the highest Aaa rating in 1997.

Through a major strategic effort known as the Michigan Mandate, described in chapter 3, we significantly altered the racial diversity of students and faculty, doubling the population of underrepresented minority students and faculty over a decade, thereby providing a laboratory for exploring the themes of a "diverse university."

We established campuses in Europe, Asia, and Latin America, linking them with robust information technology, to understand better the implications of becoming a "world university." We played leadership roles first in the building and management of the Internet and then Internet2 to explore the "cyberspace university" theme.

Not all of our experiments were successful. Some crashed in flames, in some cases spectacularly. For example, we proposed to spin off the academic health center, merging it with a large hospital system in Michigan to form an independent health care system. But the regents resisted this effort, concerned that we would be giving away a valuable asset (even though we would have netted well over $1 billion in the transaction and avoided projected $100 million annual operating losses as managed care swept across the state of Michigan).

Although we were eventually successful in winning a Supreme Court ruling that provided relief from the intrusive nature of the state's sunshine laws, efforts to improve state policies for selecting governing boards were largely ineffective. (Michigan remains one of only three states in which the governing boards of its flagship state universities are determined by popular election and partisan politics.)

We also attempted to confront our own version of *Tyrannosaurus rex* by challenging the Department of Athletics to better align its athletic activities with the university's academic priorities (e.g., recruiting true students, reshaping competitive schedules, throttling back commercialism, and even appointing an educator, a former dean, as athletic director. Yet in 2002 the university spent $100 million on skyboxes for Michigan Stadium after expanding stadium capacity two years earlier to over 110,000, reestablishing its ranking as the largest stadium in the country.

Nevertheless, in most of these cases at least we learned something—if only our ineffectiveness in dealing with nearly cosmic forces such as college sports. More specifically, all of these efforts were driven by the grassroots interests, abilities, and enthusiasm of faculty and students. While such an exploratory approach was disconcerting to some and frustrating to others, fortunately there were many on campus and beyond who viewed this phase as an exciting adventure. And all of these initiatives were important in better understanding the possible futures facing the university. They have all influenced the evolution of the university.

Our approach as leaders of the institution was to encourage strongly a "let every flower bloom" philosophy, to respond to faculty and student proposals with "Wow! That sounds great! Let's see if we can work together to make it happen. And don't worry about the risk. If you don't fail from time to time, it is because you aren't aiming high enough!" We tried to ban the word *no* from administrators' vocabularies.

Turning Threats into Opportunities

It is important for university leaders to approach issues and decisions concerning transformation not as threats but as opportunities. True, maintaining the status quo is no longer an option. Once change is accepted as inevitable, however, it can be used as a strategic opportunity to control the destiny of universities while preserving their most important values and traditions. Creative, visionary leaders can tap the energy created by threats such as the emerging for-profit marketplace and technology to engage their campuses to participate in leading their institutions in new directions that will reinforce and enhance their most important roles and values.

Final Observations

Certainly, any effort at institutional transformation will be highly influenced by the unique circumstances, challenges, and opportunities facing a university. But we can offer several general guidelines—in a sense, a recipe for institutional change.

In business, management approaches change in a highly strategic fashion, launching a comprehensive process of planning and transformation. In political circles a strong leader with a big idea can captivate the electorate, building a movement for change. Change occurs in the university through a more tenuous, sometimes tedious, process. Ideas are first floated as trial balloons, all the better if they can be perceived to have originated at the grassroots level. After what often seems like years of endless debate, challenging basic assumptions and hypotheses, decisions are made, and the first small steps are taken. For change to affect the highly entrepreneurial culture of the faculty, it must address the core issues of incentives and rewards.

Efforts to achieve change following the time-honored traditions of collegiality and consensus can sometimes be self-defeating; the process itself frequently leads right back to the status quo. As one of our exasperated presidential colleagues once noted, the university faculty may be the last constituency on Earth which believes the status quo is still an option. To some degree strong resistance to change is both understandable and appropriate. After all, the university is one of the most enduring social institutions of our civilization in part because its ancient traditions and values have been protected and sustained.

It is particularly important to prepare the academy for change and competition. Unnecessary constraints should be relaxed or removed. Greater effort should be made to link accountability with privilege on campuses, perhaps by redefining tenure as the protection of academic freedom rather than lifetime employment security or better balancing authority and responsibility in the roles of academic administrators. It is also important to begin the task of transforming the academy by considering a radical restructuring of the graduate programs that will produce the faculties of the future. There is a clear need to consider the restructuring of university governance, particularly the character of lay governing boards and the process of shared governance among boards, faculties, and administrations, so that universities are better able to respond to the changing needs of society rather than defending and perpetuating an obsolete past.

Clearly, any serious transformation effort must involve financial issues. But such changes should occur within a broader national debate concerning the nature of public support for higher education. What is the appropriate mix, for example, between public support (i.e., appropriations from tax revenues for higher education as a public good) and private support (i.e., revenues from the marketplace reflecting higher education as a personal benefit)? Considerations of public support should include both direct mechanisms such as appropriations, research grants, and student financial aid and indirect public subsidy through tax expenditures reflecting the favorable tax treatment of charitable gifts and endowment earnings. Other important policy issues include: (1) the appropriate burdens borne by each generation in the support of higher education as determined, for example, by the mix of grants versus loans in federal financial aid programs; (2) the degree to which public investment should be used to help shape powerful emerging market forces to protect the public purpose of higher education; and (3) new methods for internal resource allocation and management which enhance productivity.

We noted earlier in this chapter the importance of encouraging experimentation within the university, to explore different models of teaching and scholarship as well as different institutional policies and practices. During a time of change and uncertainty experimentation and risk taking are vital in identifying future possibilities and developing paths to these futures.

It All Comes Back to Values

In this book we have added our voices to those of many others in considering the significant shifts in national and state policies concerning public higher education which have occurred over the past half-century. Recent policy development seems largely an aftermath of image-driven politics.[6] The current political environment is dominated by media-driven strategies, fund raising, and image building. Policy is largely devoid of values or social priorities but, rather, is shaped in sound bites to achieve short-term political objectives. Perhaps as a consequence if not as a cause, U.S. society appears to have lost confidence both in government policies and in programs it once relied on. Instead, it has placed greater faith in the marketplace, depending on market competition to drive and fund the evolution of social institutions such as the university.

Those of us in higher education must share much of the blame for today's public policy vacuum. After all, for much of the last century the college curriculum has largely neglected any consideration of values. While some people might date this abdication to the trauma of the volatile 1960s, in truth it extends over much of the twentieth century, as scholarship became increasing professionalized and specialized, fragmenting any coherent sense of the purposes and principles of a university. Values such as tolerance, civility, and personal and social responsibility have been largely absent from the academic curriculum.

It is not surprising that the future of public higher education has largely been left to the valueless dynamics of the marketplace. Most undergraduates experience little discussion about values in their studies. Graduate schools focus almost entirely on research training, with little attention given to professional ethics or even the preparation for teaching careers. Faculties prefer to debate parking over principles, just as our governing boards prefer politics to policy. And in this climate university leaders keep their heads low, their values hidden, and prepare their resumes for their next institutions.

The remarkable resilience of institutions of higher education, the capacity to adapt to change in the past, has occurred because in many ways they are intensely entrepreneurial, transactional cultures. As a society, we have provided faculty the freedom, encouragement, and incentives to move toward their personal goals in highly flexible ways, and they have done so through good times and bad. The challenge is to tap the great source of creativity and energy associated with entrepreneurial activity in a way that preserves the university's fundamental mission. In one sense we need to continue to encourage the tradition of evolution and adaptation, which has been so successful in responding to a changing world.

Yet we must do so within the context of an exciting and compelling vision for the future of public institutions. We need to guide this process in such a way as to preserve core values. We must work hard to develop university communities in which uncertainty is an exhilarating opportunity for learning. The future belongs to those who face it squarely, to those who have the courage to transform themselves to serve a new society.

Institutions that can step up to this process of change will thrive. Those that rigidly defend the status quo or, even worse, some idyllic vision of a past that never even existed are at very great risk. Institutions that are micromanaged, either from within by faculty politics or governing boards or from without by government or public opinion, stand little chance of flourishing during a time of great change.

CHAPTER TEN

The Future

For over two centuries the American public university has contributed significantly to the education needs of a growing nation. The history of the public university in America is one of a social institution, created and shaped by public needs, public policy, and public investment to serve a growing nation. With an expanding population, a prosperous economy, and compelling needs such as national security, health care, and economic competitiveness, the public was willing to make massive investments in higher education. While elite private universities were important in setting the standards determining the character of higher education in America, it was the public university that provided the capacity and diversity to meet the nation's vast needs for post-secondary education.

In recent years, however, the fortunes of public higher education have been mixed. During the late 1990s a prosperous economy allowed many states to halt the erosion in appropriations for higher education which had occurred during the 1980s and early 1990s. Some states even took steps to reinvest in the capacity of their public colleges and universities in an effort to prepare them for rising enrollments driven by the echo of the postwar baby boom and the expanding higher education needs of adults in the high-performance work-place. Despite great concern about the impact of efforts to balance the federal budget, federal research support was largely spared, and research grants and contracts continued to flow to U.S. campuses.

Yet, as we enter a new century, the inevitable downturn in the economic cycle has arrived, and once again states are cutting appropriations, and public universities are tightening their belts, reducing staffing, eliminating programs, and increasing tuition.[1] There are growing concerns that the financial stresses on public colleges and universities in the early years of the new century arise from structural flaws in state budgets, such as inadequate tax rates, eroding infrastructure, and overcommitments to social services that are unlikely to disappear with the next period of prosperity. Even as the correlation between earning capacity and education level becomes more dramatic in a knowledge-driven economy, parents and students are increasingly worried about whether they can afford the rising costs of a college education.[2] Politicians are attempt-ing to respond to these concerns, but all too frequently they do so by increasing regulations and bureaucracy in the name of public accountability, rather than addressing the adequacy of public support for higher education during an era of growing enrollments. The shift of federal financial aid programs from need-based grants to loans to tax credits and deductions is clearly designed to appeal more to middle-class voters than to provide access to educational oppor-tunities for lower-income students.

In many states, particularly in the South and the West, massive increases in the population of college-age students will rapidly exceed the current capacity of public colleges and universities. In still others, the high-performance work-place has triggered a growing need for adult education at the college level. Yet the states face competing demands on resources for K-12 education, correc-tions, public health, and deteriorating public infrastructure. Furthermore, many state governments are increasingly inclined toward market philosophies that channel public tax dollars away from state appropriations to public in-stitutions and, instead, to individuals through merit-based financial aid or vouchers. Hence, there is a very real concern that public colleges and univer-sities will be asked to meet growing education needs with little additional public support.

Another harbinger of change can be found in the stresses felt by faculty members, particularly in public research universities. Forums held on univer-sity campuses across the nation reveal a growing gulf between what faculty members value about their schools and the terms dictated by those whom the universities serve.[3] Most faculty members recognize the importance of the efforts by their institutions to cut costs, raise revenues, capitalize on new technology, and increase productivity. But they also believe these activities create additional burdens on faculty members which distract them from their core academic activities of teaching and scholarship. With increasing specialization, faculty members sense a loss of scholarly community. They feel torn between the demands of grantsmanship, a reward structure emphasizing research, and a love and sense of responsibility for teaching. While today's stresses on the academy have many symptoms, they have fundamentally one major cause: change, in the world and in our institutions, which is occurring more rapidly than most in the professoriate find comfortable.

Perhaps nowhere is this change in perception of the role of higher education in society more obvious, or more disturbing, than in government itself. Without explicit policy debate—indeed, without even public awareness or an acknowledgment by government—the fundamental equation for the support of higher education in America has been changing dramatically. To some degree this transformation represents shifting public priorities during a period of limited resources. But it also represents a decided, yet generally unstated, shift in the perspectives of many elected public officials, who increasingly regard education as an individual benefit rather than a public good that addressed societal needs. We see this elsewhere—for example, the recent flurry of proposals for the use of voucher systems in K-12 education and the introduction of charter schools, both driven as much by the concept of education as an individual benefit as by a desire for school autonomy or market-driven excellence.

Finally, current policies and practices for governing, leading, and managing public universities seem increasingly incompatible with the needs of a rapidly changing world. Governing boards have become overly politicized, focusing more on oversight and accountability than on protecting and enhancing the capacity of their university to serve the changing and growing educational needs of society. Faculty governance—at least in its current shared form—is largely unworkable, and in many cases even irrelevant, to either the nature or pace of the issues facing the contemporary university. University leadership, whether at the level of chairs, deans, or presidents, has insufficient authority to meet the considerable responsibilities engendered by the powerful forces of change on higher education. And nowhere, either within the academy, at the level of governing boards, or in government policy, is there a serious discussion of the fundamental values so necessary to the nature and role of the public university. Today it seems clear that a new dialogue is needed concerning the future of the public university in America, one that balances today's economic imperatives with higher education's traditional values and roles in serving a democratic society.

The New Imperatives for a Knowledge-Driven Society

Today we are evolving rapidly—decade by decade, even year by year—into a postindustrial, knowledge-based society, experiencing a shift in culture and technology as profound as that which took place a century ago, as agrarian America evolved into an industrial nation.[4] Industrial production is steadily shifting from material- and labor-intensive products and processes to knowledge-intensive ones. A radically new system for creating wealth has evolved which depends upon the creation and application of new knowledge.

In a very real sense we are entering a new age, an age of knowledge, in which the key strategic resource necessary for prosperity has become knowledge itself in the form of educated people and their ideas.[5] Unlike natural resources such as iron and oil which have driven earlier economic transformations, knowledge is inexhaustible. The more it is used, the more it multiplies and expands. But knowledge is not available to everybody. It can be absorbed and applied only by the educated mind. Hence, as society becomes ever more knowledge intensive, it becomes ever more dependent upon social institutions such as the university which create knowledge, educate people, and provide them with knowledge and learning resources throughout their lives.[6]

The signs of such a social transformation are numerous. When asked about their state's priorities these days, governors are likely to express concern about the education and skills of their citizens. The National Governors Association stresses that "the driving force behind the 21st Century economy is knowledge, and developing human capital is the best way to ensure prosperity." The skills race of the twenty-first-century knowledge economy has become comparable to the space race of the 1960s in capturing the nation's attention. Seventy percent of Fortune 1000 CEOs cite the ability to attract and retain adequately skilled employees as the major issue for revenue growth and competitiveness. Corporate leaders now estimate that the high-performance workplace will require a culture of continuous learning in which as much as 20 percent of a worker's time will be spent in formal education to upgrade his or her knowledge and skills.[7]

People have long looked to education as the key to prosperity and social mobility, but now, more than ever, people see education as their hope for leading meaningful and fulfilling lives. One's level of education has become a primary determinant of economic well-being. Just as a high school diploma became the passport for participation in the industrial age a century ago, today a college education has become the requirement for economic security in the age of knowledge. The pay gap between high school and college graduates continues to widen, doubling from a 50 percent premium in 1980 to 111 percent today. Not so well known is an even larger earnings gap between baccalaureate degree holders and those with graduate degrees. People with professional degrees earn an average of $4.4 million over the course of their working lives, compared to $3.4 million for those with doctoral degrees, $2.5 million for master's degrees, $2.1 million for bachelor's degrees, and $1.2 million for those holding only a high school diploma.[8]

Yet here we face a major challenge, since it is increasingly clear that we are simply not providing citizens with the learning opportunities needed for a twenty-first-century knowledge economy. Recent scores from the Third International Mathematics and Science Study-Repeat *(TIMMS)* suggest that, despite school reform efforts of the past two decades, students in the United States continue to lag behind those in other nations in mathematics and science skills.[9] Even given the growing correlation between the level of one's education and earning capacity, only 21 percent of the population over the age of twenty-five have graduated from college.[10] Furthermore, enrollments in graduate programs (particularly in technical fields such as engineering and computer science) have held constant or declined over the past two decades.[11]

The growing and changing nature of educational needs of society is likely to trigger strong economic and political forces. The space race galvanized public concern and concentrated national attention on educating "the best and brightest," the elite of our society. The skills race of the twenty-first century will value instead the skills and knowledge of the entire workforce as a key to economic prosperity, national security, and social well-being. Yet traditional sources of public support for higher education such as state appropriations and federal support for student financial aid have simply not kept pace with the growing demand. This imbalance between demand and available resources is aggravated by the increasing costs of education, driven as they are by the knowledge- and people-intensive nature of the enterprise as well as by the difficulty educational institutions have in containing costs and increasing productivity. It also stimulated the entry of new for-profit competitors into the education marketplace.

It seems clear that education, broadly defined, will play a pivotal role in the coming economic transition and its impact on individuals. Previous economic transformations were closely associated with major public investment in infrastructure such as railroads, canals, electric networks, and highways. In the coming economic transition an equivalent infrastructure will be schools, colleges, universities, workplace training programs, and other learning organizations and opportunities.

A Society of Learning

As we enter the new millennium, there is an increasing sense that the social contract between the public university and American society may need to be reconsidered and perhaps even renegotiated.[12] The ultimate challenge for the public university in the twenty-first century may be to assist the nation's evolution into what one might call a "society of learning," in which opportunities for learning become ubiquitous and universal, permeating all aspects of society and empowering all citizens through education.

We have entered an era in which educated people and the knowledge they produce and use have become the keys to the nation's economic prosperity and social well-being. Education, knowledge, and skills have become primary determinants of one's personal standard of living. In such a world one might argue that it has become the responsibility of democratic societies to provide their citizens with the education and training they need throughout their lives, whenever, wherever, and however they desire it, at high quality and at an affordable cost. Of course, this has been one of the great themes of higher education in America. Each evolutionary wave of higher education has aimed at reaching a broader segment of society and creating new educational forms— public universities, land grant universities, historically black colleges and universities, tribal colleges, normal and technical colleges, community colleges, and cooperative extension programs.

What, then, would be the nature of a university of the twenty-first century which is capable of creating and sustaining such a society of learning? It would be inappropriate to suggest one particular model. The great and ever-increasing diversity characterizing U.S. higher education makes it clear that there will be many types of institutions serving the future learning and knowledge needs of society. But there are a number of themes that will almost certainly factor into the higher education enterprise.

Like other social institutions, universities must become more focused on those they serve. They must transform themselves from faculty-centered to learner-centered institutions, becoming more responsive to what students need to learn rather than what faculties wish to teach, building true learning communities on campuses and beyond. Society will also demand that universities become more affordable, providing educational opportunities that are within the means of all citizens. Whether this change occurs through greater public subsidy or dramatic restructuring of the costs of higher education, it seems increasingly clear that society, and the world, can no longer tolerate the high-cost, low-productivity paradigm that characterizes much of higher education in America today.

In an age of knowledge the need for advanced education and skills will require both a personal willingness by Americans to continue to learn throughout life and a commitment on the part of institutions to provide opportunities for lifelong learning. The concepts of student and alumnus will merge. The highly partitioned system of education will blend increasingly into a seamless web, in which primary and secondary education; undergraduate, graduate, and professional education; on-the-job training and continuing education; and lifelong enrichment become a continuum.

Already we see new forms of pedagogy: asynchronous (anytime, anyplace) learning that utilizes emerging information technology to break the constraints of time and space, making learning opportunities more compatible with lifestyles and career needs; and interactive and collaborative learning appropriate for the digital age, the plug-and-play generation. The great diversity characterizing U.S. higher education will continue, as it must to serve an increasingly diverse population with varied needs and goals.

It is clear that access to advanced learning opportunities is not only becoming a more pervasive need, but it could well become a defining domestic policy issue for a knowledge-driven society. In a society of learning people would be continually surrounded by, immersed in, and absorbed in learning experiences. As a society, we are challenged to create learning environments capable of responding to rapidly changing educational needs. Public higher education must define its relationship with these emerging possibilities in order to create a compelling vision for its future as it enters the new millennium.

Financing the Future

As we have suggested throughout this book, the current paradigm for financing public higher education seems incapable of responding to the growing educational needs of a knowledge-intensive society. In years past public investment in higher education through both state support of public colleges and universities and federal funding of student financial aid and campus-based research has been justified and accepted as a means for achieving societal goals. Today, however, both the public and its elected representatives in state and federal government see the marketplace as a more effective mechanism to address public priorities such as an educated workforce and economic vitality. The long-standing goals of access and equal opportunity have been replaced with new objectives for public universities which are more consistent with this market-driven philosophy. Both state legislatures and federal agencies increasingly demand measurable performance indicators such as graduation rates, faculty contact hours, improved productivity, and cost containment. Beyond this change in perception, there is also a sense that, as higher education falls behind other social priorities such as health care, K-12 education, and corrections in claiming public funding, public colleges and universities are expected to turn to alternative revenue sources such as tuition, fund raising, and the commercial marketplace to compensate for declining public support. As a result, students are increasingly viewed as consumers and faculty members as entrepreneurs, and universities are judged by their ability to compete in the marketplace rather than sustain their academic values.

Rather than simply accepting this mission- to market-driven evolution of the public university as an inevitable consequence of contemporary society, perhaps it is time to launch a more fundamental debate about financing public higher education. At one extreme would be a return to the perception that public higher education represents a public good, with sufficient public support to provide access to low-cost, high-quality college education to meet the growing needs of a knowledge-driven society. Here both the states and the nation would recommit themselves to providing educational opportunity to everyone with the desire and ability to learn, halting the erosion in public support of higher education and reaffirming the commitment to educational opportunity from one generation to the next.

In this "back to the future" scenario states would provide adequate appropriations to meet the true instructional costs of their public colleges and universities, and federal financial aid programs would move away from providing loans and tax benefits and back to offering grants based upon financial need. More specifically, at both the state and national levels public higher education would shift from the high tuition / high financial aid policies that have dominated much of the past several decades. The high tuition / high financial aid model may be responsible in part for public concerns and misunderstanding about the affordability of a college education, since it reinforces the belief that higher education is primarily an individual benefit rather than a social responsibility. It certainly has created the mistaken impression that public higher education is beyond the reach of students from modest economic backgrounds, discouraging them from even applying for financial aid or admission.[13]

Clearly, strengthening public support of higher education and focusing financial aid programs on those most in need seems consistent with a national strategy to broaden the opportunities for advanced learning. Yet there is a formidable challenge to this approach. The fiscal constraints faced by local, state, and federal governments will intensify in the years ahead, particularly during inevitable periods of economic weakness, since there continues to be strong public resistance against further taxation.

A sharply contrasting approach would be simply to accept a market-driven future for higher education as inevitable and remove hidden subsidies in higher education by raising prices (i.e., tuition and fees) to levels more accurately reflecting true costs so that the marketplace can operate in the most efficient fashion. Such an approach would shift even more funding away from direct public support of institutions and would channel it, instead, toward financial aid programs aimed at providing access to those with the greatest need rather than buying middle- and upper-class voting clout. A strong justification for this approach is motivated, in part, by evidence that raising prices for middle- and upper-income students in higher education does not appear to discourage enrollments in public institutions.[14] In a similar sense using federal dollars to subsidize the lending costs of middle- and upper-income students does little to create new opportunities for college enrollment.

Hence, if the intent is to utilize increasingly limited public dollars for higher education, there is some justification for raising the price of a college education in public colleges and universities so that it more accurately reflects true costs. In the process this market-driven approach would likely eliminate much of the difference between public and private higher education. It would also eliminate many public colleges and universities, which would find it very difficult to compete in such an open marketplace.

As a variation on this theme of a market-driven future, perhaps we might even question the tradition of viewing the provision of a college education as an obligation of one generation to the next and an investment in the future. In today's knowledge-driven economy a college education is becoming increasingly valuable. So, too, both taxpayers and parents are becoming increasingly resistant to supporting higher education in the face of limited resources and competing social priorities. Perhaps it is time to question the long-standing perception of higher education as an obligation from one generation to the next and shift more of the burden for its financing to those who benefit most directly, the students and their employers. After all, today an advanced education can viewed as a high-return investment both in the earning capacity of individuals and the success of their employers. Of course, this approach would require some form of financing infrastructure, perhaps similar to that of a long-term mortgage or income-contingent federal loan program. It might also require explicit recognition by business and government organizations of the importance of investing in human capital, particularly if they were assessed in part for the educational costs of those they hire. However alien the concept, recasting the financing of higher education as an investment opportunity rather than a social obligation might be more consistent with the realities of the market-driven politics of the times.

Although these steps represent dramatic departures from the current paradigms for financing higher education, it is clear that the present course may not be workable in the years ahead. If colleges and universities continue to increase tuition to compensate for the imbalance between society's demand for higher education and rising costs, on one hand, and stagnant public support, on the other, and state and federal financial aid programs continue to focus on subsidizing middle- and upper-class students rather than providing educational opportunities for those with the greatest economic need, millions of Americans will find a college education priced beyond their means.[15] While cost containment and renewed public investment are clearly needed, it seems increasingly clear that entirely new paradigms for providing and financing higher education are required for the long term.[16]

Achieving a Balance between Excellence and Elitism

We earlier expressed concern about the growing divergence between elite, highly selective private colleges and universities and public colleges and universities whose mission is to provide quality educational opportunities more broadly. An exceptionally strong economy, coupled with highly beneficial tax policies, has allowed some institutions to accumulate vast wealth through private gifts and endowment income and to focus these resources on selecting and attracting an elite class of students and faculty. We suggested earlier that the predatory practices of several of these institutions in buying the best students and raiding the top faculty members from less wealthy institutions have had a deleterious impact on higher education. Former Secretary of Labor Robert Reich has suggested that their increasingly selective student admissions policies may not be a wise social policy.[17]

In a knowledge-driven economy, clearly it is in the national interest to provide as many people as possible with advanced educational opportunities of the highest quality. To this end it should be a national objective not simply to expand educational opportunities for the entire population but also to develop more colleges and universities with the capacity to produce graduates of the very highest caliber. Yet current social policies, coupled with the competitive culture in higher education, have created a situation in which our most elite institutions focus more and more resources on fewer and fewer students and faculty. As the elite institutions use their vast wealth to buy, in effect, the very best faculty and students, they diminish the quality of the rest of the higher education enterprise.

If these were truly independent institutions operating in a highly competitive marketplace, then perhaps there would be little beyond grumbling for the have-nots to do. But, as we have pointed out, the public subsidy of elite private institutions through both direct federal programs (e.g., sponsored research, student financial aid, and health care) and beneficial tax policies (e.g., the tax-exempt status of private gifts and endowment income) is considerable. In fact, in many cases this public subsidy of private colleges and universities is substantially greater than that provided to public institutions with a mandate to serve a broader segment of the population.

Hence, it may be in the national interest to consider more progressive federal policies in which the flow of public funds to the most selective and wealthiest of colleges and universities is redirected toward building the quality and capacity of other less well-endowed institutions, both public and private. For example, perhaps there should be a cap on the level of endowment per student beyond which the tax-exempt status of endowment income would no longer apply. Or federal financial aid programs could be more limited in the amount of tuition subsidy they would provide. There are many other possibilities, but the point is clear. In an age in which knowledge and highly educated citizens have become our most important national asset, there are strong reasons to consider public policies and programs that target limited public funds to broaden the base of institutions capable of producing high-quality graduates and research, rather than channeling public funds to fill the coffers of the very few elite institutions already characterized by vast wealth. Put more succinctly, what America needs today is not a richer and richer Harvard; rather, it needs more institutions of Harvard's quality, and it needs them dispersed across the nation.

A Learn Grant Act for the Twenty-first Century

As the United States enters a new century, we face social and economic challenges triggered by globalization and technological and demographic changes which make the development of the nation's human and intellectual capital our highest domestic priority. At similarly critical periods in the nation's history the federal government took strong action to address citizens' needs for education. The Northwest Ordinances of 1785 and 1787 established the principle of government support of schools by setting aside public lands to support public schools in each new state. The Morrill Act of 1862 and the other Land-Grant Acts democratized higher education, transforming it from a privilege of the elite to an opportunity for the working class while stimulating the development of academic programs in applied areas such as agriculture and engineering to serve an industrial economy. The 1944 GI Bill provided millions of returning veterans with the opportunity for a college education. The Truman Commission of 1948 stated its belief that every high school graduate should have the opportunity for a college education and laid the foundation for the sequence of federal student loan programs which has made this dream possible for a significant portion of the population. In the years following World War II, concern for national security stimulated a research partnership between the federal government and universities which led to increased support for graduate education and research on the nation's campuses.

Hence, there are strong precedents for promoting federal policies, programs, and investments that work through colleges and universities to address national priorities. What might we expect in the decades ahead? Recall that a century and a half ago the United States was facing a similar period of tremendous change, evolving from an agrarian, frontier society into an industrial nation. At that time a social contract was developed between the federal government, the states, and public colleges and universities designed to assist the nation in making this transition. The land grant acts were based upon several commitments. First, the federal government provided federal lands for the support of higher education. Next, the states agreed to create public universities designed to serve both regional and national interests. As the final element, these public or land grant universities accepted new responsibilities to broaden educational opportunities for the working class, launching new programs in applied areas such as agriculture, engineering, and medicine aimed at serving industrial society while committing themselves to public service, engagement, and extension.

Today U.S. society is undergoing a similarly profound transition, this time from an industrial to a knowledge-based society, and thus it is time for a new social contract aimed at providing the knowledge and educated citizenry necessary for building prosperity, security, and social well-being in this new age. Perhaps it is time for a new federal act, similar to the land grant acts of the nineteenth century, which will help the higher education enterprise address the needs of the twenty-first century.

The land grant paradigm of the nineteenth and twentieth centuries was focused on developing the nation's vast natural resources by investing in its agricultural and industrial development.[18] Today, however, we have come to realize that the most important national resource for the future will be people, their talents, and their abilities. At the dawn of the age of knowledge one might well make the argument that an educated citizenry will replace natural resources or national defense as the priority for the twenty-first century. We might even conjecture that a social contract based on developing and maintaining people's abilities and talents to their fullest extent could well transform schools, colleges, and universities into new forms that would rival the research university in importance. In a sense the twenty-first-century analogue to the land grant university might be viewed as a *learn grant university*.

A learn grant university for the twenty-first century would be designed to develop our most important asset, human resources, as its top priority, along with the infrastructure necessary to sustain a knowledge-driven society. The field stations and cooperative extension programs—perhaps now as much in cyberspace as in a physical location—could be directed to the needs and development of the people in the region. Furthermore, perhaps we should discard the current obsession of research universities to control and profit from intellectual property developed on the campus through research and instruction by wrapping discoveries in layer after layer of bureaucratic regulations defended by armies of lawyers and, instead, move to something more akin to the "open source" philosophy used in some areas of software development. That is, in return for strong public support, public universities could perhaps be persuaded to regard all intellectual property developed on the campus through research and intellectual property as part of the public domain and encourage their faculty to work closely with commercial interests to enable these knowledge resources to serve society, without direct control or financial benefit to the university. MIT, itself a land grant university, has recently taken a major leadership step in this direction with its "open course learning ware" project, which aims at putting the materials for over two thousand MIT courses on the Web for public use.[19]

In an era of relative prosperity in which education plays such a pivotal role, it may be possible to build the case for new federal commitments based on just such a vision of a society of learning. These new investments, however, are unlikely to be made within the old paradigms. For example, while the federal government–research university partnership utilizing peer-reviewed and merit-based grants has been remarkably successful, this remains a system in which only a small number of elite institutions participate and benefit. The theme of a twenty-first century learn grant act would be to broaden the base, to build and distribute widely the capacity to contribute both new knowledge and educated knowledge workers to society, not simply to channel more resources into established institutions.

The National Association of State Universities and Land Grant Colleges proposes a Higher Education Millennium Partnership Act in the spirit of earlier federal enactments such as the Morrill Act and GI Bill, which have so enriched the nation.[20] The Millennium Partnership Act would draw on resources from state and federal governments and the private sector to expand the technology capacity of higher education, foster the educational progress of its citizens, and sustain the economic prosperity of the nation. In particular, it would ensure that colleges and universities have the necessary infrastructure to integrate technology into the traditional curriculum, provide more flexible educational opportunities for part-time, nonresidential students, and develop new partnerships with K-12, business, and local communities.

An interesting variation on this theme is the Millennium Education Trust Fund proposed by Lawrence Grossman and Newton Minnow.[21] This fund would be established by investing the revenues from the sale or lease of the digital communications spectrum and would serve the diverse educational, informational, and cultural needs of American society by enhancing learning opportunities, broadening the knowledge base, supporting the arts and culture, and providing the skills that are necessary for the information age. Grossman and Minnow estimate that the auctions of unused communications spectrum over the next several years could yield at least eighteen billion dollars. These revenues, placed in a Millennium Education Trust Fund, would work just as the Northwest Ordinance and Morrill Act did in past centuries, investing proceeds from the sale of public property in the nation's most valuable asset, its people.

Whatever the mechanism, the point seems clear. It is time to consider a new social contract linking federal and state investment with higher education and business to serve national and regional needs, much in the spirit of the land grant acts of the nineteenth century.

The Future of Public Higher Education

As society changes, so too must change its institutions such as the university. But change has always characterized the university, even as it has sought to preserve and propagate the intellectual achievements of U.S. culture and society. The university has endured as an important social institution for a millennium and over time has evolved in profound ways to serve a changing world. The American public university has likewise been characterized by change, embracing the concept of a secular liberal education then weaving

scholarship into its educational mission and broadening its activities to provide public service and research, in response to society's needs.

The public university has played a key role in building and sustaining the
nation. It has expanded educational opportunities dramatically, providing
affordable, high-quality college education to almost two-thirds of today's high
school graduates. It has conducted the research critical to national defense,
public health, and economic prosperity. It has served communities, states, and
the nation with an extraordinary array of services. Throughout its history
public higher education in the United States has provided a unique combination of liberal learning, practical education, and professional service, first for a
growing nation and today for an increasingly interconnected world.

To be sure, both the character and needs of the nation have changed dramatically over the past two centuries, since the founding of the first public
universities. While the details of the social contract between America and the
public university may change, its fundamental character remains intact. The
major principles that undergird public higher education remain as valid today
as they were at earlier times—manifested in a bond between the society and its
universities to educate, to discover, and to serve. Now, more than ever before,
the national interest calls for an investment in human and intellectual capital
and hence in public higher education. The fundamental mission of the public
university continues to be that of advancing the public good but in a way that
serves an ever-changing society in a new age.

Throughout its history the public university has responded quite effectively
to the perceived needs, and opportunities, of American society. It has also
evolved through different forms—the land grant college, research university,
and new forms such as the virtual university and web portal—to serve an ever-
changing society. Yet today public colleges and universities are straining to
balance public needs for greater access, high quality, and cost-effectiveness in a
period of limited resources and political turmoil. The incompatibility of the
demands placed upon the public university during a time of constrained resources, increasing market competition, and accelerating technological change
could well erode the quality, public character, and civic purpose of these
important institutions.

The nation faces a clear choice about the future of the public university. We
can accept the challenge, and the risk, of transforming institutions and policies
into new forms more appropriate to the age of knowledge, or we can accept the

near certainty of stagnation and decline as the capacity of traditional universities to serve the changing world erodes. The years ahead could represent one of the most exciting periods in the history of higher education if public universities have the capacity, and the will, to respond positively and creatively to the challenges, opportunities, and responsibilities facing our nation. They must demonstrate once again that they are willing to take the actions necessary to serve a changing society, thereby earning the renewed commitment of their many stakeholders.

Notes

ONE: A New Century

1. "Almanac Issue, 2001–2002," *Chronicle of Higher Education* 47, no. 1, August 31, 2001.

2. Frank H. T. Rhodes, *The Creation of the Future: The Role of the American University* (Ithaca, N.Y.: Cornell University Press, 2001).

3. John Seely Brown, *The Social Life of Information* (Cambridge: Harvard Business School Press, 2000).

4. Derek C. Bok, *Beyond the Ivory Tower: Social Responsibilities of the Modern University* (Cambridge: Harvard University Press, 1982).

5. Harold Bowen, *The Costs of Higher Education* (San Francisco: Jossey-Bass, 1990).

6. Carnegie Commission on Higher Education, *Higher Education: Who Pays? Who Benefits? Who Should Pay?* (New York: McGraw-Hill, 1973).

7. Frederick Rudolph, *The American College and University* (Athens: University of Georgia Press, 1962); Clark Kerr, *The Yellow and Blue: A Personal Memoir of the University of California, 1949–1967*, with a foreword by Neil J. Smelser (Berkeley: University of California Press, 2001).

8. House Committee on Science, *Unlocking Our Future: Toward a New National Science Policy*, report prepared by Vernon Ehlers, 105th Cong., September 24, 1998.

TWO: The Public University

1. Burton R. Clark, "Collegial Entrepreneurialism in Proactive Universities: Lessons from Europe," *Change* (January–February 2000).

2. Kerr, *Gold and the Blue*.

3. Cyril O. Houle, *Governing Boards* (San Francisco: Jossey-Bass, 1989).

4. Clark Kerr, *The Guardians: Boards of Trustees of American Colleges and Universities—What They Do and How Well They Do It* (Washington, D.C.: Association of Governing Boards, 1989).

5. Scott W. Blasdell, Michael S. McPherson, and Morton O. Schapiro, "Trends in Revenues and Expenditures in U.S. Higher Education: Where Does the Money Come From? Where Does It Go?" in *Paying the Piper: Productivity, Incentives, and Financing in U.S. Higher Education*, ed. Michael S. McPherson, Morton O. Schapiro, and Gordon C. Winston (Ann Arbor: University of Michigan Press, 1993); *Explaining College Costs*, National Association of College and University Business Officers, Washington, D.C., 2002.

6. Stephen Burd, "House Republicans Challenge New England Senators on Shaping Aid Policy," *Chronicle of Higher Education,* February 15, 2002, A14–A15;. F. King Alexander, "Student Tuition and the Higher Education Marketplace: Policy Implications for Public Universities," *Journal of Staff, Program, and Organization Development* (winter 1999). In 1980 public universities expended 34 percent less in Education and General expenditures per FTE and 33 percent less in instruction-related expenditures per FTE than their average private university counterparts. In 1995 public universities expended 52 percent less in education and general expenditures per FTE and 46 percent less in instruction-related expenditures per average FTE than average private universities.

7. Kellogg Commission on the Future of the State and Land-Grant Universities, *Renewing the Covenant: Learning, Discovery and Engagement in a New Age and Different World* (Washington, D.C.: National Association of State Universities and Land-Grant Colleges, 2000); James J. Duderstadt, "New Roles for the 21st Century University," *Issues in Science and Technology* 16, no. 2 (2000): 37–44.

8. Derek C. Bok, *Universities and the Future of America* (Durham, N.C.: Duke University Press, 1990).

9. Robert B. Reich, "How Selective Colleges Heighten Inequality," *Chronicle of Higher Education,* September 15, 2000, B7–B10.

10. F. King Alexander, "Student Tuition and the Higher Education Marketplace: Policy Implications for Public Universities," *Journal of Staff, Program, and Organization Development* 17, no. 2 (summer 2000): 79–93.

11. Patricia Gumport, *A Higher Education Research Agenda for the 21st Century* (Stanford: National Center for Post-Secondary Improvement, Stanford University, 2002).

12. Alexander, "Student Tuition and the Higher Education Marketplace."

T H R E E : Responding to the Changing Needs of Society

1. National Center for Education Statistics, *Projections of Education Statistics to 2011, NCES 2001–083* (Washington, D.C.: U.S. Department of Education, 2001), 47–50; see also "Almanac Issue, 2001–2002," *Chronicle of Higher Education* 47, no. 1, August 31, 2001.

2. National Center for Education Statistics, *The Condition of Education* (Washington, D.C.: U.S. Department of Education, 2002), 25–39.

3. Michael G. Dolence and Donald M. Norris, *Transforming Higher Education: A Vision for Learning in the 21st Century* (Ann Arbor: Society for College and University Planning, 1995).

4. Committee on Science, Engineering, and Public Policy, National Academy of Sciences, *Reshaping the Graduate Education of Scientists and Engineers* (Washington, D.C.: National Academy Press, 1995), 144.

5. Chris M. Golde and Timothy M. Dore, "What the Experiences of Doctoral Students Reveal about Doctoral Education," report prepared for the Pew Charitable Trusts, Philadelphia, 2001; see http://www.phd-survey.org.

6. Terrance Sandalow, "The University and the Aims of Professional Education," in *Intellectual History and Academic Culture at the University of Michigan: Fresh Explorations,* Proceedings of the Symposium Marking the 50th Birthday of the Horace H. Rackham Building, ed. Margaret A. Lourie (Ann Arbor: University of Michigan Press, 1989).

7. Dolence and Norris, *Transforming Higher Education*.

8. "Anxiety over Tuition: A Controversy in Context," *Chronicle of Higher Education*, special report, May 30, 1997, A10–A21

9. "Explaining College Costs: NACUBO's Methodology for Identifying the Costs of Delivering Undergraduate Education" (report, National Association of College and University Business Officers, Washington, D.C., February 2002).

10. Note here that this tuition is for students who are Michigan residents. Most public universities charge much higher tuition levels for students from out of state, reflecting a policy that the education of these non–state residents should not be so heavily subsidized by state taxpayers. In the case of the University of Michigan the tuition for such nonresidents is $20,000, roughly comparable to that of many private universities (the average instate tuition is $7,000).

11. Louis Menand, "Everybody Else's College Education," *New York Times Magazine*, April 20, 1997, 48–49.

12. Patrick M. Callan, *Losing Ground: A National Status Report on the Affordability of American Higher Education* (San Jose, Calif.: National Center for Public Policy and Higher Education, 2002).

13. Thomas J. Kane, "Assessing the U.S. Financial Aid System: What We Know, What We Need to Know," *Ford Policy Forum 2001 on Exploring the Economics of Higher Education* (Cambridge: Forum for the Future of Higher Education, 2001), 25–34.

14. Alexander, "Student Tuition and the Higher Education Marketplace."

15. McPherson and Schapiro, "Are We Keeping College Affordable?"

16. National Center for Education Statistics, *National Postsecondary Student Aid Study* (Washington, D.C.: Department of Education, 2001).

17. Kane, "Assessing the U.S. Financial Aid System," 25–34.

18. Patrick M. Callan, "Coping with Recession," in *Future Forum 2002: Exploring the Future of Higher Education*, ed. Maureen E. Devlin (Cambridge: Forum for the Future of Higher Education, 2002), 44–47.

19. Donald R. Kinder and Lynn M. Sanders, *Divided by Color: Racial Politics and Democratic Ideals* (Chicago: University of Chicago Press, 1996); Stanley B. Greenberg, *Middle Class Dreams: The Politics and Power of the New American Majority* (New Haven, Conn.: Yale University Press, 1996).

20. Pat Gurin, G. Lopez, and B. R. Nosda, "Context, Identity, and Intergroup Relations," in *Cultural Divides: The Social Psychology of Intergroup Contact*, ed. D. Prentice and D. Miller (New York: Russell Sage Foundation, 1999)

21. William G. Bowen and Derek Bok, *The Shape of the River: Long-Term Consequences of Considering Race in College and University Admissions* (Princeton, N.J.: Mellon Foundation, Princeton University Press, 1998).

22. Bowen and Bok, *Shape of the River*. See n. 11.

23. Claude M. Steele, "A Threat in the Air: How Stereotypes Shape Intellectual Identity and Performance," *American Psychologist* 52 (1997): 613–19. Richard C. Atkinson, "The Changing World of College Admissions Tests," paper presented at the Western Association of College Business Officers, San Diego, Calif., May 7, 2002; see also http://www.ucop.edu/pres/speeches/achieve.htm.

24. Here we should note that it was these long-standing admissions policies dating from the 1970s, in which race was one among several criteria for admission, which became the target of litigation in the federal courts in the late 1990s. Ironically, al-

though these race-conscious policies have been the focus of major court tests at the University of Michigan and elsewhere across the nation, we believe they played little role in the success of the Michigan Mandate.

25. For example, African American enrollments increased to 9.2 percent, Hispanic enrollments to 5 percent, and Native American enrollments to 1.2 percent. Altogether, minority enrollments increased to 28 percent of the student body during this period.

26. Office of Scientific Research and Development, *Science: The Endless Frontier,* report to the president on a program for postwar scientific research by Vannevar Bush, July 1945 rpt., Washington, D.C.: National Science Foundation, 1990.

27. Bok, *Universities and the Future of America.*

28. James J. Duderstadt, ed., *Observations on the President's Fiscal Year 2001 Federal Science and Technology Budget,* Committee on Science, Engineering, and Public Policy report, National Academy of Sciences (Washington, D.C.: National Academy Press, 2000).

29. Jeffrey Brainard and Ron Southwick, "A Record Year at the Federal Trough: Colleges Feast on $1.67 Billion in Earmarks," *Chronicle of Higher Education,* August 10, 2001, A20.

30. Barry Checkoway, "Reinventing the University for Public Service," *Journal of Planning Literature* 11, no. 3 (February 1997): 307–19.

FOUR: Technology

1. Steve Lohr, "The Future Came Faster in the Old Days," *New York Times,* October 5, 1997, sec. 4, pp. 1, 4.

2. Peter J. Deming and Robert M. Metcalf, *Beyond Calculation: The New Fifty Years of Computing* (New York: Springer-Verlag, 1997).

3. Ray Kurzweil, *The Age of Spiritual Machines: When Computers Exceed Human Intelligence* (New York: Viking, 1999).

4. William Gibson, *Neuromancer* (New York: Ace, 1984).

5. "Books, Bricks, and Bytes," *Daedelus: Journal of the American Academy of Arts and Sciences* 125, no. 4 (1996): v–vii.

6. John Perry Barlow, "The Economy of Ideas: A Framework for Rethinking Patents and Copyrights in the Digital Age," *Wired* 2, no. 3 (March 1994): 84–90, 126–29.

7. "On-Line Education: Learning Effectiveness and Faculty Satisfaction," in *Proceedings of the 1999 Sloan Summer Workshop on Asynchronous Learning Networks,* ed. John Bourne (Nashville, Tenn.: Center for Asynchronous Learning Networks, 2000).

8. Clayton M. Christensen, *The Innovator's Dilemma: When New Technologies Cause Great Firms to Fail* (Cambridge: Harvard Business School Press, 1997).

9. Stuart Feldman, "Technology Futures," paper presented at the Workshop on the Impact of Information Technology on the Future of the Research University, January 22, 2001; see www.researchchannel.com/programs/nas/itfru.html.

10. Stan Davis and Jim Botkin, *The Monster under the Bed: How Business Is Mastering the Opportunity of Knowledge for Profit* (New York: Touchstone, 1995); Ted Marchese, "Not-So-Distant Competitors: How New Providers Are Remaking the Postsecondary Marketplace," *AAHE Bulletin* (May 1998); David Collins, "When Industries Change: Scenarios for Higher Education," in *Forum Futures 1999* (New Haven, Conn.: Forum for the Future of Higher Education, 1999), 47–72.

11. David Collins, "New Business Models for Higher Education," in *The Internet and the University,* ed. Maureen Devlin, Richard Larson, and Joel Meyerson (Cambridge: Forum for the Future of Higher Education, 2000), 97–116.

12. Christensen, *Innovator's Dilemma.*

13. Mohan Swahney and Jeff Zahn, *The Seven Steps to Nirvana: Strategic Insights into Business Transformation* (New York: McGraw-Hill, 2001).

FIVE: Market Forces

1. David W. Breneman, Joni E. Finney, and Brian M. Roherty, *Shaping the Future: Higher Education Finance in the 1990s* (San Jose: California Higher Education Policy Center), April 1997.

2. Joseph L. Dionne and Thomas Kean, *Breaking the Social Contract: The Fiscal Crisis in Higher Education,* report of the Commission on National Investment in Higher Education (New York: Council for Aid to Education, 1997).

3. Alexander, "Student Tuition and the Higher Education Marketplace."

4. William H. Graves, "Virtual Operations: Challenges for Traditional Higher Education," *Educause Review* 36, no. 2 (March–April 2001): 46–56.

5. Davis and Botkin, *Monster under the Bed.*

6. NationsBanc Montgomery Securities, *Communications Market Quarterly Update* (December 1996).

7. Arthur Levine, "The Remaking of the American University" (paper presented at the U.S. Department of Education Symposium, Washington, D.C., August 2001).

8. Kathleen F. Kelly, *Meeting Needs and Making Profits: The Rise of For-Profit Degree-Granting Institutions* (Denver: Education Commission of the States, 2001).

9. See the website of the Michigan Virtual University: http://www.mivu.org.

10. "Almanac Issue, 2001–2002," *Chronicle of Higher Education.*

11. David Collis, "Emergents vs. Incumbents in the Higher Education Marketplace," *Forum on the Future of Higher Education* (Aspen Institute) (fall 2000).

12. Diane Oblinger and Jill Kidwell, "Distance Learning: Are We Being Realistic?" *Educause Review* (May–June 2000): 30–39.

13. Marvin W. Peterson and David Dill, "Understanding the Competitive Environment of the Postsecondary Knowledge Industry," in *Planning and Management for a Changing Environment,* ed. Marvin W. Peterson, David D. Dill, and Lisa Mets (San Francisco: Jossey-Bass, 1997), 3–29.

14. Donald N. Langenberg, "Taking Control of Change: Reinventing the Public University for the 21st Century," in *Reinventing the Research University,* ed. Kumar Patel (Los Angeles: University of California Press, 1994), 89–99.

15. Robert Zemsky, "Rumbling," *Policy Perspectives* (Pew Higher Education Roundtable, sponsored by the Pew Charitable Trusts) (April 1997); Zemsky and Wegner, "Very Public Agenda."

16. Levine, "Remaking of the American University."

SIX: Financing the Public University

1. Breneman, Finney, and Roherty, *Shaping the Future.*

2. Gumport, *Higher Education Research Agenda for the 21st Century.*

3. Duderstadt, "Observations on the President's Fiscal Year 2001 Federal Science and Technology Budget."

4. McPherson and Schapiro, *Are We Keeping College Affordable?*

5. James L. Fisher and Gary H. Quehl, *The President and Fund-Raising* (New York: American Council on Education, Macmillan, 1989).

6. Burton R. Clark, "The Entrepreneurial University: Demand and Response," *Tertiary Education and Management* 4, no. 1 (1998): 5–16; S. Slaughter and L. L. Leslie, *Academic Capitalism: Politics, Policies, and the Entrepreneurial University* (Baltimore: Johns Hopkins University Press, 1997).

7. Zemsky and Wegner, "Very Public Agenda."

8. "College and University Endowments, 2000–2001," *Chronicle of Higher Education* 48, no. 20, January 25, 2002, A23.

9. Terry W. Hartle, letter to the editor, *Wall Street Journal*, March 16, 1999.

10. Frederick E. Balderston, *Managing Today's University: Strategies for Viability, Change, and Excellence* (San Francisco: Jossey-Bass, 1995).

11. Edward L. Whalen, *Responsibility Center Management* (Bloomington: Indiana University Press, 1991).

12. Kent J. Chaboter and Philip G. Knutel, "Reengineering: A View from the Frontlines," *Planning for Higher Education* 25 (1997): 11–17.

13. Patricia J. Gumport and Brian Pusser, "Academic Restructuring: Contemporary Adaptation in Higher Education," in Peterson, Dill, and Mets, *Planning and Management for a Changing Environment.*

14. David Ellwood and Thomas J. Kane, "Who Is Getting a College Education? Family Background and the Growing Gaps in Enrollment," in *Securing the Future: Investing in Children from Birth to College*, ed. Sheldon Danziger and Jane Waldfogel (New York: Russell Sage Foundation, 2000).

15. Michael McPherson and Morton Schapiro, *The Student Aid Game* (Princeton, N.J.: Princeton University Press, 1998).

16. Zemsky, "Rumbling"; Zemsky and Wegner, "A Very Public Agenda."

17. Ben Gose, "The Fall of the Flagships," *Chronicle of Higher Education*, July 5, 2002, A19–A21.

SEVEN: University Leadership

1. National Commission on the Academic Presidency, *Renewing the Academic Presidency: Stronger Leadership for Tougher Times* (Washington, D.C.: Association of Governing Boards of Universities and Colleges, 1996).

2. National Commission on the Academic Presidency, *Renewing the Academic Presidency.*

3. Gumport and Pusser, "Academic Restructuring"; Patricia J. Gumport, *Academic Restructuring in Public Higher Education: A Framework and Research Agenda* (Stanford: National Center for Postsecondary Improvement, 1998), 111.

4. William G. Bowen and Harold T. Shapiro, eds., *Universities and Their Leadership* (Princeton: Princeton University Press, 1998).

5. Peter T. Flawn, *A Primer for University Presidents: Managing the Modern University* (Austin: University of Texas Press, 1990), 23.

6. According to Laurence J. Peter, "In an organization, each person rises to the level

of his own incompetence" (*The Peter Principle* [Cutchogue, N.Y.: Buccaneer Books, 1996]).

7. Government-University-Industry Research Roundtable, National Academy of Sciences, *Stresses on Research and Education at Colleges and Universities* (Washington, D.C.: National Academies, 1998); see http://www7.nationalacademies.org/guirr/PUBLICATIONS.html.

8. National Commission on the Academic Presidency, *Renewing the Academic Presidency.*

9. National Commission on the Academic Presidency, *Renewing the Academic Presidency,* 11.

10. *The Presidency* (American Council on Education) 3, no. 2 (spring 2000).

11. Donald Kennedy, "Making Choices in the Research University," *Daedelus: Journal of the American Academy of Arts and Sciences* 122, no. 4 (fall 1993): 127–56; Robert Birnbaum, *How Academic Leadership Works: Understanding Success and Failure in the College Presidency* (San Francisco: Jossey-Bass, 1992); Nannerl O. Keohane, "More Power to the President?" in *The Presidency* (Washington, D.C.: American Council on Education, 1998), 12–18.

EIGHT: Governance

1. National Commission on the Academic Presidency, *Renewing the Academic Presidency.*

2. Peter Schmidt, "Most States Tie Aid to Performance, Despite Little Proof That It Works," *Chronicle of Higher Education,* February 22, 2002, A20.

3. John Immerwahr, *The Price of Admission: The Growing Importance of Higher Education* (Washington, D.C.: National Center for Public Policy and Higher Education, 1998).

4. Harold T. Shapiro, *Tradition and Change: Perspectives on Education and Public Policy* (Ann Arbor: University of Michigan Press, 1987).

5. Teresa J. MacTaggart, ed., *Seeking Excellence through Independence* (San Francisco: Jossey-Bass, 1997).

6. Cyril O. Houle, *Governing Boards* (San Francisco: Jossey-Bass, 1989) 223.

7. Frederick E. Balderston, *Managing Today's University: Strategies for Viability, Change, and Excellence* (San Francisco: Jossey-Bass, 1995), 398.

8. Harold M. Williams, "An Agenda for the Governing Board," in *Governance in Higher Education: The University in a State of Flux,* ed. Werner Z. Hirsch and Luc E. Weber (London: Economica, 2001), 182–92.

9. National Commission on the Academic Presidency, "Renewing the Academic Presidency." See n. 1; Richard T. Ingram, *Transforming Public Trusteeship,* Public Policy Paper Series (Washington, D.C.: Association of Governing Boards, 1998).

10. National Commission on the Academic Presidency, *Renewing the Academic Presidency.*

11. Luc E. Weber, "Critical University Decisions and Their Appropriate Makers: Some Lessons from the Economic Theory of Federalism," in *Governance in Higher Education: The University in a State of Flux,* ed. Werner Z. Hirsch and Luc E. Weber (London: Economica, 2001), 79–93.

12. Michael E. Porter, *Competitive Strategy: Techniques for Analyzing Industries and Competitiveness* (Boston: Free Press, 1998).

13. Larry Downes and Chunka Mui, *Unleashing the Killer App: Digital Strategies for Market Dominance* (Cambridge: Harvard Business School Press, 1998).

14. National Commission on the Academic Presidency, *Renewing the Academic Presidency.*

15. Dionne and Kean, *Breaking the Social Contract.*

16. Keohane, "More Power to the President," 12–18.

NINE: University Transformation

1. C. K. Prahalad and G. Hamel, "The Core Competence of the Corporation," *Harvard Business Review* 68 (1990): 79–91.

2. Michael G. Dolence and Donald M. Norris, *Transforming Higher Education: A Vision for Learning in the 21st Century* (Ann Arbor, Mich.: Society for College and University Planning, 1995).

3. Gumport, *Academic Restructuring in Public Higher Education.*

4.Gumport and Pusser, "Academic Restructuring."

5. Kellogg Commission on the Future of State and Land-Grand Universities, *Renewing the Covenant.*

6. Zemsky and Wegner, "Very Public Agenda."

TEN: The Future

1. David W. Brenneman, "For Colleges, This Is Not Just Another Recession," *Chronicle of Higher Education,* June 14, 2002, B7–B9.

2. Immerwahr, *Price of Admission.*

3. Government-University-Industry Research Roundtable, National Academy of Sciences, *Stresses on Research and Education at Colleges and Universities: A Grass Roots Inquiry* (Washington, D.C.: National Research Council, National Academy Press, 1994); *Stresses on Research and Education at Colleges and Universities: Phase II;* see http://www4.nas.edu/pd/guirrcon.nsf.

4. Peter F. Drucker, "The Age of Social Transformation," *Atlantic Monthly,* November 1994, 53–80; *Post-Capitalist Society* (New York: HarperCollins, 1993).

5. Erich Bloch, National Science Foundation, testimony to Congress, 1988.

6. Bok, *Universities and the Future of America.*

7. Michael Moe, *The Knowledge Web: People Power—Fuel for the New Economy* (New York: Merrill-Lynch, 2000)

8. Jennifer Cheeseman Day and Eric C. Newberger, "The Big Payoff: Educational Attainment and Synthetic Estimates of Work-Life Earnings," *Current Population* reports, U.S. Census Bureau, Washington, D.C., July 2002.

9. National Science Foundation and Department of Education, *The Third International Mathematics and Science Study-Repeat* (Washington, D.C.: U.S. Department of Education, 2001).

10. Moe, *The Knowledge Web.*

11. Massey, "Higher Education and Social Mobility in the United States."

12. House Committee on Science, *Unlocking Our Future.*

13. Stephen Burd, "Rift Grows over What Keeps Low-Income Students Out of College," *Chronicle of Higher Education,* January 25, 2002, A18–A20.

14. McPherson and Schapiro, "Are We Keeping College Affordable?"

15. Dionne and Kean, *Breaking the Social Contract.*

16. Kane, "Assessing the U.S. Financial Aid System," 25–34.

17. Robert B. Reich, "How Selective Colleges Heighten Inequality," *Chronicle of Higher Education,* September 15, 2000, B7–B10.

18. Frank Rhodes, "The New American University," in *Looking to the Twenty-First Century: Higher Education in Transition* (Urbana-Champaign: University of Illinois Press, 1995).

19. Charles M. Vest, "Disturbing the Educational University: Universities in the Digital Age—Dinosaurs or Prometheans?" report of the president, MIT Press, Cambridge, Mass., 2001).

20. *The Millennium Partnership Initiative,* National Association of State Universities and Land-Grant Colleges, Washington, D.C., November 11, 2000; see http://www.na sulgc.org/initiatives.html.

21. Lawrence K. Grossman and Newton N. Minnow, *A Digital Gift to the Nation: Fulfilling the Promise of the Digital and Internet Age* (New York: Carnegie Corporation of New York, 2000).

Index